Music Wars

The Sound of the Underground

The Untold Story of Central Station Records

Copyright 2017 © Central Station Publishing Pty Ltd
PO Box 457 Pomona Qld 4568 Australia
www.centralstation.com.au
morgan@centralstation.com.au; centralstation@gmail.com

All rights reserved. Please contact the publisher for permission to reproduce or transmit any part of this book.

Cover design by Peter Coombes
Research, writing and text design by Rell Hannah
Typeset in 11 / 14 pt Adobe Marion
Printed and bound in Australia by Focus Print Group

National Library of Australia Cataloguing-in-Publication entry:
Creator: Hannah, Rell, author.
Title: Music wars : the sound of the underground / Rell Hannah ; Peter Coombes.
ISBN: 9780987619501 (paperback)
Subjects: Palumbo, Giuseppe.
Williams, Morgan.
Central Station Records.
Electronic dance music--Australia.
Electronic dance music--New Zealand.
Other Creators/Contributors:
Coombes, Peter

To the extended Central Station Records family

This book does not aim to be a definitive history of the dance music scene in Australia and New Zealand – it's a collection of memories and observations from employees, customers and associates of Central Station Records.

Much of the story takes place at a time when Australia's copyright law restricted the availability of music, especially in the early era of electronic dance genres. In those pre-internet times, there was immense frustration among DJs and independent retailers such as Central Station Records when the major recording labels under-estimated the potential of an emerging culture. Thankfully, times have moved on, and major labels are now an integral part of the dance music scene Down Under.

Contents

First Word – Jo	1
First Word – Morgan	5
1. The Source	9
2. Giuseppe Palumbo	27
3. Freedom (1979-80)	39
4. The Outlaw and the Hombre (1980-1983)	53
5. Morgan Williams	63
6. Fighting Back (1983-1986)	69
7. Evolution (1986-1989)	75
8. The Dance Scene in the 80s	95
9. The Commercial Battlefront (1989-92)	115
10. The Political Battlefront (1989-92)	131
11. The Reboot (1992-2000)	143
12. The Heyday of the Stores	155
13. The Dance Scene in the 90s	175
14. The Dance Media	197
15. The Political Finish Line (1992-98)	209
16. Devolution (2000-2007)	215
17. The Phoenix Rises	229
18. The Dance Scene 2000+	233
19. Full Circle	251
Appendix 1 – Last Word: Professor Allan Fels	261
Appendix 2 – The Players	263
Appendix 3 – Employees	277
Appendix 4 – Addresses	282

The neon sign at the first Sydney store, in Pitt Street

First Word – Jo

In the late 1970s, when I started Central Station Records, the Australian music industry was a closed market. A *suffocated* market. Under the banner of protecting the livelihoods of local talent, the major recording labels – and I'm talking for the most part about the local branches of multinational businesses – were severely restricting people's access to new music from around the world. Many young people were not allowed to buy the records they wanted, because the majors were not interested in catering to niche tastes like the emerging electronic dance music scene. In fact, the multinationals were even out of touch with mass taste. In the early 80s, CBS refused to import *It's Raining Men* by The Weather Girls until Molly Meldrum took up the cause on *Countdown*. Of course, the track proved a massive hit. Disco was not dead, as CBS believed … or wanted to believe.

At the same time, everyone was paying more for their music than was reasonable by international standards. The tax department and the general public were also missing out on tax revenue, because Australian copyright law enabled these multinational companies to transfer their profits to offshore tax havens via licensing payments. Small recording labels such as the one that Morgan Williams and I founded in 1986 struggled to compete with the giants when we were paying full tax rates.

Of course, I didn't know any of this when I started out. I was a young man wanting to make something of myself in a field that I loved. Music is more than idle entertainment for some people – it's a need. It speaks to the soul and the times. In my original little shop near Flinders Street Station in Melbourne, customers would ask for songs they'd heard on the radio but I couldn't locate them from my suppliers. Naively, I set about sourcing them directly from overseas. DJs went crazy for the new twelve-inch vinyl singles that I shipped in. It wasn't just the range of titles that appealed to people – the sound and packaging quality was also much better than what the majors were offering here.

It was a wonderful period in my life. I tasted freedom for the first time – achieving financial independence and having fun all at once. My tiny shop in Melbourne was full to the brim, with queues outside. People love to be entertained, and I just loved serving them, so it was all pretty wild and colourful. Central Station Records was diversity itself. Gays, blacks, migrants, punks, heavy metal fans – we catered for everyone. No discrimination whatsoever. We were a liberal force for freedom and enlightenment, and we rode the wave of new dance music that washed over Melbourne.

Unfortunately, the euphoria was not to last. To my astonishment and dismay, I received a threatening letter from lawyers acting for Festival Records. 'Desist or we'll sue,' the letter screamed at me. I got very depressed for a while after my first legal fight. Then I got angry. So I went underground. I continued importing records, but I kept them under the counter, only selling to people I trusted. Occasionally, though, I would trust a stooge acting for one of the major record companies. The receipts I gave them were used as evidence against me. The endless legal fights sapped my energy and emptied my pockets.

I met Morgan Williams on the night before I planned to give up the game altogether and return to Italy. As an experienced public servant, he had the political skills I needed to widen the battle. He also had the people skills to broaden the business by locating new talent and ventures. OK, to my mind, many of his ideas were ridiculous, but we often struck gold. We made a great team. Our skills were complementary.

We realised that we couldn't win through the courts – we had to get the law changed. We threw everything at the system – from employing guerrilla war tactics to hiring QCs and appearing before government hearings. For the better part of two decades, we fought on three fronts – commercial, legal and political. At the same time, we developed the Central Station business, opening many shops throughout Australia and New Zealand, branching out into distribution, recording under our own labels, selling equipment, clothing and merchandise, and exporting product around the world.

On my sixtieth birthday, someone asked me why I had taken on the multinationals and fought so hard to have the copyright laws changed and the market opened up. Why had I sacrificed my youth on such a tortuous campaign? Would I have done it again if I could roll back the years and start over?

When Morgan woke me up at five o'clock in the morning on 12 July 1998 to tell me that we'd won and the law had been changed, I was too exhausted to care. The business had moved on. It hardly mattered to us any more money-wise. Maybe it never had. The principle was always more important. In fact, if Festival Records hadn't sent me that first nasty letter, most likely I would have been happy to stay small. I had to expand to pay my legal bills. I had to lobby the politicians to get the legal monkeys off my back.

Now, at the age of sixty-seven, living at the wildlife sanctuary that Morgan and I have created in the Sunshine Coast hinterland, I am aware that there was a spiritual element to the journey as well. I had been set a challenge to help others. That is what gave me the energy to continue fighting the system and developing talent.

The simple fact is that the majors here in Australia didn't want us to have dance music. They didn't get it. It was too gay, too woggy, too do-it-yourself, and too *new*. They wanted us to stick to their pop star creations from the USA. We had to fight them – not only to save our business, but also to save our whole scene.

At the beginning of this project, I just needed to get this story off my chest, to lay some ghosts to rest. As Zen as I had become, I was wondering how much more I could have achieved in life if I hadn't spent so many years battling the system. What did it all mean, now that technology has made our battle seem like a blip in history? As the project went on, I found my answers. I am very grateful to the many people who have given their time so generously to make this book happen. Your passion, humour and insight have reminded me of what an amazing experience we shared – the eruption of the dance music scene in Australia. It wasn't just about fun. It was also a force for social change, for celebration of our diversity as human beings.

I am also grateful to the many public figures who stuck their necks out to support opening up the music market – among others being Professor Allan Fels, then chairman of the ACCC and still a fearless champion of competition. I felt deeply honoured when he responded to our request for his current take on the struggle, and we've given him the last word in this book (appendix 1) because his reply is a beautiful read.

One thing people often forget to do is thank those behind the scenes, in accounting and administration. Brian Riseley, Melbourne CPA accountant, was instrumental in getting our systems up and running and helped me to structure the business and handle affairs with the tax department. Pam Verity stood by me for many years as we tidied up outstanding business issues during the low point of our business story. And my assistant, Annie Luo, is magnificently attentive and fast, and she has introduced new software with ease. I want to thank them for their dedicated work, together with all customers and employees who helped us to achieve and succeed.

All in all, this book is crowd-created. A collective gift to the vast extended family of our scene. I really enjoyed reading it and I hope you do too. It brought some tears as well as laughs. We have done our best to get names and dates right. If we've made any errors, we apologise. Please let us know and we will update the electronic version and any reprint that occurs down the track.

Central Station Records used a number of slogans over the years, but my personal favourite seems to fit the scope of this wide-ranging story: Everything to Dance To ... Everything to Dance For!

Giuseppe Palumbo
(But you can call me Jo – I prefer it without the 'e' on the end)

A lot of work went into Central Station's best-seller charts. This one dates from around 1989.

First Word – Morgan

The more things change, the more they stay the same. On a drizzly Melbourne day in June 2016, Jo and I pulled up outside a brand new vinyl store. A poignant sense of déjà vu washed over us as we walked inside. The man about to greet us was Greg Molinaro, the owner of HUB301 Records, an employee at one stage and a competitor at another. Now here he was – committing to selling vinyl again. And new vinyl at that, not the recycled stuff. It felt like we were returning to our roots. Especially when hearing tunes that sampled others we'd sold in our previous life.

It struck me that nothing had really changed. Dance music has always recycled old favourites. People still want to buy and sell vinyl. And Melbourne, where Jo opened his first Central Station Records store forty years ago, still puts on a classic drizzly day.

It has been a crazy roller coaster ride in the thirty-three years since I met Jo (aka Giuseppe, Joe and Master Joe) at an underground gay disco in St Kilda. He's an Italian alpha male – most likely affected by the (self-diagnosed) Asperger's syndrome that he semi-boasts about. And I'm a Kiwi who happily admits to having ADHD (also self-diagnosed). Putting us together was always going to make for a madly unpredictable trajectory.

This is Giuseppe's story, the story of a highly motivated, creative and spiritual soul who was committed to doing good deeds and ended up making a difference in this country. To me, he exemplifies the classic Australian immigrant, and his story is too good a yarn not to share. He left Naples reluctantly, aged seventeen, departing by ship with his family in 1967. With very little proficiency in English on arrival at Port

Melbourne, he was obliged to shoulder the burden of being the eldest son. The family owed a huge amount to Italian mafia figures who had put up cash to pay for the Palumbos' fares and their modest suburban house in Melbourne. The only route to survival was through hard work. That meant labouring in factories as well as going to school. It meant learning English in front of the TV, where the whole family tried to copy the newsreader Brian Naylor. It meant growing veges in the garden and making wine on the first day of summer, a family tradition back in Torre di Passeri. It was a stressful time, with two adults and five energetic kids in a three-bedroom home.

University beckoned for Jo, but family responsibilities took

Top: Greg Molinaro when he was a Central Station employee at Chapel Street in the 90s Above: Greg at HUB301 Records in 2016

precedence. After a short spell at university in Canberra, he came back to Melbourne to contribute to the family coffers and make the tough decisions. Living in dreary suburban Melbourne drove him crazy, but he bought a car and headed to the city. Exploring the gay underworld (as it was back then) introduced him to disco music – a revolutionary change from the rock music he'd heard on radio and television but had never related to. One thing led to another and he founded a disco record store. The rest is history, our history.

I feel privileged to have played a part in the story of Central Station Records under the creative direction of Giuseppe Palumbo. I was only a bit player, with no prior experience in business and no knowledge of the machinations of the music industry. I went through a baptism of fire. Within the first few hours of meeting Jo, I was corralled into the business. I had a day job selling export insurance, and an evening one trying to help a burgeoning record store chain in the throes of growing pains.

Compared with the excitement and energy of the new dance music industry, my day job soon seemed boring and dead-end. Within five years, I'd become a full-time employee. With the innocence of youth (always relative, we were in our mid-thirties), we took on the establishment. We fought the major recording companies who refused to share the market with upstarts promoting new-fangled music genres. We tackled unscrupulous landlords. We set up a record label from scratch and we spread out from Melbourne. We travelled the globe chasing new music.

In the course of all of this mayhem, Jo had the foresight to collect stuff – boxes and boxes of material tracking the rise and fall and rise again of our business and the music we focused on. All of these boxes sat in a shed on our farm in Queensland. Just waiting for the day we could find the time to commit to writing this memoir.

And here it is at long last ...

Morgan Williams

As a recording label, the original Central Station Records (and sub-labels) kicked off with vinyl releases and moved on to CDs

1. The Source

DJs talk about taking people on a journey – of lifting them up, bringing them down, and ultimately taking them to the peak. Clubbers talk about finding a haven of like-mindedness and liberation, where they can be as wild and weird as they like while feeling safe and in sync. Ravers talk about the sheer fun and physicality of sharing pills, pounding beats and pulsating light with thousands of other revellers in illicit locations. Words like 'soul', 'community' and 'experience' come up again and again. It all reeks of a religious experience – something very primitive and tribal. Dance music demands engagement. It bypasses the intellect and goes straight for the blood and nervous systems. You have to move. Sweat. Lose yourself in the moment.

How ironic then that it's all built on technology – synthesisers, drum machines, lasers and sophisticated pharmacology. But that's the beauty of it too. The marriage of our most primitive instincts and our most boundary-busting tools. As much as we sometimes bemoan more innocent days before Spotify and Auto-Tune, technology allows us to keep magic alive. There are Facebook pages with huge followings, not just for posting old pictures but also promoting parties for the forty-plus crowd who want to dance again to retro classics. And there are fifty-plus producers teaming up with kids on the other side of the world to release new tracks and find new audiences.

By general agreement, it all started with disco and we wouldn't have had disco without technology. 'In Australia, we could only experience disco as recorded music because people like Loleatta Holloway and productions with forty-piece orchestras were never going to come here,' points out Stephen Allkins, a towering figure in Sydney's unique dance scene. Starting in the late 70s, he played his own eclectic mix – 'anything you can dance to' – at Oxford Street clubs, Mardi Gras parties and Hordern Pavilion extravaganzas. The man has a fierce intellect and a take-no-prisoners style. When asked about the state of music today, he acknowledges the benefits of technology before launching into a scathing attack on the SYNC button and the dumbed-down output that American industry moguls catalogue as EDM (for 'electronic dance music'). 'There's no rhythm or melody,' he says. 'There is no music being played on ninety per cent of those tracks. It's all programmed and even then it's all a baseline and a kick. That's not music.'

Technology is a subject that sparks strong opinions and emotions in the DJ world. Vinyl stirs deep feelings, even among those like Steve Hill who happily show up to gigs these days with a USB stick. He's hard to pin down for an interview, travelling extensively to play and produce his hard dance, hard trance and hard style. Fresh from a trip to the UK and Europe, he says his shoulders are grateful for no longer having to haul around crates of vinyl, and he certainly doesn't miss being hostage to airlines losing his precious luggage. But he still loves his vinyl. 'I've got 14,500 in storage,' he says. 'It's too much to have in the house. But I've got them all racked up and I go visit my babies once or twice a month. I go say hi, let them know I'm still here.'

As a young DJ in Wellington, New Zealand, Steve even made a pilgrimage to Melbourne to check out the store that many friends had told him about. He laughs when recalling how he spent all of his play money on the first day, leaving nothing for the rest of his trip. After a stellar career in the UK as a DJ and producer, Steve moved to Sydney in 2003. 'Vinyl was still very popular when I got here,' he says. 'The phase-over to CDs was starting to happen, but the Central Station record store was huge. And they still had the influence. They were the tastemakers, the ones making the local dance music compilations that the punters were listening to. They made so many hits, and broke so many acts.'

For devotees, vinyl means much more than a simple delivery system for music. 'Nothing is like vinyl. It's the ultimate analogue music form,' says Stephan Győry who runs The Record Store in Crown Street (Darlinghurst, Sydney), one of the new-breed of vinyl shops that have sprung up in recent years. 'The internet has moved all consumption online. The only things left for retail to sell are either experiences or things that people still want to engage with. Vinyl is functional art. To make a record, it's not just the musicians. You need the cover artists.

Stephan Győry (right) with Giles Peterson in The Record Store (courtesy of Stephan Győry)

Even the gatefold cardboard sleeve – that is an art form; there's someone who does that for a living. There are so many different people who make a living in records. I think that's what makes them so human. And they're human-sized. Have you seen that web site Sleeveface? Check it out. It's pictures of people holding record covers in front of their heads … Hilarious.'

Stephan is contemptuous of media articles that attribute the so-called vinyl resurgence to hipster collectors. He says there is no demographic and storeowners aren't 'targeting' anyone. 'It's like we're a community and we all buy and sell records from each other,' he says. 'The thing is, if you treat records well, they don't wear out.'

Melbourne-based DJ Ken Walker – who has worked alongside the likes of Grandmaster Flash, Calvin Harris and DJ Jazzy Jeff – says that he has always welcomed new technology. He 'copped shit' for being one of the first DJs to play CDs, for example. But he owns more than 15,000 records and is positively poetic when describing the thrill of shipment day at Central Station. 'It was the smell, the imagery, the whole experience,' he says. 'There's nothing like opening a box – it might sound freakish, a fetish – and maybe it was! You'd crack open the vinyl. It was such an experience listening to a track for the first time. You don't have the same connection and love affair with an mp3 as you do with vinyl. You don't have that warmth, that beauty of the artwork, of pulling out the sleeve. Each record is a piece of your memory. I can pull out any record and remember a time playing it, which shop I bought it from.'

Most of the DJs interviewed for this book were vinyl fanatics as teenagers and got their first break because of their collections. They were also voracious readers and listeners, picking up everything they could about new music from magazines, radio programs and record store staff. Sooner or later, they discovered Central Station Records and a whole new world opened up. It was the source – the place where you could find twelve-inch singles of cutting-edge music from far and wide, the wellspring of inspiration, information and camaraderie.

When Gavin Campbell (of Razor Club and Razor Recordings fame) started DJing in 1983, he went straight to the 'really cool record shop at the City Square' and spent his entire student allowance cheque. Jo was the first person he met, and that day introduced him to a song called *White Horse* by Laid Back, something Gavin still plays to this day. 'Jo was central to the whole scene, not just in terms of the records he sourced but also the people he chose to give first access. His record shop was the place you went to find out what was happening. We all knew that Jo was breaking the law by stocking under-the-counter imports, but the music was incredible and he was such a lovable cowboy,' he says. 'There was another guy, Ray, who was the shop's funk expert. I didn't know what beat mixing was until I heard Ray mix together two copies of the same Madonna song. I knew the song, so pricked up my ears to what was going on. I was like a babe in the woods there for probably four years even though I had the coolest club in town, because I was coming from the alternative mentality of purely programming, not mixing. The shop had two massive tables, like roulette wheels, with rows of records organised alphabetically. It took me weeks to go through it all before my first gig.'

Taken at face value, Gavin could come across as a touch arrogant – as he spontaneously confesses, adding that it had more to do with his 'shyness in the presence of such musical knowledge' – but he's clearly a sweet and sensitive character with loads of creative flair. It's no surprise that fashion people and art-house musicians flocked to his clubs in the 80s and 90s. Nor that he should have gone on to co-producing a massive hit like the dance remix of Yothu Yindi's *Treaty*.

While Gavin was rubbing shoulders with the ultra-cool crowd in inner-Melbourne, John Course was a kid from the outer suburbs riding the rails into town to visit the source. 'I still remember Andy Van and I going back to Frankston and listening to the new music we'd bought – things like *Slice Me Nice* by Fancy and *Happy Song* by Boney M – that Italo disco movement thing. You went to Central Station to get records you couldn't get at Brashs at Frankston. And then the house music boom happened and Andy and I were DJing in the city more. For my first ever gig in the city, which was 1986, my records stayed at the club and I worked there five nights a week. I spent half of my pay at Central ... I built my classics catalogue there. You couldn't be a credible DJ unless you shopped at places like that.'

When interviewed for this book, John radiated gravitas. It's soon apparent that he knows his shit when it comes to music and music history. But he's still that passionate young kid when performing for a crowd, whether at a huge festival or an intimate club. He obviously enjoys what he does. In fact, passion for underground danceable music is what unites everyone interviewed. And Central Station was where they could – and did – share that passion. Even sub-teens.

'My love affair with Central Station Records started way back in 1985, when I was barely twelve years old,' remembers singer, songwriter and producer Peter Wilson. After discovering *Pulsation Club Show* and also *Dance Til Dawn* on Melbourne's 3RRR radio station, he became obsessed with visiting the source of the twelve-inch singles he'd heard – from Madonna's *Lucky Star* to Dead Or Alive's *My Heart Goes Bang*.

'Arriving at City Square and seeing the store for the first time was like pure magic. There was a buzz in the air, from getting out of Dad's car to walking through the walkway to the store. My first memory was approaching the store and hearing a freestyle mix of Divine's *Native Love* blasting loudly. Outside the store were four young break-dancer kids, and the atmosphere was electric. I can't explain it other than to say that it was like coming home.'

Peter Wilson in 1988 with Central Station purchases (courtesy of Peter Wilson)

From its Melbourne origins, Central branched out across Australia and New Zealand with physical stores, a thriving mail-order operation and a successful recording label that brought the whole dance music community together. Although DJs and vinyl remained at the core of the business, Central thrived by broadening the market and the offer, selling everything from turntables to party tickets, record bags and rave pants.

Sydney was the first city in the expansion program and ultimately its home base. Mark Vick (aka Mark Dynamix) was a teenager when he discovered the original store there. 'Walking around Pitt Street one day, I heard music coming out from a basement and was curious,' he remembers. 'Oh, there's another record store. This was in the day when there were plentiful record stores – one on every block at least – so it wasn't anything out of the ordinary. But when I got in there, it just felt like a whole new world was happening. I wasn't part of it, but I wanted to be. It was 1989 or 90, the days of really bright neon colour. Everything was very bold – the posters on the walls, the record sleeves. It was a visual feast as you walked down the stairs. And the ceiling was very low, so it kind of felt like a subterranean world. I had an instant compulsion to find out more.'

Mark went on to become a highly rated DJ and producer. Ever restless to go where his changing taste takes him, he's also acutely conscious of past buzzes and giving respect where due. In 2016, he took the lead in organising a tribute party for Paul Holden at Home nightclub in Sydney, after the legendary DJ's accidental death. 'I wondered what

DJs Mark Dynamix (left) and Paul Holden at a Sydney rave in 1998 (courtesy of Mark Vick)

The Source

we could do for Paul to show how appreciated he was,' he says. 'He gave so much to all of us. I was one of his little followers when I was sixteen years old and I learned much about mixing records together from watching him.'

Like Mark, Jesse Desenberg (aka Kid Kenobi) was very young when he began shopping at the Pitt Street store. 'When I was about thirteen or fourteen, I would skip lunch every now and again and save up money to buy records,' he recalls. 'I was really into hip hop, like New Jack Swing. You had to get that stuff on import and the only place I knew where to go was Central Station. When I went down the stairs at Pitt Street, I actually felt I was being transported to New York. It was in a cool, almost-warehouse space, with wooden floors. I'd go up to the counter and say, "I'm into hip hop. What's the latest you've got?" and they'd pull out this folder and you'd look through it and say, "Can I have a listen to that?" Far out. It was the coolest thing I could think of.'

Someone who definitely doesn't fit the classic DJ mould is Maynard – the former Triple J radio host formerly known as Maynard F# Crabbes. These days, he 'still does retro sets all around the place'. In fact, he had just returned from being the MC and host for the Vengaboys' 2016 tour of Australia when interviewed for this history. With his cultured-sounding voice and acute sense of irony, he manages to sound both authoritative and irreverent at the same time. 'If I'd been able to sing, I probably would never have been a DJ,' he says. 'It was just a way of performing. I can't mix to save my life. Most DJs don't want to talk, whereas I'm very happy to talk. In fact, it often hides the very bad joins of my mixes.'

In the mid 80s – when he was doing a Saturday morning program (*Radio Stupid*) on 2SER – Maynard was impressed by the new Pitt Street store's generosity in lending records to community radio presenters. Later at Triple J, he headed to the Oxford Street store for twelve-inch imports ranging from Kylie Minogue's *Better the Devil You Know* to Capella's *Helyon Halib* (otherwise known as *Work it to the Bone*). Having found his way into radio via cabaret, Maynard didn't take himself or his playlist too seriously. 'I really enjoyed being able to play dance music in the morning and I would have been one of the few people doing that at that time,' he says. 'Sometimes I'd play twelve-inches in the morning which was also an unusual thing. And a couple of times – if I liked a song – I'd pick up the needle and play it again immediately, which nobody does on radio.'

Belying his madcap image, Maynard prepared himself well for

our wander down memory lane. His list of must-mentions included the 'legendary' status of Central Station's Christmas parties, the 'petty jealousy going on among DJs about who would get the best stuff' on shipment days, and the 'social milieu' at Oxford Street. 'When everyone was together for the opening of the import crate, it was the who's who of the DJing circuit,' he says. 'It was always a bit of a Saturday morning there as well. If you were going for a wander up Oxford Street, it was always good to drop in there with your date and hang around and see who else was there with their date.'

But Maynard's most revealing story is about encountering one of his listeners in the store. 'I was doing Free FM breakfast at the time and I'd said something on air about Barbra Streisand after playing the Pet Shop Boys' cover of her song, *Somewhere*. Suddenly someone charged up to me and said at the top of his lungs, "How come you don't like Barbra Streisand?" I admitted, "Well I do like Barbra Streisand. I just don't like her ballads." Then he said, "So you don't actually hate Barbra Streisand?" I told him, "No, my favourite song of hers is *Don't Rain On My Parade*. But I hate *Evergreen*." He looked at me and said, "Well that's OK then" and he turned on his heel and went back to what he was doing. So I would have encounters like that at Central Station. It was a place where my listeners could meet me and have a chat to me about stuff.'

John Ferris is one of three big-name DJ brothers (the others being

Maynard with DJ Sveta at the 1993 Sydney Gay & Lesbian Fair Day at Jubilee Park, Glebe (Photo by Mazz Image, www.mazzimage.com, courtesy of Maynard)

John Ferris hamming it up to promote (via his Facebook page) the Keep Sydney Open rally in October 2016 (courtesy of John Ferris)

Stephen and Pee Wee Ferris) who were high in the pecking order on shipment days. Their upbringing made them natural party animals. 'Our mother had six kids in seven years,' says John. 'We always felt like it was a party at our house – especially when we were teenagers. We had friends over all the time, so lots of dogs, lots of kids and lots of group activity. I remember buying music from ages six or seven, but I think that was because of the social aspect to it. People would come to our place and we would say, "Listen to this music." We were pretty big consumers of music and we wanted to talk about it.'

In 1986, John was living in a share house in Darlinghurst, throwing parties for friends and playing the music he'd picked up while travelling around Europe and America – when acts like David Bowie, Talking Heads and Public Image Limited were experimenting with disco or African sounds. 'Dancing was coming into it. It wasn't just music to listen to. So I bought a twenty-eight-piece vinyl box set called *The History of Disco (1973-1983)* and it was a great tool to have,' he says.

One memorable night, John was playing these tunes when all hell broke loose. 'The party was so rammed and busy at one stage that the whole crowd just collapsed on top of me. A light fell down and completely destroyed the turntable and speakers ... we all thought it was hilarious. Then somebody managed to get a shopping trolley up through the terrace house to the top floor, put my fish bowl and other things in it, and ram the trolley through the balcony so that it landed on a car below. There was smashed glass everywhere. That was when I decided that I couldn't keep doing this. It was out of control.' So John and his friends found 'empty' venues in Kings Cross that were happy to host their parties. From there, he built an illustrious DJing career, which culminated in being recognised for his 'Outstanding Contribution To Dance Music' in the inaugural Australian Dance Music Awards in 2000.

'The thing about Central Station is that it changed the game,' he says. 'Up until they opened in Sydney, it was a very tight little circle of relationships between DJs and the import store buyers. The stores didn't bring in much disco. Generally they'd get in five records of something they knew would sell and that was it. So it was a big shit fight between a small group of people who liked that kind of music. Often the stores gave preference to gay DJs because most of the disco venues were gay. Then Central Station came in and completely upset that working model. They ordered a lot of stock and didn't really care if you were gay or straight. They knew their stuff. And they didn't stock any rock. It was just disco and they got all the different styles. It meant that I wasn't playing the second best records; I was playing the records I wanted to play.'

Another big-name DJ and producer, Simon Lewicki (aka Groove Terminator) would travel to Melbourne to buy records from Central before a store opened in his hometown, and he credits its eventual Adelaide presence with stimulating the local scene. 'In the late 80s, early 90s when Central opened, there was a proliferation of clubs because you could get access to the music. It was like a meeting ground. You could go there and hang.' Simon is still hanging with the Central crowd. After living in the US for a decade producing film scores for movie houses, he married an Adelaide woman, came back to Sydney and now runs the publishing arm of Ministry of Sound Australia, working at the same location where the current incarnation of Central Station is based.

Trent Rackus, who is part of this very crew nowadays, paints the picture: 'I always think of Jo as the godfather of dance music in Sydney. He comes to a Ministry lunch and there will be myself, Jamie, Tim and Simon sitting there thinking all of this was born out of something that Jo did. Tim is now running Ministry of Sound Australia; Simon is still out there DJing and working as a music publisher; Jamie is running Central Station that Jo and Morgan have a share in, as does Tim; and I'm running arguably the largest electronic DJ agency in Australia. Quite interesting that he was the seed for us to grow into what we are today.'

[Editor's note: Sony Entertainment acquired the Ministry of Sound trademark in 2016.]

Brisbane was the fourth city to benefit from Central's arrival. A former DJ, Central Station employee and store-owner, Murray Brown, remembers his first encounter with the Elizabeth Street store: 'As you walked up the stairwell next to Hungry Jacks and started going up the first flight of stairs, you could hear the base – doof, doof – coming down the stairs. As you got up higher and higher, the base got louder and louder. Then you opened the door and there was this oasis of people who were on the same level of love for music. There was just this energy in the shop. All the hardcore guys would be in the hardcore quarter, and the breaks guys would be all in their section. It was just really special.'

Cadell Bradnock has been a full-time working DJ for more than twenty years. He believes art and passion are still alive in the scene, but misses the old 'hands on' days when music was more valued. He started playing happy hardcore and breakbeat at friends' houses in 1994, the year after he arrived in Sydney. Nothing he'd seen in his native New Zealand had prepared him for the scale and intensity of the shopping experience that was Central's Oxford Street store in Sydney. 'Chaos! That's the best word to describe it,' he says. 'You came in on Tuesday or Wednesday when the shipments arrived and people were like cockroaches – DJs appearing out of nowhere and rummaging through vinyl. It used to be an awesome, awesome buzz. But it was organised chaos. There were not that many copies of a particular track. A lot of stuff was very exclusive. If you didn't get a copy – and there might be five or ten altogether – you wouldn't be able to get it again until two, three, maybe four weeks later. So you were in a hurry to get down there and make sure you got a good listen to this stuff. It was a lot of fun. The music playing. Everyone talking. It was very social. These days, there is nowhere near the social aspect that there used to be. What they've been doing, where they're at, where they're playing. It was really cool. It felt like a community.'

In record store culture, it didn't matter what you looked like or where you hailed from. All that mattered was that you could talk music. And rave culture was even more inclusive. The euphoria went past drugs and youth. People felt that all sorts of possibilities were opening up.

A young Rebecca Poulsen (aka BeXta) was studying at the Conservatorium of Music in 1993, when fellow students introduced her to Central and Brisbane's club scene. She immediately fell in love. 'I liked the alternative of going to a place and dancing for hours,' she says.

Music Wars

'You'd go to pubs and get pushed around and stood on and picked up ... it just didn't work for me. There was such a positive energy around the rave scene. There were no punch-ups and I don't think it was because people may have been on pills. It was because of the music and the connections that were happening. There was heaps of passion about an emerging genre.' After landing her first gig via the Brisbane store, Rebecca became the first female DJ to tour nationally. She also released a series of successful CDs on the Central label.

Nicole Fossati was editor of Sydney's 'dance music bible', *3D World*, from 1994 to 1997. 'It was such a magical time in history,' she says. 'We were part of something. The only thing I can draw a similarity to is maybe the 60s summer-of-love type revolution. We were involved in a movement – electronic music, dance music, rave music, club music ... whatever you want to call it. It was new, it was visceral, it was subversive, it was hugely misunderstood and we were fantastically grateful for that.'

As a professional wordsmith and multi-media maven, Nicole can string words together well – no surprises there. But even by email she crackles with energy and passion. 'We started radio stations, we formed organisations, we lobbied councils, we fought police, we were tight knit, we learned heaps and we forged friendships that have lasted until

The May 2006 edition of '3D World' featured Central Station's 30th birthday celebrations on the cover, with BeXta cutting the cake. (Reproduced with the permission of Street Press Australia P/L)

today, literally,' she writes. 'So many of the people I associated with professionally back in those days have forged great careers as heads of industries, organisations, corporations, media, marketing, entertainment. I was just speaking earlier with Rebekah Horne, who's just left her post as the Chief Digital Officer at Ten to head up that role at the NRL. I met her twenty years ago when she was a new label rep for Warner Music with Michael Richardson. He's now the Head of Spotify. Tim McGee, the store manager from Central Station Records, now runs Ministry of Sound Australia. Mark Poston was an EMI rep; he's been the head of EMI, and then Warner, he's on the ARIA board and god knows what else. It was a very unique time for Gen X.'

From the very beginning, Central Station was shaped by the underground dance culture emerging around the world. But it was also a catalyst for the diverse and cutting-edge scene we've developed in our part of the globe.

After working for Central Station as A&R (artists and repertoire) manager from 2000 to 2009, Ashley Gay started Xelon Entertainment, a Melbourne-based company that provides global digital music distribution services for artists. He shopped at Central's Flinders Street store in Melbourne from age fourteen, volunteered at Kiss FM from age sixteen, and had a go at DJing before getting into A&R. In the process he built up a strong network of DJs and artists and a broad perspective of the music industry. 'The stores used to get weekly shipments from the UK, Germany, US, Holland, Italy, France etcetera, so the DJs were influenced by all types of records and sounds coming from all parts of the world,' he points out. 'This was never the case if you went into record shops in other countries. They basically stocked what was released only out of their home territory. This one point alone is the reason why the Australian dance music scene has always been strong and diverse, and influenced so many people to start playing out.'

Mark Vick and Rebecca Poulsen back up this view. Both have toured and produced extensively, so they're in a position to compare scenes. Mark puts it this way: 'Central Station Records took all of these influences from around the world and we were getting exposed to equal amounts of records from the UK, USA and Europe, especially Italy and Germany. If you go to Germany even now, they mostly play all German music. But we got records from all around the world. This place was like a melting pot of world music.' Rebecca makes a similar point: 'At the beginning, there were big differences between the European countries and the UK. Musically they were quite different, and a fair way ahead of Australia. There were people like Central who worked really hard to get Australia on the map – knowing what was going on, getting the latest releases, touring artists, building the scene here to be part of that international movement.'

The music movement went hand in hand with a social change movement. Dance culture grew out of separate marginalised sub-cultures, and when it became so popular that it crossed over into mainstream success, barriers broke down and cross-cultural acceptance became the norm. Nowhere was that more apparent than in Central Station stores. Describing himself as a 'socially awkward person', Jon Wicks sums up a sentiment that many people express one way or the other: 'Central Station was the anchor of a particular vibe that happened. Everyone was welcome there. You had your hardcore music and your gay handbag music. It was really indicative of those early years of inclusion and excitement.'

Although the Central Station stores are no longer with us, the spirit lives on in the recording label, which Jo and Morgan resurrected from the ashes of an ill-fated sale. It also lives on in the extended family of creatives who have ongoing professional and social links with them. Matt Nugent, a popular DJ in Brisbane in the 90s, now runs an artist management service in Sydney. Once upon a time, he managed Central's Brisbane store. 'They are such lovely, down-to-earth guys,' he says of his former employers. 'They've got that thing for life, that passion to try things out, do things. That's what this era is about. Parties, fun, happy times. Music bringing people together. And they were very good at bringing people together. They still are.'

In 2005, Mark Gerber and his friends took over the site of Central Station's most iconic store – 46 Oxford Street – after it had lain vacant for a year. After a major refurbishment, they opened as the Oxford Art Factory in 2007 – a unique and artsy venue for live and electronic music. 'Coming down here after purchasing vinyl for years in this space was quite surreal,' says Mark. 'The dance scene and electronic world of music would not have grown exponentially as it did without Jo and Morgan. They had everything down there ... clothing, hip hop ... That's very important for an art industry to get a leg up. You couldn't really foresee the Australian community growing as fast as it did without places like Central offering a connection to the rest of the world. You were able to pick up your European and American imports, and some rare ones at that. Morgan's and Jo's passion and knowledge were absolutely vital.'

Thinking back to Central's contribution to the dance scene, Mark wonders whether the site itself may have affected its tenants. 'Maybe there's something in the building that makes people want to be creative and think about the community. Maybe it's because we're underground and below Oxford Street. Maybe it's also the fact that I'm not that much younger than Jo and Morgan, and have a history with the area as well.'

So much for the macro picture. What about the micro level? Without prompting, most former staffers say Central Station was massively important in their lives. People met promoters, DJ friends and future life partners. They learned from Jo's work ethic and business nous. They benefited from Morgan's social skills and market-reading abilities. And they saw how people could have fun and still be successful.

Mikel Goodman (aka DJ Fenix) worked for Central for a short time in the 90s while making his mark as 'a superstar DJ/rave promoter'. He packs a lot of personality into his emailed answers, and now runs a promotional gear company, so it's not hard to imagine how sensational his space-themed parties must have been. 'Morgan (and Jo) were instrumental in my career,' he writes between emoticons. 'I remember being out the back of Central Station interviewing international acts for a TV show on Channel 31 and Morgan came out and asked what time I was playing at that night's big rave party. I told him I wasn't actually playing for that promoter and within thirty minutes I was doing the warm-up set for the main international act. Now that's called "pulling strings" and I am forever grateful to Morgan (and Jo) for all they did for me. I looked to Morgan and still do as a mentor and his advice and guidance have *really* helped.'

But Harry's story takes the cake. Nowadays, Harry Katsanevas (aka Hakka or Harry K) runs the Family super-club in Brisbane and was recently voted DJ of the Year by the local LGBTI community. With his chiselled jaw and buffed-up body, he's described as 'a Greek god'. Back in the 90s, when he started working for Central, he was anything but. 'I didn't know I was gay,' Harry explains. 'I think that's why they wanted me to work there, because I was very straight-laced. I didn't drink. My passion was music. I come from a very Greek family, and there was no gayness around. Working with Jo and Morgan, it clicked. It was OK to be gay and you can be successful and live a happy normal life. They were always very forward thinkers and they had their fingers on the pulse on a lot of different things.'

Former customers and staff volunteer many stories about Jo and Morgan – mostly about outrageous behaviour or stunning acts of generosity. Nick Dunshea offers two that run to type. Nick has only had three jobs in his life and the first two involved Central. He worked in the South Melbourne distribution centre fresh out of high school in the late 80s, and later went to Shock Records where Central was one of his biggest labels. Now running Liberator Music within The Mushroom Group, he fields phone calls and makes launch decisions while being interviewed. 'They're unique individuals,' he says. 'I used to travel with them overseas. I always felt that if you were ever going to have a weird night out, it would be with them.

From left: Nick Dunshea, Morgan Williams and Charles Caldas in the south of France, before the infamous trip to Bangkok (courtesy of Nick Dunshea)

'There was a time when Charles Caldas, who was the CEO of Shock (he's now the head of Merlin in London), Joel Whitford (who was the head of Shock Exports) and myself, happened to be in Bangkok with Morgan and Jo. We said we'd go out for dinner and they invited us down to where they were staying. Suffice to say that we were a little surprised that the idea was that we would have dinner there, just wearing towels. Then they took us into a nightclub, which was in the complex, and it soon became apparent that we were well and truly outside our comfort zone. So Morgan said, "You know what, guys? I think you should go. You said you were up for something crazy, but we think we've shown you enough. Right?"'

'Morgan and Jo came to my wedding fifteen years ago,' he adds later. 'They were late. They looked a little dishevelled. They handed me an envelope which, from memory, just had "Nick" written on it, not "Nick and Margarita", my new wife. I said thanks and they said, "When you open it, you'll find one joint. There were supposed be two but we smoked one on the way here." Then I opened it and there was a thousand dollars cash inside and one joint. I think they were so stoned that they left pretty quickly.'

Surprisingly, few people talk about the legal and political side of Central Station's history. Most people were unaware of the troubles that almost cost Jo and Morgan the business. Morgan didn't bother to raise the subject when talking to Jon Wicks about setting up a store in Canberra, even though that was when and where the most intense campaigning occurred. Although Jo did his best to raise hell about the issues wherever and whenever he could, DJs generally had little interest in how the records were sourced ... only that they were. Much of this book will be unfamiliar territory for even close associates of Jo and Morgan in the dance music scene. It's time the whole story was told.

Special thanks must go to Mike Kerry for helping to broaden the scope of this project with his passionate arguments about the social significance of the dance movement, and to George Klestinis (aka DJ George Vagas) for his many insights and his treasure trove of pictures.

Seeing his whole life as 'a transition', George is the ultimate genre-jumper, multi-tasker and new wave spotter. 'I've done a lot of things where I was the first one to bring changes,' he says. 'I admire all sorts of music, whether it be punk, acid house, disco, techno, rockabilly, psychobilly, hard core, gabber.' In his hometown of Adelaide, he had been the drummer for a punk band, Grong Grong, which was on the verge of touring America with the Dead Kennedys when the lead singer over-dosed on heroin. Then he DJd punk and ska at a club called the Electric Torture Room. 'It was weird. I'm European – Macedonian – and here I am playing all this skinhead stuff to neo-Nazi skinheads! They were the nicest lads who loved their music.' Later, in 1988, he met Danny Rampling at Shoom in London, along with Paul Oakenfold and Steve Jervier, after which George became a pioneer of acid house in Australia. He also met Paul Lekakis (famous for *Boom Boom Boom Let's Go to Your Room*) at a club in New York in the late 80s.

But George Vagas, the 'godfather of Australian hardcore', has never limited himself to music. Fashion and film are other strings to his bow.

He became Flipside's sales manager at Central's Oxford Street store after creating, developing and pitching the idea itself. Later, he went on to become a top rave DJ, touring all capital cities and producing the hardcore hit track *Hyperdome*. In 1994, he also founded a successful touring company, booking and touring all the hardcore gabber DJs to Australia. He now makes short films. 'George Vegas was the best. We sold thousands of his hardcore tapes,' says Jo. 'He also used to bring in hard core bands from Holland and pack them into his parties.'

Many fascinating characters are yet to be introduced. If you get lost following who's who, go to appendix 2 where you'll find mini-bios of key players. Sadly, many people have passed away or proved untraceable. VALE John Cassar, Paul Jackson, Paul Holden, Angus Galloway (aka DJ Angus, DJ Bribe) and Edwin Morrow (aka DJ Edwin). Where are you, Ray Herd and Vivien Rogers? You are all missed.

But our two leading characters have most of the speaking parts – it's their story after all. Others usually see Jo as a crazy Italian, a risk-taker and reveller who's also shrewd, caring and full of integrity. He's the alpha one. Morgan's the calm one, the social connector, the one who smooths over Jo's bluntness and brings reality to bear from his risky ideas. They don't see themselves exactly that way. Jo complains about having to make Morgan's crazy ideas work, and Morgan sees himself as the lowly blow-in who was thrust into taking strategic action when the boss-man (Jo) told him to do some real work for a change.

Together they were – and are – a formidable team. Enjoy the ride with them and the far-reaching Central Station Records network.

George Klestinis (aka DJ George Vagas) circa 1995 (courtesy of George)

2. Giuseppe Palumbo

An activist is made, not born. Temperament plays its part, of course, but circumstances are crucial. Early experiences in life moulded Giuseppe Palumbo into an agitator – like a record press stamping hot vinyl.

He was born in 1950 in the small town of Torre di Passeri, in the province of Abruzzi, in central Italy. His family was dirt-poor, and he had a few medical problems and personal eccentricities that set him apart and alienated some teachers. Throughout childhood, he felt misunderstood, neglected and exploited. Strangely enough, he says that he was quite happy (between fits of temper and indignation), because three things inspired him – maths, music and Mother Nature.

The second of five children and the first son, he was in a hurry to come into the world. 'My mother told me that she was screaming with pain a short time into labour. Then, kaboom! I just popped out.'

Chaos greeted the newborn. 'Our back yard was full of animals on the loose – from pigs, donkeys and chickens to feral cats. From my point of view, the world was completely mad. One of my earliest memories is of smashing glassware in the family buffet at age six. Mum asked me, "Why did you do that?" I told her that I couldn't help myself. I felt the need for destruction. "I don't want to be here, Mum," I wailed. She didn't hit me. She was a kind and loving mother and I'm very grateful for her patience, because I was really angry as a child. Looking back now, I suspect I had a touch of Asperger's syndrome – a few exceptional talents and a major dose of issues around fitting in.'

Because of problems with his lungs, left leg and possibly malnutrition, Giuseppe needed regular injections, hundreds of them. He hated those needles and fought against them with all of his might.

One time he was so nervous and bucked so hard, that he made the nurse break the syringe in his rump. Ouch.

As a member of the Communist Party, his father was barred from jobs where Christian Democrats were doing the hiring. 'I loved him because he was my father but I didn't have a lot to do with him,' Giuseppe recalls. 'He wasn't around much, preferring to sit in cafes – smoking, drinking and playing cards until late at night.'

In his father's absence, the eldest son went overboard on responsibility, assuming the role of protector for his mother and siblings. In this respect, he tended to take after Grandpa Giuseppe, his father's father, who was highly regarded in the village as a good family man, a decent provider and a strong man of honour. Their temperaments were also similar – tending towards loner.

Giuseppe's love of music came from the other grandfather, his mother's father, a civil engineer who specialised in power stations. 'I used to spend a lot of time with him, watching him draft designs and listening to classical music. All these beautiful operas he had. I'd sneak in to his office to rifle through his vinyl collection – old 33s and 78s of classical music and Neapolitan songs. The female voices were my favourites. I never listened to the words, only the way the voice followed the melody and spoke to the soul.'

An early photo of Giuseppe's mother

Giuseppe's parents on their wedding day

The grandmothers were very influential too. From his father's mother, Giuseppe inherited the excitability and emotion that he tries to suppress (and often can't). His mother's mother was his role model for working hard. 'She was the most active and energetic woman I've ever met,' he says. 'She would happily bake cakes and cook for fifty people – even people you could kill, they were so annoying – and then wash all of the dishes by herself, stacking them up against the wall.'

His mother was less secretive than most of his relatives. One day he said to her, 'You know. I'm totally different in this family. Are you sure that Dad is my father?' To his surprise, she slapped him. 'Don't you ever talk to me like that ever again!' she said, with hurt in her eyes. Giuseppe had no clue that she would interpret his words as questioning her honour. It was a spontaneous remark, intended as a joke. But the truth was that he did feel like an outsider in his own family. Where had he come from? Was he some sort of avatar? Had he come back to this planet at the wrong time and place?

There was never enough to eat at home, so he went into the fields and took what he could find – apricots, peaches, cherries and figs. Thousands of figs were rotting on the ground. Big ones, small ones. He came to love figs, and still does, but he didn't love feeling like a scrounger. In town, he would hustle for leftover pasta and bread, broken eggs and other stuff that market stalls or restaurants would normally throw away. He would wrap up the haul and take it home to his mother.

He was always badly dressed and dirty because there was no running water at home, let alone hot water. That was tough. The weather was confronting for most of the year. In winter, the temperature might drop as low as minus ten. Spring was nasty and windy, Summer was hot, and Autumn was cold and miserable. It was pleasant for only about four months of the year. The area was prone to earthquakes too – with a couple of tremors a week – and deep cracks ran through and around the walls of his ancient school.

Cracks or not, school should have been a sanctuary, a haven for his developing mind, but the system worked against that. 'Rich kids were given books and help, while poor kids got a kick in the arse and fuck all else,' he says. Being poor was only part of his problem, though. He was different. His brain worked differently. By the age of three he was thinking about mathematical equations and by six or seven he was dreaming about Einstein formulas. His body had a few kinks too – he was left-handed and had a hearing impediment.

Teachers forced him to switch to his right hand, tying his left behind his back so that he couldn't use it. 'My right hand became very angry. I used to push the pen so hard that I would perforate every page of the endless writing exercises that teachers made me do. My protests were ignored. The left hand grew weaker, and my handwriting remains abysmal to this day.'

His hearing problem went undiagnosed, but not unnoticed. Unable to afford textbooks or even notepads, he had to listen intently in class, watching the teacher's lips and committing everything to memory. But he had a tendency to turn his head sideways to favour the better ear. He would be focusing deeply on the subject – taking it to multiple combinations and permutations – then SLAP! The teacher would smack his face. 'Why did you do that?' he'd ask. 'Because you were staring at me,' came the reply. He would counter, 'I wasn't staring at you. I was thinking.' It was all to no avail. Some teachers took a set against him – convinced that he was challenging their authority. Later on he began to do exactly that, but not at the beginning.

For some years, Giuseppe wore equipment to balance his hearing. 'I recognised the problem ages ago, but I didn't do anything about it for a long time,' he admits with a laugh. 'I can't imagine how many people

Giuseppe on his confirmation day, aged about seven

I've freaked out in my life by giving them the side face! It's off-putting, I know. But nowadays I'm more concerned about tinnitus, caused by listening to too much loud music. People say it's incurable, but it can be controlled through sound therapy and meditation. There is a lot of information on the internet now that I've used to reduce my problems dramatically. The Chinese say that the function of the left kidney is linked, so you must address that with certain herbs they prescribe. The ringing in the inner ears is also an alarm from the body telling you that your head is not aligned, balanced.'

In a sense, he was an accidental rebel. Some things came easily to him, like numbers and patterns. On the other hand, the simple idea of holding back from saying what he really thought never occurred to him. He has never been any good at toeing the diplomatic line, but he was a rebel with plenty of cause. (I was unfairly provoked, Your Honour!) The more teachers underestimated him, the more he sought to show them up and the cockier his attitude appeared. He was incapable of bending to authority or grovelling to keep the peace. It wasn't a power or ego thing. What drove him then (and still does) was to learn, achieve and feel free.

One episode in his years at intermediary school shows how blithely he would get himself into hot water. He was about fifteen. His Italian language and literature teacher had ignored him for nine months. Even though he would be waving his hand around energetically, she would look expectantly at everyone else until finally groaning, 'OK, fine, Giuseppe'.

One cold, dark and miserable day, he boarded the Pullman bus after school. It was full, and he found himself facing this teacher. For half an hour, he looked at her calmly and said nothing. 'What did I have to lose? She already hated me.' The standoff only finished when the teacher left the bus at her stop and he continued to the railway station. The following day he had a religious class. The priest was talking about Michelangelo and homosexuality, and his obvious distaste offended Giuseppe's sense of logic. So he said, 'Excuse me. You've been saying all along that God made us in his image, equal to himself. We are his creation. Therefore, God must accept homosexuals as much as anyone else.'

The aftermath of this innocent argument caught Giuseppe by surprise. The class fell completely silent to begin with. Then chaos erupted. Desks were thrown over and papers flew around. What had he said? He was a sheltered boy. He didn't understand the concept of sexuality. Nor did many of his classmates, most likely, but they understood well enough that the priest had no comeback. His authority had been undermined. While he stood there speechless, the female Italian teacher – the one that Giuseppe had ignored on the bus – stormed in from the next room. Everybody ran for their chairs. 'You have no idea how wonderful it was to watch the chaos from the back of the room,' he remembers.

His enemy slammed a bundle of examination papers down, and humiliated the priest by restoring the order he had lost. Looking straight at Giuseppe, she said, 'Yesterday, some of you on the Pullman ignored me. You didn't say hello. You didn't say one word'. He put his hand up. 'Excuse me. I am the person you are referring to. For the last nine months, you've helped everybody else but ignored me. So that's exactly what I did to you.' Again, he thought this was a perfectly legitimate and logical point to make. For his contribution, he was presented with a 'Fail' in Italian at the end of the year. 'OK, to be fair, I probably deserved to fail anyway because I didn't like the subject much – unlike Latin, French and English – but I still bristle at the memory of her treatment of me.'

Nor did he lack for things that affronted him outside of the classroom. From a very young age, he was expected to work after school.

He first job was with a distributor, packing buttons. 'The only thing I got out of that gig was a meal, and a crap one at that. Later, I worked in a poultry factory, where I'd do the job of three men, cleaning thousands of chooks a week, and get just two bucks for my efforts in today's money. Others would take home fifty!'

To a fair-minded person, this was outrageously unjust: 'I always felt used by the system, the family and the mafia. As a little kid, mafia types would make me run errands, delivering parcels that I must not look at, often five kilometres away there and back. Life was hard. When it got too much, I would run away from home. I'd tell my mother, "I'm going away for a few days. Don't look for me. I'll be in the bush". My friend, Dante, and I would wade across rivers and roam the mountains, often climbing trees to escape wolves. We'd just hang around on the branches until they disappeared – sometimes twenty-four hours. Those were great times.'

Grandpa Giuseppe insisted that his grandson learn a few trades. The first one was helping in the garden. The boy hated it. Pulling weeds, picking vegetables, and carrying baskets of grapes on his head was hard labour. Didn't his grandfather realise that he could do more than that? Later on, he was obliged to learn hairdressing, welding, carpentry and printing, the latter being the only one he liked. But his intention was to go to university and study mathematics and applied science. He had an affinity for physics, and was fascinated by the structure of atoms and the forces of magnetism and gravity.

In 1967, the year that he turned seventeen and was due to choose his path at tertiary level, the family decided to emigrate to Australia. His father had been working in a timber mill when he severed his hand in a terrible accident and was laid off. A friend of his suggested moving to Australia. 'We'll find jobs for you and your five children,' he promised.

'So Dad went to Melbourne and stayed with his friend for about six months until he'd found a house. Then the rest of us followed. After going to Rome to get photo identities and health checks, I started to have second thoughts. Grandpa Palumbo was dead by this time and Grandma was devastated about losing us too. I found myself promising to stay. As well as feeling sorry for her, I had been accepted into university and was looking forward to it.'

Back at intermediary school, though, Giuseppe found that he couldn't understand one word the teacher was saying. He had missed half a dozen lessons because of the trip to Rome and his mind was distracted. All he could think about was his family shipping out. One day, he realised what he had to do. He said to himself, 'Dad is maimed and Mum can't cope providing for my younger brother and sisters on her own. My older sister is capable but not as strong as I am. What the fuck am I doing? I'm the only one who can save my family from hell'. So he simply sneaked away, told nobody, met his family in Rome, got on the boat and left. His grandma 'screamed and screamed' when she found out.

Mother and children arrived in Australia in December 1967 and moved straight into the three-bedroom house in Glen Waverley that the father had bought. 'I remember that it was a really hot day. Forty degrees,' remembers Jo. 'I was lying on the grass and somebody gave me a beer to drink. I'd never tried beer before. I didn't like the taste, but I still managed to get drunk, and that made me become very moderate in the consumption of alcohol for the rest of my life.'

The house was cramped for a family of seven, but there was bushland close by and abundant bird life in the front garden, so Giuseppe was rapt. He would spend hours watching the birds through the windows. Across the road, the neighbour's garden – brimming with hydrangeas, a floral favourite in Melbourne suburbia – was also a source of fascination. One day, this very neighbour knocked on the Palumbos' door, bearing a huge bunch of flowers for Giuseppe's mother. 'Welcome to Australia,' she said before hugging everyone in the family one by one.

Giuseppe Palumbo, about eighteen years old, in the garden of the family house at Glen Waverley

'It was the strangest feeling in my life,' remembers Giuseppe. 'I was really taken by her warmth. And that made me fall in love with Australian people. No one had ever hugged me before!'

The neighbour offered free English lessons twice a week. At a family meeting, the Palumbos agreed to stick to English at home, so they made good progress. With plenty of factories nearby, a national shortage of labour and a government in favour of immigration – for whites and Christians in any case – the family found their feet in their adopted land. Giuseppe's father got a job with the Country Road Board, pulling apart tractor and heavy machinery engines and cleaning them. His mother worked in a factory in Glen Waverley, making moulds for Old Spice aftershave. Giuseppe worked there too for a few months. The family had to repay their borrowings over eight years, and the lender's rep would visit the house every month to collect installments. 'We also gave to the church,' Giuseppe remembers. 'I was a good Catholic boy in those days. I accepted that if you wanted to get along in life you had to get along with the church. You'd kiss the archbishop's shoes if you had to.'

On the boat, he had dreamed of becoming a singer, but in Melbourne he did the sensible thing and enrolled at Glen Waverley High School to study for his matriculation. As in Italy, he divided the teachers into two camps. His English teacher, for instance, was very supportive. He recognised that the teenager had arrived only two months before, and that he was making a huge effort to learn the language. His maths teacher, on the other hand, was not a fan. In retrospect, Giuseppe recognises that he rubbed him up the wrong way by being such a smart aleck in class.

On one occasion, this maths teacher set the class a challenge – to resolve a question first published in the Monash University Year Book of 1915, and uncracked ever since. Giuseppe took the problem home to have a go. Luckily, his parents were away at the time, and he had the whole house to myself. After a twelve-hour night shift at the factory, he stayed up scribbling away with butcher's paper and black chalk. Assuming that the solution would be complex, he went through dozens of sheets of paper trying to work it out, getting very frustrated in the process. Two nights later, though, he realised that the solution was blindingly simple.

'My brain is usually best at three o'clock in the morning, when everyone else is asleep and I can tap into the universal energy. Since I was a kid, I've used a technique that I call "ten-minute Zen-ism". I take deep breaths and focus on whatever subject is troubling me. My subconscious always works it out. Breathe in, breathe out. Relax and then suddenly kachung! The answer comes.'

He was over the roof with excitement. A high school student had cracked a puzzle that all those university students couldn't! At maths class the next day, he shot up his hand eagerly.

'Yeah, what do you want?'

'You know that question from 1915? I think I've resolved it.'

'Nah, you couldn't have done that one,' the teacher sneered.

After Giuseppe showed his solution, the teacher cold-shouldered him even more obviously. Much worse than that, other kids in the class started calling him names. 'I had a thick accent and looked like a wog. Maybe I looked gay too, because they would whistle at me in the street and yell ugly homophobic stuff. I felt even more isolated than in Italy.'

After matriculating, he enrolled at the Australian National University in Canberra to study political science and applied maths. For a short time, he delivered milk in the morning before lectures. Then he started worrying about the expense and his family complaining about his absence, so he dropped out and went back to Melbourne. To begin with, he worked in factories while he brushed up on his English. Then he landed a job as a teller with the National Bank in Fitzroy North. Banks appealed to him because he wanted to learn how the financial system worked. Watching his family's accountant as he went through the figures – his machine going 'click, click, click' – had always fascinated him. Balance sheets and profit and loss statements were as entertaining to him as Graham Kennedy on *In Melbourne Tonight* on the family's old Astor TV.

Working at the bank taught him about exchange rates, money lending, and accounting for every cent. He had to balance the books every day. If one cent was out, he had to find it. He excelled at finding errors in thousands of entries. He could see the pattern. After three years, though, the bank wanted him to study economics – which didn't interest him much – so he left for a job at the General Motors Acceptance Corporation, better known as GMAC. With sixty per cent share of the national motorcar financing market, it was called 'the university of financing' so that seemed a good next step in his education.

In 1973, he was invited to give talks. He was so embarrassed about his accent that he shook with nerves and could barely speak. One of the managers at GMAC sent him to a speech therapist. She explained that, by age seventeen, the palate has hardened, adjusting to the vowels a speaker has become accustomed to, so it takes a long time to control those sounds in English like 'th' that Latin languages don't use. 'I want you to do something for yourself,' she suggested. 'Record Brian Naylor reading the news, write down what he says, and then put your headphones on, and run through the reel trying to match his voice.' So Giuseppe bought a reel-to-reel tape recorder ('a beautiful thing,' he says) and recorded Brian Naylor from the TV using a microphone. Then he would spend hours transcribing the report and copying Naylor's speech patterns. Little by little, he lost his fear of speaking the English language.

One day, many years later, Jo was reliably informed that former prime minister Paul Keating advised his enemies in the major recording companies to back off provoking him. 'Just leave that man and his business alone,' Keating reportedly said. 'He squeals too much.' Insult him, ignore him, threaten him? Go ahead. Giuseppe won't back down if he believes his cause is just. His early years were tough, but they were just what he needed to take on the biggest struggle of his life – changing Australia's copyright law.

Giuseppe, now better known Jo, standing on the rooftop of Central Station's South Melbourne warehouse in the late 1980s

Music Wars

Throughout its history, Central Station Records has stood for freedom.

Right: This 1988 chart from the 'Pran' store reflected the e-infused times

Below: Street-style artwork on the wall of the 340 Flinders Street store

3. Freedom (1979-80)

Cast yourself back in time. If you aren't old enough to remember 1979, imagine a world before personal computers, the worldwide web and smart phones. There were no mp3 files. No iTunes. Not even CDs. Music was bought on vinyl discs or audio-cassettes. And music lovers relied on record shops and DJs as much as the media to discover new sounds. Record shops were meeting places and temples of worship. DJs were shamans and missionaries.

Back then, information moved slowly and trends lasted longer. Pop culture was more homogeneous than now, but the process of fragmentation had already begun. By 1979, the idealism of the 60s had slipped away. Flower power had withered, and cynicism and gloom had taken root. Punk expressed the mood perfectly in The Sex Pistols' song *Pretty Vacant* – 'I don't believe illusions 'cos too much is real'.

The world was troubled and divided. In Iran, the US-backed Shah was deposed and the Ayatollah Khomeini assumed power. Amid widespread panic about oil supplies, fuel prices spiked and economies slowed down. Conservatives ousted the Labour government in the UK, and Margaret Thatcher became the country's first female Prime Minister after the 'winter of discontent' was plagued by industrial strikes, severe unemployment and high inflation. A conservative government was also in power in Australia, with Malcolm Fraser as PM. And it would not be long before conservatives took over in the US – Republican Ronald Reagan became President in 1981.

In terms of social issues, one of the big frontiers in 1979 was gay liberation. In the US, Dan White got off with a light sentence for killing Supervisor Harvey Milk, the first openly gay man elected to public office in California. Outrage within San Francisco's gay community sparked the city's White Night Riots. Australia had its own watershed moment in 1978 when Sydney's first Mardi Gras march ended in violence and mass arrests. Police tried to disperse the crowd, ignoring the official permit the organisers had obtained. It's hard to believe now, but in 1979 homosexuality was still illegal in most Australian States. (Only South Australia and the Australian Capital Territory had moved to decriminalisation.) Gay characters had started to appear on Australian TV – notably Don Finlayson in *Number 96* – but social acceptance of gays was still a long way off.

How did all this turmoil manifest in music? Not surprisingly, escapism was bigger than open-eyed social comment. In the US, disco ruled. The genre developed out of the gay, African American, Italian American and Latino communities before spreading to the mainstream. At the end of July 1979, its popularity peaked on the *Billboard* Hot 100 chart, with disco accounting for seven of the top ten songs, beginning with Donna Summer's *Bad Girls*. The backlash from rock fans reached a crescendo in the same month with the Disco Demolition Night publicity stunt at a baseball game in Chicago. Fans were invited to bring disco records along and destroy them. Amid the mayhem of 'Disco Sucks' banners and burning vinyl, the game had to be cancelled.

Disco was popular in the UK too – *YMCA* (Village People), *Tragedy* (Bee Gees) and *I Will Survive* (Gloria Gaynor) all made number one. Australia and New Zealand took to disco too, but the hits happened many weeks after the US and UK.

The Australian music market was dominated by the big six recording companies – CBS, EMI, Festival, RCA, Warner and Polygram – who could afford the luxury of waiting to see what worked elsewhere before manufacturing locally. These companies' appetite for market control bordered on self-destructiveness. In a stunning example of poor judgment, they decided in 1970 (shortly after the Copyright Act 1968 was enacted) to take on a battle with commercial radio stations over royalties. During a six-month standoff, the big six stopped supplying free promotional records and the radio stations retaliated by boycotting all new major label releases by UK or Australian artists. Radio won the day and the old system was reinstated, but local artists suffered in the Australian charts for several years after the debacle.

A twenty-nine year old Italian immigrant now known as Jo Palumbo first stepped into this aggressive environment in 1975. While working

Freedom (1979-80)

Jo in the original JIST record store in Chapel Street, Windsor circa 1976

full-time in finance, he partnered up with two friends to open JIST Records, a store at 77 Chapel Street in the inner Melbourne suburb of Windsor. But he stayed in the background, doing the books and tax returns in his spare time, only rarely dealing with customers and suppliers. When JIST started losing money, Jo figured that it was a simple problem – his partners weren't putting enough effort into customer service. They were sleeping in after big nights out, failing to open the store for the all-important weekend trade. After a few years of frustration, he bought out his friends' shares and hired someone else to run the store. But the idea of getting behind the counter at his own place grew on him. By the troubled year of 1979, he had become disillusioned with his employer, because GMAC was making too many wrong decisions for his liking.

Every weekday, he took a train from Glen Waverly to the city, arriving at Flinders Street Station and walking up a ramp into the Princes Gate Arcade, under what is now Federation Square. Along the way, he passed a record store. 'It was a funny little place, about four metres by four, run by a middle-aged man,' he remembers. 'His stock was basic – mostly country music and Australian rock – but I liked talking to him about music.' One day, Jo noticed a sign in the shop's window: 'This business is for sale'. So he went inside and asked the price.

'Six hundred dollars,' came the reply. Looking around, it didn't take Jo long to recognise a bargain – the value of the stock and fittings was well above the asking price. 'I've taken a job at TDK Australia selling blank cassette tapes,' explained the vendor. 'I need to get out. I'm happy to sell cheaply.'

Deal done, Jo quit his job and began running the store. It was a big leap of faith. He had been making good money selling motorcar finance and insurance and he was a relative novice in the record business. The vendor's new job had given him an idea, though, and he put in a big order for TDK blank tapes to sell in his new shop. That would prove a good decision, as the do-it-yourself mix tape was taking off in a big way. The appearance of the boom box in the mid 70s had allowed people to record from radio to cassette on the one portable device.

In the tiny space, Jo began mulling over a new name. JIST was too much associated with other people, other times. Aware that great cities around the world had central stations, he decided to purloin that term. The funny little store's best asset was its location – a stone's throw from Flinders Street Station, the hub of Melbourne's suburban rail lines. After a search at the registry office showed availability, he registered 'Central

The original tiny shop in Princes Gate Arcade, Melbourne, with Jo the shadowy figure behind the counter

Freedom (1979-80)

Station Records and Tapes' (and variants) as business names. The next step was commissioning a logo. A French graphic artist from Heidelberg in Melbourne was paid $50 for the original design, which resembled the symbol used by the London Underground. Without twigging to the visual reference, Jo registered the artwork as his trademark. A wooden sign bearing the name, Central Station Records and Tapes, was hung on chains in the window.

To begin with, the new store carried top forty singles and albums, including by disco divas Donna Summer and Diana Ross, as well as earlier gay icons from Barbra Streisand to Peggy Lee. But customers started asking for titles Jo had never heard of, like *La Bamba* by Antonio Rodriguez, *Love Attack* by Ferrara, *Holy Ghost* by The Bar-Kays and *Rapper's Delight* by The Sugarhill Gang. Jo rang all of the obvious suppliers – the local branches of multinational recording companies – but none of them had heard or cared about these songs. The innocent that he was in those days, he made no progress discovering more until a customer suggested *Billboard* magazine as a good source of info. The magazine was a revelation. All of the songs people had been asking for appeared on its charts of top-selling American music.

This was the end of the 70s, when Casey Kasem's *American Top 40* radio show was syndicated across Australian airwaves. Jo started listening to it at one o'clock each afternoon on 3KZ in Melbourne. In Muswellbrook, a country town in the Hunter Valley, New South Wales, a teenager by the name of Paul Taylor (aka Paul 'flex' Taylor) listened to the same program late at night when the local station switched over to 2NX in Newcastle. 'Australian radio was so white,' remembers Paul. 'DJs had to stick to sanitised playlists. The only reason I knew about the Jacksons was because I watched the cartoon series on TV. Those glimpses of blackness late at night got me hooked. OK, I like this. It's funky. Let's hear some more black music.'

But how did a record store get hold of this music if the majors weren't interested in releasing it here? One day, poring over *Billboard*, Jo noticed a tiny dodgy-looking advertisement for a Miami company offering 'DJ equipment and promotional vinyl'. So he worked out the time difference and called the number at four o'clock in the morning Melbourne time.

'I can't help you. I don't carry the titles you're looking for,' said the Puerto Rican guy who answered. 'All I have are some boxes out the back full of promotional twelve-inches. I don't even know what's in there.'

Paul 'flex' Taylor at 2NM studios in 1975 aged fourteen. 'From age eleven, I knew I wanted to be a DJ radio announcer,' says Paul. 'My Dad paid one of the local DJs, Tommy Tucker, to train me. (Photo by Tommy Tucker, courtesy of Paul 'flex' Taylor)

'How many have you got?'
'About eight boxes. A hundred records in each.'
'How much do you want?'
'Oh, about fifty cents a piece.'
'Fine, I'll buy the lot.'

With wider groove spacing than the traditional seven-inch single, the twelve-inch allowed for better (and louder) sound quality as well as the extended length suited to dance floors, so the format quickly became popular with reggae and disco club DJs in America in the late 70s. No major record supplier was making them available in Australia. But Jo's new contact in Miami had promotional stock that had probably been given away to American radio jocks or record store buyers who later sold them on to middlemen.

Taking a punt, Jo transferred the funds and organised shipment by sea because airfreight was too costly. When the lucky-dip boxes arrived about a month later, he found only three or four copies of sought-after songs, rather than the fifty plus copies of each that he needed to meet demand. However, the rest of the contents turned out to be even better – exceptional material by new American artists. After factoring in costs and wastage, he figured he had to charge $10 a piece to make a modest profit.

Freedom (1979-80)

Considering that LPs retailed at $7.99 back then, $10 was a steep price for a single. To his surprise, though, customers were not only prepared to pay that price – they also fought for the privilege!

His first twelve-inch sale – *Gimme Back My Love Affair* by Sister Power – was to Ken Walker. Nowadays, Ken is a legendary DJ with a long list of top-selling remixes on Soundcloud. Back then, he was a young engineering cadet and part-time DJ. At lunchtime, he would often take the train from South Melbourne to the city to escape his boring workplace and shop at Gaslight Records. One day, he'd missed his return train, so he'd decided to fill in time by crossing the road to the Princes Gate Arcade. There he'd discovered the little shop and the big personality who ran it. They'd started chatting.

'What do you do?' Jo had asked.

'Been DJing for a couple of years,' Ken had replied.

'Funny, you should say that. I've got a contact in the States who wants to send me old disco records to sell. My first shipment is coming in next week.'

Ken had been stoked. Disco Oasis in Elsternwick had recently closed its doors, and all of the other import stores in the city had been focusing on funk and R&B. Opportunities for DJs to source dance music had been few and far between, so next week he'd come back to check out Jo's first imports.

'I bought the first ever twelves that he sold and I've still got them,' he says. 'Jo and I became friends and I spread the word to the other DJs. The next thing you knew you had people queuing up to buy vinyl from him. The American and UK pressings sounded thirty or forty per cent better than the local pressings. If you were working on a sound system that didn't have very good amps or output, you would really notice the difference.'

Another young DJ found the micro shop by accident too. Like his mate Ken, Cameron Stirling was a child when he emigrated from Scotland with his family. He grew up in Port Adelaide and came to Melbourne to play soccer for Croydon City. The club found him a flat and a job while he trained. On his way home from work one day, he happened upon Central Station Records. 'I found this little place no one knew about and a couple of these twelve-inch singles I was after,' he recalls. 'I collected records and came from a musical family. I just loved it – R&B, funk and some disco – and Jo had really good product for such a limited space. But it wasn't really about that. You could just see that he was a lovely guy who had a real passion. He was always going to make money – not tons – but you could see at that point that it wasn't a money thing. He just wanted a bit of freedom. He was having a ball, and it showed!'

So you could make money, have fun and make customers deliriously happy at the same time? It was a no-brainer for Jo. He found another vinyl distributor in New York, put in more orders and opened more boxes. Word soon spread among DJs and Central Station Records became the place to shop. Other import stores were popular with DJs, but Jo developed a reputation for being ahead of the pack.

'We put a lot of effort into cultivating suppliers, including paying them on time,' says Jo. 'We wanted continuity of supply at the fastest speed possible. If you're first in the market, DJs have to come to you.'

Kevin Attwood was one of the early customers. On Sunday nights, he was the resident DJ at Pokies, a high-profile club at the Prince of Wales hotel in St Kilda. During the week, he was a senior buyer working in the head office of Coles, the supermarket chain. Like so many people, he discovered Central Station on his daily commute from the suburbs to the city. As a teenager in Frankston, a coastal suburb in Melbourne's outer southeast, he'd become an avid record collector, concentrating on rock and pop hits from the early 70s. He became a disco fanatic when he saw a twelve-inch single for the first time.

'The first time I came out as a gay man, I went to a club called Smarties in Spencer Street,' he recalls. 'A DJ was playing Dan Hartman's *Instant Replay*. In the middle of the record, there were all of these extra drumbeats, stuff that didn't exist on the single I owned. From that moment forth, I started hunting where to buy twelve-inches. I found a couple of little shops like Disco Oasis in Glenhuntly Road in Elwood and Mighty Music Machine in Chapel Street, Windsor. Then Jo came along. We both used to go crazy for everything that came out on a twelve.'

Paul 'flex' Taylor also shopped at Jo's. In 1979, he was doing a short stint as DJ at Mickey's nightclub on the waterfront at St Kilda. A few years earlier, after leaving Muswellbrook for Sydney, he had enrolled in a radio and TV school course, determined to become a radio announcer. But a visit to The Zoo nightclub – in William Street, Kings Cross – had set him on a different path. Watching Rusty Nails, later of Triple J fame, drop a record and instantly transform the dance floor had changed his life. 'Once I found out that you could play music to people right in front of you and get a reaction straight away, I knew what I wanted to do. You

Freedom (1979-80)

could whip people up, pull them down, lift them back up again, and basically have control over a captive audience. It was an amazing feeling.'

Paul had hung around The Zoo, acting as Rusty's sidekick, until he'd got the chance to DJ there himself. When that club had closed down, he had been poached by another King Cross nightclub, Mickey's at the Hampton Court hotel. One day the manager from the sister (and main) club in Melbourne had heard him play. 'You're excellent,' he'd said, 'I want you to come to Melbourne.'

That's how Paul met Jo. 'He took me to the original shop and then back to his house,' he recalls. 'He had all of these records in the garage as well. He was just totally immersed in vinyl and so excited and passionate about music. I thought he was a really cool guy.'

More and more customers began crowding into the tiny shop near Flinders Street Station. Needing someone to run the place when he was out lining up supply or taking care of paperwork, Jo put a sign in the window: 'Staff wanted'. Greta Tate walked in to apply.

'I've been working in record shops for almost ten years,' she said. 'I'm over the place where I am right now, and one of the record company reps told me there's a job going here, so I thought I'd drop by.'

'What music do you listen to?' asked Jo.

'Heavy metal,' she said.

'OK, you're hired ... as long as you can fit behind the counter.'

Greta laughs when she recalls the interview: 'I wasn't skinny and Jo wasn't tactful.'

Greta Tate in shop 12, 181 Flinders Street in the mid to late 80s (courtesy of Greta Tate)

Imagine this four-by-four metre shop. On one side, the shelves groaned under the weight of disco, funk and other dance music. On the other side, it was all pop and rock – Kiss, ACDC and whatever else was big at the moment. The shop started operating from seven o'clock in the morning to seven in the evening, because most customers wanted to call in on their way to or from work. At peak commuter times, the place was packed and long queues waited outside to get in.

'I didn't like Greta much at first,' says Jo. 'She dressed like a witch, all in black from head to toe. At first she ran the shop while I did the admin side. Then everything became so busy that we had to start working together at the counter. I came to appreciate Greta and loved what we were both doing. The rock customers mixed with the dance music ones amazingly well. Diversity was at its best. It was magic. The money was coming in and I was paying my bills. But it was a love affair more than a business for me.'

As the imports rolled in, the dance market took off and Jo had to look for another space. Luckily a bigger shop was available nearby in the arcade – further up the ramp at street level, the base of the ugly (now vanished) Gas & Fuel Corporation Towers.

One day Cameron Stirling came in.

'Do you enjoy the public service?' Jo asked him.

Cameron was living out in Boronia in Melbourne's eastern fringe, working at the Department of Transport in the city during the week, and DJing in Collingwood on Friday and Saturday nights.

'My job's boring, to be quite frank with you,' he replied. 'But I'm doing this DJing at Skate City in Johnston Street, and I've been offered a full-time gig at a new club when it opens next year.'

'That shop will be finished in two weeks,' said Jo, showing him his new premises. 'Do you want to work in it? All it's going to be is disco twelve-inches and albums. All imports. All from the States.'

Cameron asked for some time to think it over, and called his father in Adelaide that evening to seek his support.

'Look, I want to do this,' he told the former professional double-bass player who'd been part of some big jazz acts in post-war Britain.

'Absolutely, if music's what you want to do,' said his dad.

So Cameron – employee number three (after John Cassar at Chapel Street and Greta Tate in the city) – agreed to work for Jo in the new shop until September 1980 when he was due at Sheiks nightclub.

Greta stayed on in the original location. It was lonely and dull for her. 'I was down in that little shop late at night, when the passing traffic had dried up. He had DJs coming in and out of his shop all the time. It was jumping up there and I thought, "Nah, I can't handle this." So I said to Jo, "You've got your favourite up there. Can I try mine down here?" And he agreed, as long as it worked.'

As simple as that, Central Station branched out into heavy metal. Greta scoured the local catalogues for suitable stock and was excited to see Angel's debut album in Polygram's listings. Discovered by Gene Simmons of Kiss, the white-wearing band failed to achieve the mass commercial success of its black-clad mentor but had developed something of a cult following. Greta ordered twenty copies of the record and showcased it to a few loyal customers who worked in the Gas & Fuel Towers. The reaction was positive and she soon sold out. When she went to Polygram to order more, however, she was told that the record had been deleted and no more stock was available. One by one, she went to each of the companies and grabbed whatever heavy metal they had. Back then, the genre was fairly new and not well known or accepted in Australia. 'To the mainstream, it was devil music,' says Greta. 'The local record companies were not interested in pressing records here to supply the small but devoted local market.'

Meanwhile, in the dance store, Jo and Cameron were bumping into each other when they were both serving. 'Jo and I had slightly different tastes in disco and dance music,' says Cameron. 'He has always loved 130 bpm and up. Boom boom boom. Really quick. Hi NRG. Preferably with an Italo, European feel. I was always more R&B, 115, 120 bpm. Together, we doubled the potential of people coming in. Some people would say, "When's Jo coming back?" I'd go, "An hour, hour and a half. He's down at Windsor, or organising a shipment." And they'd say, "No problem. We'll have a listen and wait." That was cool. I had people coming in who'd just want to be served by me. And it worked really well.'

In the spirit of the times, Jo found himself swept up in the craft of DJing. At a gay sauna in Caulfield, he became friendly with a DJ who went by the nickname of Hilda. 'One day, I heard Hilda merging two songs,' says Jo. 'I asked him how he'd managed to do that with no gap between and he showed me one of the earliest mixing machines. He would have music going on each of two channels and use the crossfader to move from one to the other seamlessly. That got me interested in dance music more than anything else. When I asked mobile DJs why they got into the scene, they would all tell me about their love of mixing.'

Central Station's elite customers were 'fixed' professional DJs, who either ran their own clubs or were hired by venues. But Jo made a point of cultivating the 'mobile' DJs, the enthusiastic amateurs who ferried their own equipment around the suburbs, entertaining crowds at birthday parties, weddings and community functions, usually for glory as much as for money. The fixed DJs were often gay. The mobile ones were usually of Mediterranean background. As an Italian-born gay man, Jo related to both sets of customers. He loved to talk to them in the store, picking up ideas and learning what appealed to people. He also went to nightclubs. Right there in the thick of things, he could sense the increasing excitement for dance music and was in a far better position to know what was happening than record company executives in their corporate offices.

Angie Young, who would later work for Central Station as promotions manager in the early 2000s, was a child when her Greek-born parents and aunts were out and about at discos in the 80s. 'My parents were only nineteen when I was born,' she recalls. 'So I had aunties who were five or so years older than me – like big sisters really – and I would watch them getting ready to go to discotheques, playing records while they did their hair and make-up. My parents would have parties at their house too. My mother had a microphone and used to sing on top of the disco music and I would sing along in the background. Music is a very big part of Greek culture.'

What is it about dance music that appeals to Mediterranean sensibilities? Angie, who now has her own successful promotion business in the music industry, believes it's the soul vibe. 'When I was a teenager, there was definitely a divide in terms of musical tastes. Australian-born kids were into traditional pub rock bands, whereas Europeans preferred anything with a soul vibe. It has nothing to do with racist issues. It's just what you're used to and like. Something in the music that grabs you. Whether it's a vocal hook or a baseline, there has to be soul in it for me.'

For Jo himself, the attraction was freedom and fun. The music brought him financial independence and social connection. One day in late March 1980 – about a year after he'd opened in the city – he felt a sweet sense of euphoria wash over him. No more exploitation. The anger at old wounds slipped away. With a few smart decisions and a lot of hard work, he had won his freedom. 'Thank you, God,' he said out loud. 'I've finally found something I love to do. What can I do for you?'

The following day, Jo received a hand-delivered letter from solicitors acting for Festival Records. 'We have been instructed that you are selling and offering for sale in infringement of our client's copyright, the imported records: Noel – "Dancing is Dangerous" – Cat. No. DK4806; and Slick – "Sexy Cream"/"The Whole World's Dancing" – Cat. No. D-122.'

In four pages of legalese, the letter demanded written undertakings within seven days – in essence, to stop importing and selling the 'infringing records' and any other record licensed by Festival, to deliver up remaining stocks and to provide the name of the supplier and all transaction details. Failure to do so would result in legal action without further notice.

At first, Jo felt as if he'd been dowsed with a bucket of ice water. Then his mood dipped alarmingly. He felt like a prisoner on death row, his dreams of freedom dashed.

Check or checkmate? Festival Records had put the king of the DJs in deadly jeopardy.

The Central Station Records and Tapes stall at Gay Day, Melbourne 1983
(Photo by Jay Watchorn, courtesy of Australian Lesbian and Gay Archives)

Left: Heavy metal chart produced by Greta Tate, dated 22 January 1985. After hand-writing her earliest charts, she began using Letraset, a rub-down transfer system for lettering that was used by graphic artists in pre-computer days. 'It would take me all weekend to do those,' she says. (courtesy of Greta Tate)

Right: Few customers were aware of Central Station's legal problems and later lobbying efforts. This 90s flyer for an in-store appearance at 340 Flinders Street highlights the cheeky optimism that prevailed at store level, belying the stress and anguish felt by the owners.

4. The Outlaw and the Hombre (1980-1983)

All three of Jo's stores (two in Melbourne's city centre, one in suburban Windsor) were doing well. Buzzing, in fact. He kept on playing the showman, spinning records on request or to promote a new release. Only a handful of customers had any idea of how deeply unhappy and angry he was behind the theatrical bravado. 'Thank you. Come again,' he'd say as the cash register rang after another sale. It was April 1980, and Festival Records was threatening his livelihood and life passion. When he could get away from the store, he combed Collins and Bourke Streets looking for a lawyer to represent him. Nobody was prepared to take on the case – claiming that they weren't familiar with copyright law, were too busy, or were already representing other parties. Lawyers know a bucket of money when they see one – Jo's opponent, Festival Records, was a wholly owned subsidiary of the giant News Limited corporation.

By the time Jo found a firm willing to help him – common-and-garden solicitors in suburban Carlton – the deadline for the original demands had passed. In a scenario reminiscent of *The Castle*, the 1997 Australian movie about a blue-collar home-owner and his clueless lawyer taking on big developers, Jo's under-powered champions wrote to Festival's high-calibre legal guns, seeking clarification of the licensing agreements being held over Central Station's head. The reply came two weeks later with more details in legalese and an updated seven-day deadline for written undertakings. Failure to comply would mean that Festival would 'have no alternative but to take such proceedings as are necessary to protect its rights'.

'You need to hire a barrister, mate,' said the Carlton crew. 'They're not backing down, and you need someone to represent you in court.'

'How much will that cost?' asked Jo.

'You're looking at $2,000 minimum.'

Knowing he couldn't afford a fight, Jo decided to do nothing. Wait and see. He would represent himself if necessary. He carried on importing, but warily, selling under the counter to people he trusted (or thought he could). Sympathetic to Greta's difficulties in sourcing heavy metal locally – because he'd been through the same frustration with dance titles – Jo even handed her some releases sheets and told her she could import what she was after.

The new wave of British heavy metal was underway in 1980, with the rise of Iron Maiden, Saxon, Judas Priest and others. 'I was dead against imports being illegal,' says Greta. 'The big six recording companies didn't think they'd sell enough of those records so they didn't release them. In other words, the companies were telling me that I wasn't allowed to listen to the music I was into. I thought that was absolutely disgusting. Anyway, I would have to run up to the main post office in the city and send a telex order, wait a few weeks and get one little box. Then I'd ring up one of my customers at Gas & Fuel and he'd tell the others and they would all come down. Service was very personalised back then.'

When the Gas & Fuel Corporation decided to renovate, Jo was faced with a dilemma. The original Central shop in Princes Gate Arcade was slated to disappear, so he had to find a new location for Greta. He knew that the Melbourne City Council was also in a pickle, because earlier in the year the Builders Labourers Federation had put an indefinite black ban on the redevelopment of the City Square in support of the Save the Regent Theatre movement.

'All these beautiful shops had been vacated ahead of the stalled project,' remembers Jo. 'The whole place was empty. Two or three thousand square metres of shops under the fountain, with gates locked every day and nothing happening. Such a shame. So I went to see the Council and told them I wanted to open a music store there for young people. Why don't you let me move in?'

The Council agreed and gave Central Station a lease. So in October 1981, Jo took his dance operation into the City Square and moved Greta into his former location. Her shop was stripped of the pop singles that weren't selling in any case. 'People who wanted that kind of music wouldn't come in,' she says. 'By then we looked too heavy for them.'

Meanwhile, in his new space, Jo set up an office behind a little partition at the back and installed a telex machine. He spent all of his time researching product and putting in orders, while staff served customers out the front. Overseas suppliers provided information of what was available. Jo marked the titles he wanted and telexed his orders. When they arrived, he taped the tracks and listened to them when he had time. If he particularly liked anything, he would order more.

According to Jo, the secret of his success was the speed and security of supply that he achieved through sheer hard work and conscientious account management: 'I used to sit in my office, using the telex for fucking hours. Click, click, click. My business grew quickly because I paid on time. I made contacts in London, New York, Italy, Spain, Germany, Holland. Not even accounts, but agreements on credit for thirty-five days. If you do the right thing by suppliers, they respect you and they talk to each other. Swish, boom. Right, you buy, you hit the market, and you beat everybody else because you're consistent and efficient. Orders twice a week sometimes from London. Quick, quick, it's on the floor.'

Not long after the City Square move, and seemingly out of the blue, the sheriff of the Supreme Court of Victoria delivered Jo a thick letter in November 1981. 'Sorry,' he said as he handed over the official-looking packet. Almost eighteen months after the last correspondence from lawyers, and with no further notice to him, the court had ordered that

The forecourt area of Melbourne's City Square in the 80s

Central Station Records be restrained from importing and selling records licensed exclusively to Festival Records. A long list of labels was attached. Adding financial insult to psychological injury, Jo was also ordered to pay the plaintiff's costs – not just legal fees but photocopying and courier charges. He felt shocked and devastated. Not only had he been stomped on, but he also had to pay for the privilege! It would be another six months before a bill for $2,221.94 arrived.

Feeling he had no alternative, Jo removed the labels listed in the court order. He and Greta continued working together in their respective stores, surrounded by shelves of vinyl right up to the ceiling, being as friendly and professional as ever. But Jo couldn't contain his feelings altogether, and he started telling customers how distressed he was about the situation. What was wrong with Australia? Why was the country letting these multinational recording companies damage little businesses importing records they could very well release but didn't want to? Who were they to tell kids they couldn't have the music they loved? And why was the quality of imported product so much better than the locally manufactured version?

An enormous amount of moral support came his way, to the extent that he believed many people were buying from him just to keep the store afloat. All the same, depression set in. It was the end of a road. He knew that he couldn't go backwards – there was no money to be made in the legally sanctioned model. And he felt he couldn't go forward – the fines the court had threatened him with would be ruinous.

What eventually broke the impasse in his mind was escalating demand for emerging music – rap, electro-funk and electro-pop – the sounds of New York streets, Chicago clubs and European beach parties, all with driving synthesized beats. Although Gen X would not be defined in the popular imagination until 1991 when Douglas Coupland's novel *Generation X: Tales For An Accelerated Culture* appeared, the generation born between 1963 and 1980 didn't grow up in the buoyant socio-economic environment that the baby boomers enjoyed. Theirs was a tougher, more cynical world, but also a more technologically savvy one. Like every generation, they rejected their elders' taste in favour of sounds that spoke to their times, their reality. But the big six recording companies in Australia didn't know or care about the changing of the guard.

When the law is an ass – rigid, stupid and outdated – people tend to disobey. And Jo was super-sensitive to injustice. He resolved to keep his customers happy, despite the risks. 'I didn't want to sell the business and I couldn't afford the fines. Going back was not a good idea. So I thought, "Fuck it. I'm going to import everything and see what happens". So I took all the imports off the shelves. I kept importing, but I sold that product under the counter or from the boot of my old Toyota Crown car. I analysed my customers and if they'd been there a few times and didn't look like lawyers or company stooges, I'd sell to them. Every so often, I'd trust the wrong person, but I never wrote the names of titles on receipts, so they couldn't do much.'

Aware of this under-counter trade, the majors regularly raided import stores. Cameron Stirling remembers one occasion vividly. It was a Saturday, when Cameron was usually left to run the city shop on his own while Jo took over the Chapel Street store. In walked a bunch of people from Festival Records. They quickly commandeered some stock from A&M, an associated label.

'Can't you go and find some real criminals?' Cameron shouted at them. 'You're idiots. All we've got is a handful of a records you're not even promoting!'

After the raiders left, Cameron felt so incensed that he phoned A&M's head office in LA. Somehow he got through to a senior figure in the marketing division and explained the situation.

'I'm about to start at a club and I can't get copies of your records. I work in a highly regarded record shop and we're not allowed to sell them.'

'Who are the artists?'

Cameron listed the records.

The marketing honcho was surprised. 'Why isn't A&M down there releasing them?' he asked. 'We're sending them promos. Why aren't they giving them to you? What's your address?'

Within two days, Cameron received a box from LA. 'I really do believe it came down to a couple of people being jealous, personality stuff,' he says of Festival's attitude. 'Other companies couldn't give a shit.'

EMI was another company that *did* give a shit. They threatened to close Jo's account and take legal action unless Central Station gave immediate written assurance that it wasn't importing and selling product EMI had licensed. Jo wrote back, giving such assurance. He said that he had imported single copies of three albums (by Duran Duran, Peter Tosh and Kraftwerk) simply to assess their suitability for the disco market because EMI had failed to provide information and promo copies. He had learned from the masters how to counter-attack: 'Should you close our account you will leave us with no alternative but to import all your product from other sources and will let the Trade Practices Commissioner and yourself resolve your monopolistic attitude in this matter.'

But Festival was a bigger worry – because they had won that court order. A month or so after receiving the bill for that injury, Jo met up with two senior managers at Festival's Melbourne office. It was May 1982, and he wanted to agree a peace deal. Why not see him and his DJ customers as a promotional force for Festival product? To Jo, the argument was compelling – it was in Festival's interest to allow the DJs to have their precious twelve-inch imported singles. The DJs created hits in the nightclubs with their extended versions of singles, and then their audiences bought locally produced albums. The general public wasn't interested in buying Jo's imports. Why pay $10 or $12 for a twelve-inch imported single when you could get an entire local album for less?

He urged Festival Records to work with him to develop the market, and the meeting appeared to go well, so Jo followed up with a letter, floating a proposal for discussion at a subsequent meeting with top brass. But Festival ignored Jo's olive branch. In May 1982, the company's high-priced lawyers again targeted Central Station, this time about three records advertised for sale in a May 1982 edition of *Juke* magazine. The threat of legal action was later withdrawn because the records were not in fact licensed to Festival. But the financial and emotional cost of disputing the matter was onerous.

Business has always been a chess game for Jo. After the rude shock of the court order against him, he had been continually scanning the board for threats and opportunities, trying to avoid being checkmated again. His next move was to travel to Los Angeles and New York, to find better and more reliable suppliers. His friend, Ken Walker, had told him about warehouses in America where retailers would ship unsold vinyl for return to their suppliers, the recording companies. And Jo discovered just such a warehouse in Los Angeles.

'There were about a thousand boxes lying around the floor,' he says. 'The owner had no idea what was in them, but was happy to let me dig around.' Inside the boxes, Jo found hundreds of the music titles that he was looking for. It was a bonanza. After a few hours of sifting, he'd amassed more than 9,000 pieces of vinyl in LP and twelve-inch format. The owner wanted forty cents apiece. Jo offered him half that. It took half an hour of negotiation to settle on twenty-eight cents apiece.

The Outlaw & the Hombre (1980-1983)

A freight forwarder collected the haul that evening and loaded it onto a ship. By the time the Los Angeles haul arrived in Melbourne about forty days later, Jo had spread the word that a huge shipment of rare old titles in twelve-inch format were on the way to his Windsor store. The rarest recordings – *The Message* (Grandmaster Flash), *Mandolay* (La Flavour) and *Catch Me* (Pockets) – were displayed high on the store walls with ridiculously high prices ($100, $300, even $600 apiece). The remainder of the vinyl was stacked on the floor against the walls. DJs stormed the store as soon as the doors were opened.

'There were all these records that had never found their way to Australia, and DJs wanted the vinyl,' says Ken. 'It just took things to a whole new level. Jo had been focused on new music, so when he got access to this old music, it went gangbusters.'

As English dance-pop bands such as Duran Duran, Wham and Culture Club soared in popularity, Jo opened another shop in City Square devoted to this style of music. He hired Vivien Rogers as the manager. 'She was amazing,' he says. 'She knew everything about seven-inch singles. We used to buy 5,000 at a time and she would sell them like hotcakes.'

Greta's heavy metal imports caused the next headache for Jo when Van Halen's *Diver Down* triggered a dispute with the Australian branch of the American giant, Warner Brothers Records. Managing director Paul Turner was still at the helm after twelve years since the company had been established in Sydney in 1970. Lawyers acting for Warner wrote to Jo in September 1982, threatening the usual stuff. In response, Jo sent a hand-written letter, apologising for breaching a promise he'd made in early 1982 – to stay away from importing Warner's 'bread and butter lines'. He then offered to pay compensation for any lost revenue on the twelve guilty import copies. Lawyers responded on Turner's behalf – restating demands for the usual undertakings and disclosures, before insisting on payment of $21.24 to cover lost royalties. Jo's accountant sent off a cheque for the petty sum.

Pettiness was the order of the day. Undeterred by the failure of his charm offensive, Jo tried another conciliatory tactic with Festival Records. He sent a bundle of form letters to the managing director, Jim White, requesting confirmation that Festival held no copyright or license for a range of records he wanted to import. Jim White wrote back. He wanted no bar of Jo's carefully constructed forms. Instead, he demanded that Jo 'immediately furnish to us' a complete list of all records that

Central Station had imported in the past or intended to in the future.

By August 1983, Jo's mood had hit rock bottom. One night, near closing time, he arrived at Mandate, a gay nightclub in St Kilda, Melbourne's bayside playground. Hanging out there was his only diversion from work. He'd usually arrive around midnight and leave at three o'clock in the morning to walk his nearby apartment in William Street, Windsor and then start calling distributors in Los Angeles or New York. Not much of a drinker, he would sit on a glass of whisky for hours listening to the music and rebuffing any proposition that came his way. Sex was of no more interest to him than alcohol or drugs. He was doped up on Valium and Serepax, and too preoccupied with his legal battles to bother with anything else.

As he sat at the back of the club on this particular night, he made up his mind to ditch Australia and return to Italy. Every cent he was making was going to lawyers. His apartment was worth no more than the mortgage. And a recent break-up felt like the last straw. 'I was totally unhappy, dragging my feet, complaining all the time,' he recalls. 'I thought, "Fuck this, forget Australia, forget the multinationals. I'll find a way back to Italy, get married and do whatever other Italian gay men do. I'll leave my family here. I don't care. I'll go insane if I stay."'

The music wound up and the crowd drifted off. The club was almost empty when in walked a short guy with long, mousy-coloured hair and a moustache. Fresh from a Lena Lovich concert and high on magic mushrooms, Morgan Williams spotted Jo and swaggered over. His opening line fell well short of his customary charm.

'Do you speak English?'

Maybe it was the mushrooms speaking, or maybe Jo looked more like a foreign tourist than a 'new Australian'. Whatever the reason for the strange intro, Jo felt insulted.

'How dare you speak to me like that. Fuck off!'

Morgan ambled off.

'That was a pretty pathetic entrée, wasn't it?' he observes now. 'Because I'm not sure *I* was even speaking English at the time, considering the condition I was in.'

Being a social creature by nature, Morgan tried again. 'Can I offer you some amyl?' he asked as he pulled out a tube of amyl nitrate.

Again, Jo was horrified. Amyl was a popular stimulant on dance floors at the time, but he hated the smell ('like rotten socks') and the headaches it promised.

'Put that away. Get out of my sight,' he snapped.

As Morgan staggered off a second time, Jo suddenly felt either a twinge of interest or a surge of disgust. He grabbed the persistent stranger by the belt and pulled him back.

'Do you know the trouble with you?' he demanded. 'You're weak!'

'Well, I suppose that means you won't come back to my place.'

'Of course not.'

A few minutes later, Jo changed his mind: 'OK, but only on condition that you don't touch me until I give you permission.'

They walked to Morgan's house in Gurner Street, St Kilda. Jo was not impressed with the décor – 'carpets everywhere and a cheap electric heater' – but he was certainly impressed by the news that Morgan was buying the place. Everyone in his circle was a vagabond and wastrel to him – always partying, smashing their cars and flat broke before payday came around again.

'I was surprised,' says Jo. 'I didn't know anyone else with property in his name. Then he told me that he worked for a government agency and came from New Zealand. I said, "Shit. You're a bunch of crooks."'

That's Jo – straight out with whatever he's thinking. But Morgan was a people person – as he still is – and soon drew out the story behind Jo's foul mood. They talked for two or three hours.

'I let myself go,' says Jo. 'I wanted to talk about my problems, my agony. And he was a very good listener. People love him because of that. Then he told me he had done some social work in New Zealand. Anyway, we spent the night together.'

The tone was set for the relationship. Jo the talker, Morgan the listener. Jo, the man of vision and intensity. Morgan, the man of pragmatism and empathy. Jo the tough boss man, Morgan the influencer and networker.

The first thing that Jo did the next day was to launch a credit search on his new friend. Contacts in the finance industry confirmed that Morgan did indeed have a mortgage on his home. Morgan was irritated to learn that he'd been sussed out, but Jo was unrepentant: 'I wanted to make sure you were telling the truth. That I could trust you.'

The following night, Morgan was due at a dinner party with friends of his who lived on Beaconsfield Parade, St Kilda. 'I thought I'd take a punt and bring Jo along,' he says. 'My friends were fairly posh. Jo was wearing leathers, and they freaked out. They liked him but they thought he was pretty bizarre. Anyway, they eventually became good friends.'

Jo and Morgan differ in their accounts of what happened next. Jo tells a vivid story about Morgan promptly showing up with a suitcase at his apartment, and insisting on moving in. On hearing this version, Morgan says Jo was being tongue-in-cheek: 'Good story, but actually he moved into *my* place, and it wasn't straight away. I gave it a week or two, and only overnight to begin with.'

It was not an auspicious beginning to a lifelong partnership, but the match was sealed on mutual need and complementary skills. The universe had delivered to Jo someone with the political and people skills to become his lieutenant in the music wars. And Morgan had found a partner he respected. Also known as Master Joe and the Horny Hombre, the pair would go on to do something few can claim – help change the law of the land.

Morgan (in glasses) and Jo (next to him) with Colin Sarantis and another friend in a San Francisco bar after a Divine concert in the mid 80s

5. Morgan Williams

Whereas the dominant themes of Jo's childhood were protectiveness of family and outrage at injustice, the distinguishing features of Morgan's early life were pragmatic survivalism and social adaptability.

The middle child of three, Morgan Evan Williams was born in 1952 in the tiny town of Geraldine on the South Island of New Zealand. His mother left the father, an alcoholic, when Morgan was only eighteen months old. With three children under the age of four, she moved in with her parents in the little coastal town of Haumoana on the North Island. The plus-side of the split was that Morgan didn't experience growing up with an abusive drunk. The downside was that he missed out on having a father figure. Making matters worse, his mother suffered from bipolar disorder.

'I had a very dysfunctional childhood, with a mad mother and two out-of-control siblings,' he says, with no hint of self-pity. 'In a sense, the family dodged a bullet when Mum left Dad. In moments of enlightenment, she was empathetic, loving and generous. Then she'd blow it all when she went crazy. In retrospect, I think she suffered from severe post-natal depression and never quite recovered from it. As difficult as it was, her affliction helped me to cope with some pretty crazy situations later in life.'

Fortunately, his maternal grandparents provided some of the stability and leadership that his parents failed to offer. 'My mother's mother was very important,' he says. 'She was from South Australia originally and very smart and bookish. Her father had been a Methodist clergyman. Middle class. And she mentored me. I've still got all her letters. She met my Kiwi grandfather, who had a Portuguese background, when he was on leave in Fiji after serving at Gallipoli. She was a nurse there.'

All three siblings found themselves in welfare care at various stages throughout their childhoods. When Morgan was twelve, authorities put him in touch with his father. At the time, his mother wasn't coping at all, whereas his father had remarried and sired a second set of children. He'd joined Alcoholics Anonymous, stopped drinking and settled down with his new family.

'He had been paying family support all along so there had always been some degree of contact through the courts. When he invited me down to Christchurch to stay with him and his second family, it was quite an emotional time for everyone. He and my mother still hated each other – although they did reconcile many years later when Jo and I decided to bring all the family together over a long weekend in Waiwera, a small spa town north of Auckland. But I have always been a bit adventurous socially, and became as close to my father's side as to my original family. I found out that my two half-siblings had gone through some terrible times before he'd sobered up. I'd been half-envious of them until that realisation.'

Morgan inherited his social adventurism and political nous from his father, who was of Welsh extraction. 'He made a career as the secretary of organisations like the Commonwealth Games Association, the South Island promotion association and the hotels association. He was

Morgan (front, centre) with his older sister and younger brother in Napier on the day in 1966 when they were reunited with their father (at back) after more than a decade apart

A happy moment in Morgan's years boarding at Dannevirke high school. Leading the horse, he is about fifteen years old

instrumental in bringing the Commonwealth Games to Christchurch. He was quite involved politically.' The reunion also introduced Morgan to his paternal grandparents. But it didn't set him on the straight and narrow. By age fourteen, he was getting into trouble with authorities.

'I was drinking and pinching stuff,' says Morgan. 'I was just out of control. Thanks to a charity called Birthright, I was sent off to Dannevirke High School in a rural community. The charity covered my boarding fees. I had no affinity with the other kids, so I just put my head down and thought, "Fuck it. I'll make it work". I was there for two years. Then I got chucked out when I was sixteen. Bizarrely, that was because I was caught in bed with a girl. She really liked me and initiated that.'

After being expelled from boarding school, Morgan went back to Hasting Boys' High School (which had eased him out two years before) to do his final year. Then the teenage delinquent decided to go to university. The mother of a boarding school pal had studied anthropology and inspired him to follow suit. Thanks to a government scholarship and part-time jobs in bars, factories and cleaning firms, he was able to complete an arts degree at Victoria University of Wellington.

When he began his course in 1970, he chose to board with an old lady a long way from the university. 'I didn't trust myself living in a college dormitory. I thought I'd lose my concentration and I really enjoyed studying,' he says.

In his second year, he flatted with a girlfriend and a mate. When that household drifted apart, he hooked up with another woman and moved in together. 'I had a good relationships with her, but when I look back at it, I think I was trying to avoid the hard decision,' he observes. 'Then all of a sudden it dawned on me. I remember sitting at the university and thinking, "Fuck, you're gay". It hit me like a ton of bricks. I remembered perving at guys, but I'd never acknowledged a sexual component to it. I was just admiring a good-looking person. So here I was, about twenty years old. I'd never had sex with guys. I didn't know what I was up for. But I started exploring.'

After finishing his undergraduate degree, Morgan spent a year as a social worker before returning to university to do his honours year in anthropology. Armed with that qualification, he landed a job with New Zealand's Department of Trade and Industry. 'That's when I started to get involved with the political process,' he says. 'I was briefing ministers, writing speeches, and doing some interesting political work, which I really enjoyed. I was just a shit kicker, but I did reasonably well and had hopes of becoming a trade commissioner one day.'

The trade field appealed to him, so he gained a Diploma in Export Marketing. But Morgan's 'exploring' field trips resulted in his first boyfriend and first heartbreak. The boyfriend, David, chose to move to London. Morgan was distraught and followed him there a year later. 'Everybody was going to London in those days and the department was giving people two years' leave to get it out of their system. It was called OE (overseas experience) in Kiwi parlance,' he says. 'All my contemporaries were doing that, so I requested leave for a couple of years to go to London. But it all got a bit messy. I didn't get back with David. The relationship had lost its magic, although we remained really good friends until he died.

How very Morgan. He's a middle child. Always harmonising.

He's also a survivor. Lovelorn or not, he gets on with the

Morgan's first passport photo taken in 1973 when he was a social worker in New Zealand

practicalities of life. Literally off the plane to London, he went to an employment agency, Gabbitas Thring, in Piccadilly Circus. 'It was quite a famous agency, really Dickensian with men sitting at rows of desks. I got a job living with Lord and Lady Rothemere, tutoring their nine-year-old son in Latin amongst other subjects. You know the character in Little Britain, Bubbles de Vere? That character was based on Lady Rothemere. She was known as Bubbles Rothemere. We went out partying together. She was a wild woman. I thought at the time she must have been a bit desperate for company, but I got into the swing of things. I just morphed into it pretty easily. I've always had an open mind, always liked people who live on the edge and she certainly did.'

After not one Latin lesson, but many football games and almost as many parties, Bubbles twigged that Morgan didn't speak a word of the Classic language and sacked him. Asked what he learned from this experience, Morgan shrugs. 'Well I learned that I much preferred working with real people and that things can change pretty quickly. It's wise to be adaptable and just get onto a different playing field. When I went from being a social welfare kid to being in a middle class boarding school, I had to change my world vision overnight. I just did the same in London.'

Unruffled, Morgan looked in *Time Out*, saw an ad for a social worker position, applied and got a job working for Brent Council. 'We were all Aussies and Kiwis because it was tough work, and the locals didn't want to do it. We were doing assessments of kids that came into care. Often they were in trouble with the law, and we'd have to liaise with their families, psychologists and doctors. It affected me.'

Morgan's last and favourite job in London was running an old ladies' hostel: 'I loved dealing with all these fabulous old ladies, hearing their stories.' In 1979, after two years in London, he returned to Wellington and the New Zealand public service. 'I initially got a job with the Commerce Commission, as it was called in those days, doing trade practices work. Then I got moved to the Minister's office as private secretary. I also did some campaigning work for a Labor Party friend who just missed out on a seat in parliament after a recount. He was a very high-profile gay guy but very closeted in those days. As everybody was. You had to be discreet about your public behaviour.'

In fact, it was backward social attitudes that ultimately drove Morgan away from his birth country. Having adapted to the extremes of high life and low life in London, he wasn't prepared to accept Wellington's restrictions any longer. 'We had a function at the parliament and I walked home as I often did,' he says, recalling the final trigger for his departure. 'I went past the one gay sauna in Wellington, and decided to go inside. I was in the steam room, when suddenly all hell broke loose. The police raided the place. I thought the establishment was legal but perhaps it wasn't in those days. All these police were literally throwing us around. They were being really aggressive and unpleasant and I was half pissed so I said to everybody, "Don't give them any information. You don't have to. You can get your solicitor involved". The guy in charge said, "Just get rid of him", and this constable picked me up and threw me down the stairs. In one way, that was good because I didn't have to go through the whole legal palaver. I guess people were charged with indecency. But I thought, "I just don't want to live in a situation like this." So I handed in my notice, put my house on the market, said goodbye to my family and within two months I was on a plane to Melbourne. Even though I had good friends in New Zealand, enjoyed my job, and was well established on a career path, I was really upset by the circumstances and didn't go back there for five years.'

By 1981, Morgan's 'closeted' friend was living in Melbourne where he had a very senior role in the Victorian public service. Morgan accepted an invitation to stay with him until he got on his feet, and quickly found a job with Reark Research. 'I'd done some research projects at university, which just seemed to gel with a survey project they were working on,' he says. 'Then I landed a job with the Export Finance and Insurance Corporation, a government agency that is now part of Austrade. It was a fantastic job that really suited my qualifications. We were doing underwriting and credit insurance with clients like BHP and Rio Tinto. I was literally on the road selling insurance policies.'

Morgan prefers to underplay his abilities and contributions. He pokes fun at Jo's much more flamboyant and swaggering style, joking for example that this book should be entitled *One Hundred Years of Humility*. But appearances can be deceptive. Yes, Morgan tends to be as mellow, thoughtful and go-with-the-flow as Jo is passionate, blunt and driven. But occasionally Morgan reveals a wilier, more pre-meditated side to his nature – the political side. At what stage did Jo make use of this aspect? 'Immediately,' answers Morgan. 'He brought a manila folder around and said, "I've got this problem. Write me a letter". Jo's letters were very emotional and we started to make them more formal, more businesslike. Certainly to get into politicians' ears, we had to tone it down.'

And so the partnership began ...

6. Fighting Back (1983-1986)

Jo had been a mess when he'd met Morgan. Anxious and depressed, he'd sought help from doctors, only to find himself dependent on prescription drugs. Morgan had listened to his woes and given the advice that would soon set them on a long and agonising campaign: 'You can't win this battle in the courts. Your best hope is trying to get the law changed.'

The Australian Labor Party had recently won the national election in a landslide, after the eleventh-hour leadership switch from Bill Hayden to Bob Hawke. Hawke had been sworn in as Prime Minister on 11 March 1983, ending seven years of Coalition government. The country was fed up with the recession of the early 80s and consumer confidence had begun to lift as the new government embarked on an ambitious program of economic reform, made possible by the 'Accord' that Hawke had concluded with trade unions. Morgan's argument made sense to Jo. This new bunch of politicians might be sympathetic to his complaints.

To prepare for the lobbying task, Jo did some homework on his opponents. Chatting with a friendly contact from one of the major recording companies, he learned how the company managed to make such paltry profits as far as the Australian tax office was concerned. The parent company, using affiliates registered in notorious tax havens, would charge the Australian branch excessive licensing or service fees. Effectively, the parent would bleed the branch dry – in line with its annual budget target – one fee at a time. Then the branch was obliged to borrow funds from the parent at high interest rates to sustain its operations.

'When I discovered that this company turning over millions of dollars a year was only declaring a tiny profit one year and a loss the next, I realised that it was pitching record prices at the profit the parent expected and then transferring all the money overseas,' says Jo. 'It wasn't illegal. I could have done something similar when I started my label later on. Accountants were urging me to get into minimisation schemes but I feared the tax office more than death, so I avoided all those complications.'

He decided to write to the new Attorney General, Gareth Evans, a bearded former law academic and civil libertarian. 'My sister, Leonarda, typed a short letter for me,' he says. 'If you read my letter, you might need forty-five analysts to work out what the fuck I was trying to say. It was half English, half Italian. Yet somehow he understood me and replied in a very short time. He gave me hope that the government understood how the copyright act of 1968 was restricting Australian businesses.'

When Jo takes an interest in a subject, he goes in deep and keeps going. He then flew to Canberra to visit the parliamentary library where he bought books about copyright and trade practices laws. After studying these books back in Melbourne, it dawned on him that the two sets of law were not in sync. Trade practices legislation provided stiff penalties for anti-competitive behaviour, such as big businesses abusing market power to harass small ones. On the other hand, the copyright law appeared to sanction such behaviour in the case of the music industry. He felt he had found a powerful new weapon in his battle with the big six companies (CBS, EMI, Festival, Polygram, Warner and RCA).

It wouldn't take long before he needed to apply this weapon. Dance music culture was evolving rapidly around the world. Techno, Italo disco, electro funk and other sub-genre recordings were often crossing over into mainstream success. And mainstream stars were sounding more dance by the day. By late 1983, Jo's biggest sellers were no longer limited to underground hits by obscure American artists. He had imported twelve-inch remixes of singles by major international acts (such as Prince's *Controversy* and Madonna's *Holiday*) before the local branch of Warner Brothers was even aware of the titles in its American parent's catalogue.

In this context, Warner and other members of the 'big six' began seeing Jo's imports as a serious threat. Festival Records might have been the first to throw ice water on his ambitions, but it was by no means the last. Indeed, Warner launched the biggest and nastiest of all disputes.

As already covered, Warner opened the legal intimidation in December 1982 over twelve imported copies of a Van Halen LP. That

Fighting Back (1983-86)

problem appeared to have been solved by a cheque for $21.24, but in September 1983, the company began pursuing Central Station over three records: *Morning* (Al Jarreau), *Lady Love Me* (George Benson) and *Branigan 2* (Laura Branigan). When Jo received a summons to appear in the Supreme Court in Melbourne, he decided to escalate the issue to the chairman and president of the parent company in Burbank, California. Attaching copies of this correspondence, Jo then wrote to Warner's Australian boss, Paul Turner, accusing him of over-reacting. On the same day, he also began seeking help from politicians over the dispute. His first ports of call were the Minister for Consumer Affairs in Victoria (Peter Spyker) and his local MP (Clyde Holding, Member for Melbourne Ports and Minister for Aboriginal Affairs).

Central Station survived round one of the intimidation process when the Supreme Court listed the Warner case against him in 'miscellaneous causes', meaning that it didn't fit into any simple category and judgment would most likely be postponed for up to eighteen months, depending on the caseload. Encouraged by the fact that Spyker and Holding had at least replied, the Central Station campaign team then targeted Gareth Evans again. He responded promptly, notifying them that he had referred their complaint to the Copyright Law Review Committee that he had recently established to advise on priorities for reform.

Hallelujah! There was hope!

Central Station was not the only independent record seller with reason to feel heartened by the committee's formation. Peter Snow had started importing records while a student at Monash University in the early 70s. He and a friend had opened a stall at the Friday market at Monash and had soon expanded to the La Trobe and Melbourne University campuses. After graduating, the pair had bought Gaslight (at the top end of Bourke Street) and then started Collectors Corner nearby.

'In that era, Melbourne had fifteen to twenty very good independent record shops,' Peter remembers. 'There was Missing Link for punk music, Central Station for dance, and Daniel for metal. You even had an Italian shop, Mondo Music, on Lygon Street. Then there was Euphoria, Archie 'n' Jugheads, and Readings. The copyright issue drew a lot of independents together even though we were in friendly opposition.'

Peter Snow received his first threatening letter not long after starting in the trade. 'It was an ongoing war and the big companies would go hot and cold about fighting. Their thing was to divide and rule – attack individual importers. But we would ring each other and say, "Hey, I hear you've got a letter." Customers would come in and ask for something like *Cold Fact* by Rodriguez or *Never Mind* by Nirvana. If ten people asked for the same record, I'd telex or fax a supplier in America and ask whether they had it. Independent stores did very well when underground acts first came out and the big companies were asleep.'

What sort of tactics did the companies employ against him?

'They were nasty and threatening. They had spy shoppers. You could often pick them – like plains clothes cops. They'd buy the record, you'd give them a receipt and then you'd get a letter from a fancy lawyer in Sydney. The spy would sign an affidavit that he'd purchased the record from your shop. If you fought back through the courts, they would use intimidation – cut off your account, not supply you for a while. So we'd go to another shop that would be sympathetic and the owner would order in for us.'

The letter from Attorney General, Senator Gareth Evans, that gave Central Station hope of change – the Copyright Law Review Committee had been established

Like Jo and Morgan, Peter spent a fortune battling the big six. Why? 'Because I'm a fighter type of guy,' he says. 'It was a principle. I was just trying to help my customers. I didn't see that I was a criminal. It's tricky. You do want the artists to make something, but the big companies were running a racket, making a record for one dollar and charging us five. I had a meeting once with Festival, and I said to the MD, "This issue is business. I hope you don't take it personally". And he said, "As a matter of fact, I do". In that era, the bosses all wore bomber jackets and got to go backstage with Madonna or Prince, the Stones or Fleetwood Mac. It was all very groovy, they had incredible entertainment budgets, and records sold so well they could get away with it.'

In February 1984, Jo and Morgan brokered peace with Paul Turner over lunch. Warner cancelled the court action and agreed to let Central Station import records so long as it paid royalties.

But Jo and Morgan clearly didn't expect the peace to hold. A few months later, they sent a confidential submission to the Copyright Law Review Committee. With other independent storeowners (including Peter Snow), they also formed a group called the Australian Recordsellers Association – ARA for short – to make a separate joint submission.

Hearings were held in Melbourne in May 1986. At Jo's request – because he feared further victimisation by the big six – he made his appearance in private. At the outset, chairman Justice Sheppard assured him that his testimony would be confidential and the transcript would not be released to the public.

In his excitement and frustration, Jo rambled on, jumping from one issue to another. The chairman tried to focus on the main game – how the importation restrictions were affecting his business. Eventually, Jo settled down and started talking about how much better imports were compared with locally made records. To illustrate his point, he'd brought along two versions of *Borderline* by Madonna.

'Well, now, tell us the difference,' said the chairman.

'Well, the difference, first of all, is the cover. Madonna has got the ability to be sleazy and innocent at the same time and appeals to a lot of people and ...'

The chairman interrupted: 'You mean to say they ought to have a sort of calendar girl on the record cover instead of a plain one?'

Ignoring the trivialisation of his argument, Jo tried to explain that DJs were prepared to pay more for the American version because Madonna's voice was clearer and the remix was better. Unfortunately, his expression was jumbled and long-winded.

The chairman cut to the chase: 'They want to buy the import?'

Suddenly, Jo got his act together: 'Yes, better quality, better presentation, stronger cover, good feel ... you have got to make the customer come out with that money and the American seems to be able to do it. The Australian record companies do not. They are slothful, they are slow, they are hopeless. They do not want to know about new ideas. They still think about Frank Sinatra or Bing Crosby.'

'Some of us do, you know,' returned Justice Sheppard.

The transcript of the proceedings is painful to read. Jo struggled to convey how the majors frustrated his every move in the record-selling business. The chairman repeatedly told him he was straying from the committee's terms of reference. All committee members tried putting his arguments back to him in succinct form to clarify what he was saying. You can't help feeling sorry for everyone concerned.

But the most unfortunate part of the story was yet to come – Jo's cover was blown. Because of an administrative error, his name was recorded at the end of the previous public session as the next witness to appear. He believes that this slip-up enraged the majors and contributed to the complete shutdown of supply they collectively delivered in June 1989.

7. Evolution (1986-1989)

'They were a blooming business that took Sydney and Australia by storm. And they were big sellers of our [RAT Party] tickets ... They are an extraordinary couple of people. They did something groundbreaking in Australia and New Zealand ... I was a bit shocked and mesmerised by how fast it grew.'
Jac Vidgen

Central Station grew rapidly in the second half of the 80s. These were fun and fast-changing times.

Melbourne shuffle

By this time, there were three stores in Melbourne's central business district. Two were in the City Square (dance, alternative), and one was at the second Princes Gate Arcade site (heavy metal).

The dance shop occupied a large space of about 500 square metres in the interior of the City Square shopping complex. Jo had fittings custom-built for vinyl, and bought eight huge JBL speakers: 'They were American-made, specifically for disco and dance music, and created a wonderfully round sound. Four on this side and four that side. They were pumping music at six hundred watts. The sound was just immaculate. Every time I played a song, it sold. The shop had more than 100,000 pieces of vinyl by then. Everything was catalogued – by the artist's name for major stars like Prince and Madonna, and by song title for the rest.'

The alternative music shop (featuring the new era of British bands) operated on the outside of the complex, on the frontage to the plaza. To promote a new record by Culture Club, Jo put an eye-catching display in the window. The centrepiece was a sculpture (made by one of Morgan's friends) of a green kangaroo with a human head and a sizeable penis. The controversial body part was 'concealed' by a Culture Club banner, but there was no doubt about its size and readiness for action. It was ghastly to look at, but attracted crowds of onlookers. One cold morning, about seven o'clock, a group of elderly people in cardigans stopped Jo as he was entering the store.

'Are you the owner?' they asked.

'Yes, what's your problem?'

'That statue is offensive to our religion. We want you to remove it.'

'Well, I don't think much of your religion, and I don't think I should remove the statue.'

Jo forced his way past, but the protesters insisted they were going to stay there until action was taken. When he left in the evening, they were still there, with candles. Next morning, their vigil persisted.

'Being me, compromising, I decided to remove the display,' Jo says.

At the dance shop, he offered free classes to teach mobile DJs how to mix. 'When you mix, there are two ways of doing it,' he explains. 'You start with two turntables and a mixing console. The easier way is to use a cross-fader in the middle, but the better way is to synchronise the beats as you bring one song up in volume and the other down. You listen to the monitors, and adjust the speeds on one or both channels until the beats synchronise. Sometimes, you let both songs play in sync for half a minute because it's such a rich and beautiful new wave of sound. Then you pull the first one back gently, and the second one takes over. I used to show the mobile DJs how to count the beats. They'd be amazed, buy the equipment, and keep coming back for vinyl.'

Dance scene technology was still very primitive by today's standards, but it was evolving rapidly. The Technics SL-1200, a series manufactured by Japanese company Matsushita from 1972 to 2010, was the most popular turntable among DJs at the time. The 1200s were very robust and stable, allowing for scratching and other manipulations, but they were also expensive and difficult to source. 'For me to expand into the DJ market, I had to offer something that was affordable,' says Jo. 'Initially, they were very rare in Australia, so we used to buy them from the United States. We packaged them up with a transformer and a cartridge, and sold the lot at cost. I sold my first batch of ten, then more and more, until supply dried up. The more I sold of these 1200s, the more vinyl I sold. The mobile DJs would come in at least once a month and buy twenty or thirty records at a time.

'Later, we bought a hundred pieces of this big mixing console, one of the first available from Taiwan. They were ugly, so they took a long time to sell. Eventually, I discounted them well below cost just to get rid of them. But, by doing that, I developed more and more DJs and they came back to the store. On the one hand, I was giving, but I was also getting back from people.'

Jo also created a DJ association. After completing a form, applicants received an identifying key ring, which gave them access to clubs and discounts at various shops that participated. 'I didn't give a shit about

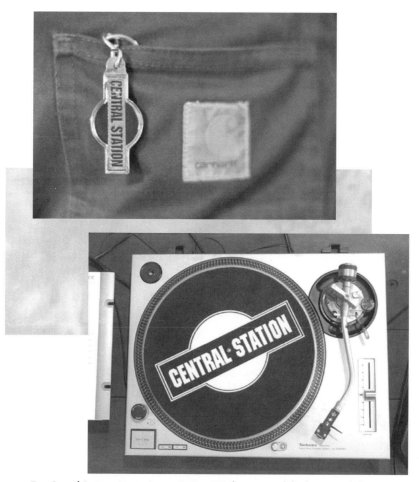

Top: Central Station set up a DJ Association. Members received this key-ring which gave them access to clubs and discounts. Above: The Technics SL-1200 turntable with a Central-branded slipmat (Photos by David Hannah)

credentials. If a young person wanted to become a DJ, I gave them the key ring,' says Jo.

Radio was crucial for promotion. Paul Jackson ran a show, *Blame it on Disco*, on 3RRR on Friday nights, and became friendly with Jo when he came to the shop to borrow records for his popular four-hour slot. 'Paul often asked me to go into the studio and bring some records,' recalls Jo. 'I always picked esoteric ones. I never went for commercial sounds, always something different. He'd ask me what I liked about the songs. It was like describing food. Not easy to do. One day I came up with the idea for a competition. I had a four-track tape recorder, a Tascam, and I took excerpts of thirteen songs, mainly instrumental sections, and put them all on a three-minute recording. I offered a set of Technics 1200s with cartridges, plus a mixer and a couple of hundred dollars worth of records, to anyone who could identify all thirteen songs. The last excerpt was the very end of a song, so it was particularly hard to pick. Paul Jackson played this tape every Friday night for a long time. No one could work it out. Then one night I was at the studio and this guy calls up. He got them all. So we invited him to come in. I expected him to be young, but he was a middle-aged man, and I was shocked that the dance audience went that far.'

Outside in the City Square plaza, Jo sponsored break-dancing competitions, and live telecasts to DJ competitions. On Friday nights, huge crowds of teenagers would gather to watch the informal contests, picking the winners with their applause. The phenomenon even inspired a special event at Moomba one year – when the Danz on Streetz Mardi Gras replaced the traditional Latin American event. Jo was quoted in a newspaper article: 'This is street music. It is unity and socialism. Kids are expressing their feelings about society by dancing in the streets. It is not rebellion. They express themselves peacefully through their body motion.'

The Melbourne City Council liked what Jo was doing because he was bringing thousands of kids into the controversial square. Ever since its opening in 1980, the pedestrian plaza and civic centre had been a hot topic on talkback radio, with many people considering it to be barren, noisy and ugly. A large yellow steel sculpture, dubbed the 'Yellow Peril', was moved to Batman Park in July 1981 after being singled out for particular criticism.

Then another 400 square metres of vacant space under the cascades caught Jo's eyes. He asked the Council if he could use that as well, and

Evolution (1986-1989)

they agreed. With hundreds of interstate calls coming in, Jo decided to establish a mail-order system there. Paul Jackson, the 3RRR DJ and friend, started to work there, along with others, answering phone calls and preparing parcels. Jo moved his office in too.

Central Station was not just about friends – it was also about family. As the business grew, Jo brought in sister Leonie and brother Emilio. Leonie worked in accounts and Emilio on the retail side. 'I've always been in the motor trade, but around 1983 I got sick and tired of what I was doing, so Jo said to come and work with him,' says Emilio. 'He wanted me to take charge, but I said I couldn't do that unless I learned first. So I would do the banking and the running around. Then I started setting up the stores.'

In May 1985, ahead of the demolition of the Gas & Fuel Towers, Jo moved Metal for Melbourne to shop 12, 181 Flinders Street, just around the corner. 'About this time, I broke my right elbow,' remembers Greta Tate. 'Jo dropped an old typewriter on the desk for me to type letters for the mail-order side. I'd never used one before. I typed left-handed for a while until my elbow healed. By then I'd really got into the typing, and Jo got me an electric typewriter. I thought, "Cool". So I typed my charts until he dumped a computer on my desk later on!'

Central Station sponsored break-dancing competitions in the City Square plaza

The heavy metal store 'upstairs' from Princes Gate Arcade – shop 12, 181 Flinders Street (courtesy of Greta Tate)

'Metal for Melbourne was a very important business for me,' says Jo. 'We released several underground vinyl pieces and CDs, even exporting albums. Greta did amazing things, including hosting heavy metal performances in the city. They were always jam-packed.'

Greta elaborates: 'Taipan was our first release, just a seven-inch with *Tired of You* on the A side, and *The Cellar* on the B-side. Bullet Records in England later took that up and released it as a twelve-inch single. Then we did a twelve-inch vinyl EP by Blackjack, our first on the Metal For Melbourne label. Next were two albums by Taramis – *Queen of Thieves* and *Stretch of the Imagination*. Both were picked up by Metal Blade in the USA and another label in Europe, and have since been re-released on CD with bonus tracks.'

A magnet for metal fans, Greta's Facebook page includes albums of photos, all carefully labeled and dated, of the many in-store appearances and annual gigs she organised. When those in-stores became so popular that Greta was obliged to notify police for crowd-control purposes, her underground tribe suddenly became very visible indeed.

On one occasion, however, Greta didn't bother alerting the police. A Christian metal band called Stryper was doing an in-store on a Saturday afternoon, and she didn't expect much of a crowd. 'I totally underestimated this one,' she says. 'About 700 to 800 people showed up, and they were all over Flinders Street, disrupting traffic. The band arrived and made it into the shop, but we had to lock the door as there was no controlling the crowd. The shop backed onto the arcade and our front and back glass walls were heaving back and forth with the force of the crowd! One guy went through the glass window of the travel agents next door. We rang the police for help, but were stuck in that shop for a few hours before they could come. They weren't amused, because most of the police were on duty at a big footy match. The police drove very carefully through the crowd, and backed a divi van right up to our door. We unlocked it, the band jumped in, and they were off. So no one got any signatures or talked to the band that day except for us. A few years later, in an interview in a metal magazine, Stryper members were asked about the scariest time they'd had as a band. They said that soldiers with machine guns had stood in the aisles at one of their gigs, but their scariest memory was of our in-store!!'

'We were doing good business by the mid-80s,' Jo recalls. 'Profit wasn't high, because I was putting everything back into stock, but I saw the future developing, and I had a long-term view. I wanted the multinationals off my back. I wanted to build an integrated business with production, distribution and sales.'

Blackie Lawless made a promotional visit to Metal for Melbourne in November 1985 to test the waters for his band, WASP, to tour Down Under from the US. The in-store appearance attracted a huge crowd. (courtesy of Greta Tate)

Sydney offshoot

While Jo was fighting the big end of town, Morgan was rising through its ranks. At the Export Finance and Insurance Corporation – EFIC for short – he was promoted to the level of assistant manager in Victoria, before being tapped for an even bigger role in Sydney. 'I was working on overseas projects, so it was a whole new ball game,' he says. 'Instead of insurance, we were getting consortia together to bid on big capital projects overseas.'

On top of his new job, Morgan set about establishing a beachhead in Sydney. He and Jo were aware of many DJs wanting Central Station to set up in other cities. Some would even drive from Sydney, Adelaide and Brisbane to buy records in bulk from the Melbourne store.

Sydney was the obvious choice for the first interstate store – not only was it Australia's biggest population centre, but also Morgan would be based there and able to keep an eye on things. Once Morgan had found a suitable location, Emilio Palumbo arranged all of the fixtures and fittings, and the late Paul Jackson opted to leave Melbourne to manage the operation. The new store, under Phantom Records in Pitt Street in the city, opened on 12 October 1987. 'It was underground. Mould, rats and dust,' remembers Jo. 'But we were an underground

A chart produced by the new store in Pitt Street, Sydney in 1988

Evolution (1986-1989)

brand and it suited our image. So we opened the store and promoted it in *3D* and a few other magazines. But it didn't take off. It proved to be a very difficult market when we first opened up. I expected it to be much like Melbourne, but it was totally different. It was exclusive, secretive, underground. There was a shop called Disco City, very well known. We had to crack into his market, but the local DJs weren't buying the stuff we were importing. We had a lot of initial losses.'

To make sure Central wasn't trailing its competitor time-wise, Jo asked suppliers to forward stock directly to Sydney, bypassing Melbourne. 'It cost more, but it meant we got shipments first, before Disco City.' The next thing Jo did was to truck in almost 20,000 records from his personal collection in Melbourne and put the word out through advertisements. 'Suddenly all the DJs took notice.'

One more piece of the puzzle was yet to come: finding out that Sydney was more oriented to house, hip hop and R&B than Melbourne was (the southern capital favouring Euro disco and dance). 'Paul Jackson started focusing on hip hop,' says Jo. 'That was what he liked and what Sydney liked.'

With all the corporate side of the music industry concentrated in Sydney, Morgan was convinced that Central Station should be headquartered there too. He bought a house at McMahons Point, which served as party headquarters for the business as well as a home base. But Jo had many business issues requiring his presence in Melbourne, so he and Morgan did a lot of flying between the two cities for many years.

Morgan on board

Meanwhile, back in Melbourne, a part-time law clerk working for RCA's lawyers walked into Central Station's shop at Prahran Central. Pretending to be a regular consumer, he asked if the store had a CD copy of Lionel Ritchie's hit album, *Dancing on the Ceiling*. The sales assistant told him it hadn't been released locally yet, but Central Station had imported copies from Britain and Germany. The spy left, phoned his boss and got the nod to collect evidence. So he returned to the store and handed over $35 in cash. The sales assistant reached under the counter for the 'guilty' CD, and popped it in a paper bag. 'Can I have a receipt?' asked the spy. This was duly given, and yet another court skirmish began.

RCA's managing director at the time, Brian Smith, was pissed off. In August 1986, his company had released the album on locally made cassette and vinyl, but there was no CD manufacturing plant in Australia at this stage, so he had to wait until October to source the CD version from America, and then package it up locally and get it out to retailers. There was a worldwide shortage of manufacturing capability for the new format, and Australia was well back in the queue for his American parent company. He had a raft of production and marketing schedules to juggle. How dare these Italian boys from Melbourne jump ahead of his timeline? From his Sydney office, Smith authorised legal proceedings against Jo and Emilio Palumbo.

The warring parties were ordered to appear at the Federal Court in Melbourne in October 1986. Jo flew down from Sydney to take care of the matter. Although Emilio took no part, he remembers the occasion to this day, because his best suit disappeared. 'I got it dry-cleaned because I was going out that night,' he says. 'When I went to put it on, it had gone. So I rang Sydney and said, "Wesley, is my brother in the shop? Is he wearing a suit? What colour is it?" It was mine! I think it was a Pierre Cardin. I paid a fortune for it. "You might as well have it now!" I told him later.'

Despite the fancy new suit, Jo was ordered to stop selling those CDs, and to pay RCA's legal costs of $2,000. By this stage, though, lawyers acting for both sides had worked out a general three-year agreement. At the cost of $1,000 for the first year, Central Station would be allowed to import RCA-licensed recordings providing they were marked with 'authorisation stickers' for display and sale. Central Station had survived yet another legal fight, but there was no elation, barely even relief. The process was too draining for that. It sapped energy, screwed up health and guzzled money.

In early 1987, Morgan suggested an Easter break from the ordeal. He was still working at the government export agency so wasn't involved with Central Station on a day-to-day basis as yet, but naturally he was affected by Jo's anxieties. The pair decided to rent a house at Port Fairy with some friends.

One day during the long weekend, Jo was sitting down listening to the thunder as an electrical storm approached. He remembers the occasion vividly: 'It was a beautiful, warm, stormy day. I took a deep breath and meditated. Suddenly, I felt like a bolt of lightning had hit the chair. My body went into a white spectrum. A warm energy entered me, starting with my feet and rising straight through my spine. Just for a few seconds. No pain, just total bliss. Everything clicked together. I knew all at once why I was fighting so hard to change the law. Not for myself, but to help other people. I went to the mirror. "Fuck," I thought. What had happened? My face had changed. My whole energy had changed. I felt like Jesus Christ, because of my upbringing. Then I began a quest to discover more about reaching a higher level of understanding. It took me a long time to evolve. Now I get just how powerful an activist can be when he or she believes in the fair-go, shares knowledge with others and lets the smarter ones do better.'

After his 'white-light' moment, Jo had a heart-to-heart with Morgan. 'Getting through this next stage isn't going to be easy,' he said. 'I don't want you working at another job, flitting off overseas while I'm stuck here working all hours, seven days a week. Let's share the burden, the profits, everything. Leave your job. Work for Central Station full-time. I'll give you half of my share, before it becomes too big and I won't be able to afford the transfer costs. I want to make sure our relationship is sustainable. We have to base it on working together to change the copyright law. No matter how hard, we can't let go.'

Morgan was committed to Jo, and could see the potential of the business, but he was also reluctant to ditch his career and Sydney lifestyle. 'Why don't I try to negotiate leave of absence for a while?' he suggested. 'We can live between Sydney and Melbourne. You focus on managing the business. and I'll focus on development ... all that stuff you don't have the time or interest for.'

Was that a marriage proposal? If so, it doesn't appear any more romantic than their meeting. As Morgan says these days, 'Ours was a love story within a business story ... or maybe a business story within a love story'. Jo is much less sentimental – on the surface at least. Here's what he says about life priorities: 'I always put my work first, my dogs second, my mum and dad third, my lifestyle fourth and my partnership on the bottom. You can quote that!'

Luckily Morgan managed to swing a two-year leave of absence from EFIC. So he joined Central Station as business manager, and began shaping a role for himself. Being a scribe, spin doctor and cheerleader for the business wasn't enough to keep him amused or to keep Jo off his back. He walked into a business in upheaval. No sooner had he joined than scuffles broke out with five different companies – Warner, EMI, Festival Records, CBS and Liberation Records (part of the Mushroom empire). A new issue had arisen. From the get-go, Jo had claimed that his shops were actually helping the majors by making hits of songs in their international catalogues that they had under-estimated or been slow off the mark with. Now some majors were stitching up licensing agreements with the independent labels that Central had cultivated, leaving Central out in the cold.

Distribution

Then bad news came from another quarter – Melbourne City Council had cooked up a new and simpler plan for the controversial City Square. The Regent Theatre would be saved. A new hotel would be built on one end of the space, and the retail centre would be demolished. Despite having signed a lease, and having done an extraordinary job of bringing young people into the complex, Central Station would have to move, because of a demolition clause in the lease.

'At this point, we decided to buy a warehouse in South Melbourne, and borrowed from Colonial Mutual,' says Jo. Morgan remembers: 'We bought this big warehouse in Market Street. It was huge, massive. It's been pulled down now. Beautiful two-storey building. We built basic accommodation for ourselves in the ceiling, with a bedroom, shower and toilet. We used the general staff kitchen downstairs.'

More moves

In August 1989, Central Station moved from the City Square to 340 Flinders Street, and from Prahran Central to 336 Chapel Street. The premises were good and the rent was reasonable. Naively, though, Jo signed personal guarantees to secure the space. 'Stupid me. I shouldn't have done that,' he says, recalling a move he would come to regret. 'I wasn't that smart.'

'I spent a fortune developing 340 Flinders Street,' he continues. 'We installed the most expensive screens to run videos, the first time anyone had done that in Melbourne. We moved to metal display fittings, specially designed for us by a Melbourne firm. And we promoted the store on TV. It became a very successful shop.'

The job of setting up 340 Flinders Street had fallen to Emilio Palumbo. Jo had sent him to Myer to check out their steel browsers. 'We used to have wooden ones, and we wanted to modernise,' says Emilio. 'The Myer ones looked fantastic, and we found the company that did them, but they quoted too much for what we wanted. So I found someone else to do the job for both Flinders Street in Melbourne and Pitt Street in Sydney. That was my job, saving Central Station a lot of money. I got the TV monitors hooked up, organised tilers and painters, anything we needed. I've always been practical. Then I ran the 340 Flinders Street store with Vivien. She was more experienced than I was, so she was in charge of all the ordering, but I got involved, and I learned the music and started to get the ear for what people liked.'

From left: Morgan, Emilio, an unidentified man and Vivien during the relocation to 340 Flinders Street in 1989

Not to be left out of the mayhem, Metal for Melbourne moved to one of the 'vaults' in Banana Alley, a stretch of shops below street-level running along Flinders Street southwards from the station.

The label

Meanwhile, Jo's dream of building a vertically integrated business had come together one random step at a time. There had been no cost-benefit analysis, critical-path planning or project scheduling, but he and Morgan had expanded rapidly between 1987 and 1989 – both upwardly in the supply chain and outwardly into the market. This was an exciting time for dance music. The Chicago house sound that was being played in European summer resorts like Ibiza had crossed the waters to the UK, flowered into the second 'Summer of Love', and inspired the acid house movement. Exciting new sounds, drugs and looks were spreading far and wide from the UK.

Being a compulsive traveller and socialiser, Morgan and Jo soon picked up what was happening around the world – dance was on the rise. They made a point every year of going to MIDEM, the major record industry trade event, held in Cannes in France and attended by musicians, producers, agents, lawyers and business people from recording companies of all sizes. Meeting independent label owners and distributors, Morgan felt that Central Station was in an unbeatable position to join their ranks. Central was the pioneer. It had nurtured and developed the market for dance in Australia. Why not develop the supply side of the equation? Start a Central Station label? Of course.

'In the early days, we went to New York and grabbed some albums from indie labels,' says Morgan. 'The Jungle Brothers' first album, *Straight Out of the Jungle*, was one of our earliest hits. We met the guys and their label, and did the deal. We had no idea how it all worked. We just winged it. We toured them in 1989, and that went really well. *White Lines* was also a big single for us. But what put us on the map was *Jack to the Sound of the Underground*. That came from Holland. The DJ who produced it, Peter Slaghuis, died in a car crash soon after he made it, and there's a Facebook page commemorating him. That was 1989, and people still remember him. Some of those dance hits certainly ignited people's passions.'

Jo remembers playing soccer with the Jungle Brothers in the street outside the warehouse during the tour of 1989. 'We were just kicking in the street and they loved that. Then Sam Burwell said to me, "I know you've done a lot for us and we're very thankful, but Warner Music have offered us a big deal with a huge advance". I said, "Take it. I'm very happy for you". We were glad to have done their first album. Our intention was to take unknowns and make them big. At that point, they become too problematic for a small label.'

Sam invited Jo and Morgan to New York. He took them around the city and a couple of clubs in African-American neighbourhoods. Jo considered it a privilege to witness the scene: 'Everywhere we went, all the guys yelled out, "Hey, Sam" as we passed by. Then he took us to another party at The Tunnel nightclub. Morgan and I were the only whites there apart from the DJ. We went upstairs. People were packed in like sardines, even hanging from the pipes above. In a claustrophobic panic, I stood near the DJ. Suddenly, a guy came on with a microphone and said, "OK, now do you want some pussy?" The audience whooped. Then six gorgeous strippers came out on stage. The crowd went completely wild. Then 2 Live Crew played *We Want Some Pussy*.'

During the late 80s, Central Station had other hits with *Pop Muzik* by English re-mixers All Systems Go, *Jack to the Sound of the Underground* by

Hithouse, *Can You Party* by US hip hop act Royal House, and *House Energy Revenge* by Italian Euro dance act Capella.

In these early days, Morgan did the entire label PR on his own, including dropping VHS copies of videos at Channel 10's popular *Video Hits* show. 'I got very friendly with the guy at Channel 10, Gary Dunstan. They would have little competitions, so I did some digging and Dell Computers gave us a computer to give away. We had some pretty interesting campaigns. As part of the deal, Gary would give our videos a

Above, top: The poster for the 'black is black' tour. Above: The Jungle Brothers (at left, with Sam Burwell third from left) during the 1989 tour

A page from Central Station News spruiking 'Jack to the Sound of the Underground'

couple of spins. It was all about networking.'

Typically, Morgan would pick up hits from shop sales and staff recommendations. If an import was selling really well, he would try to secure the licence and release it locally under the Central Station label.

Having come from an export mentality, Morgan also began thinking about signing local acts with potential for overseas sales. He appointed an A&R manager, Stephen Robinson, who had some contacts in the pop world. Backing singer Lisa Edwards, most famous for her work with John Farnham's band, signed with Central Station in 1988, and two singles were released to general acclaim: *Burning for You Hot Mix* and *Waiting for the Big One*. Actor Stefan Dennis – famous for playing Paul Robinson in *Neighbours*, Melbourne's own TV soapie and export success – had always been a keen musician. Stephen Robinson made contact, Jo agreed to fund a video, and the resulting single, *Don't It Make You Feel Good?*, reached number sixteen in the UK charts in 1989.

Inter-state expansion

The next logical step was branching out on the retail front. 'We felt we needed outlets in every city to promote our record label, so DJs could get hold of the latest stuff and our material,' Morgan explains. 'Our Sydney store was doing well, and we had a strong mail-order business. We knew that the demand was out there.'

One day in 1989, he happened to answer the phone when a mobile DJ from Adelaide, Tony Caraccia, called to make a phone order. Both talkers by nature, they started chatting about music. 'I'm not your normal traditional mobile DJ top forty,' Tony explained. 'Ever since I discovered Central Station, I only play dance music – what I get from you. The scene is really strong here. You should come over and see for yourself. Set up a store. I reckon it would work.'

Morgan already had another reason to fly to Adelaide, so he agreed to meet. 'We had a customer with an imports shop in Gays Arcade. He owed us a lot of money, so I had to go over there to collect,' recalls Morgan. He went straight from the airport to rendezvous with Tony. As they walked about, checking out stores and nightclubs, they bumped into many locals who supported Tony's view: 'Fuck, we really need a record shop in this town.'

In Gays Arcade, they saw a note on the door of the debt-owing customer: 'Sorry. Closed Down.' Central Station had found its second inter-state premises. 'We forgave the debt and took over the fittings and the lease,' says Morgan. 'It was a beautiful shop, so intimate. And Tony jumped at the chance to run it.'

That he did. Tony quit his job with AMP, and moved into the tiny space on the ground floor of Gays Arcade. Within a few weeks, he needed to find a bigger store. Demand was so high, that he couldn't fit people in. Luckily, there was a much bigger space available upstairs in the same arcade, so Tony relocated to that spot for the next two years.

'We thought, "Fuck, this is working. Let's keep doing it",' says Morgan. 'Brisbane was the obvious next step.' The first Brisbane shop opened in Fortitude Valley in November 1989. A Canberra store followed in 1990. Perth had to wait until 1996; Auckland until 1997. There were even outposts in Darwin, Newcastle and Cairns.

The number of people working at the South Melbourne distribution centre was ramped up each time a new store opened. Nick Dunshea came to work there in 1988, when the operation was in its infancy. He'd landed the role after going to see Alan Thompson, then manager of the City Square store, about a job. Although he'd been an avid record collector at high school, and knew that he wanted to work in music in the long term, his intention had been to start a university course in the New Year. So all he wanted was something temporary.

Alan said the business needed some people to work in the warehouse. So he organised an interview with Jo. 'My memory of the interview process was just talking to Jo in his office,' says Nick. 'He showed me what I think was a stock list of what they had down in the warehouse, and he asked me if I knew those acts. I knew almost none of them, but I told him I did, and bluffed my way through. He asked me when I could start. I was doing something else at the time, and I said I would give two weeks' notice. He wanted me to start sooner, so I got out of the other thing, and went straight there.'

Nick's first job was to alphabetise everything in the warehouse by artist name. As a junior member of staff, he felt shocked by the level of volatility in the workplace, especially the sharp moments between his bosses. Jo would call Morgan into his office, and call him out on issues the same way he would with any other employee. 'I remember a lot of raised voices and them standing toe-to-toe. Jo was very passionate and animated in the way he tried to get a point across. And they were living above the office at the time also.'

James Fraser started with Central Station in 1989, initially doing accounts in the South Melbourne distribution centre before moving into the retail side. He remains friends to this day with people he met there. 'It was a very eclectic mix of people from diverse music backgrounds, and they were all passionate about their own little genres,' he says. 'Central Station was a bit of a magnet for what I call "the oddballs". I was an oddball, because I'd come from a commercial banking background. But I had a thorough knowledge of dance and pop music, because I'd been collecting records for over a decade. This meant that I could fit in easily, as I knew my stuff.'

Exports

Exporting other labels' products was another line of business. Through their overseas wholesaler contacts, the Central Station team discovered that there was potential for reciprocal deals – selling back to the people supplying them. 'It was mostly product from major labels, although there was also some independent product too,' says Morgan. 'Sometimes there were special editions that only came out in Australia – like the *Beatles Greatest Hits* might have an extra track or something else that made it special – so fans in the UK would want copies. Or the artwork might be different. It didn't take much for a special edition to attract collectors. We started exporting to the USA, UK, Germany, Italy and Belgium. Just as we were importing special editions from them, for our market here. The majors in the UK took a commercial view. They were happy if they got more sales. But their counterparts here took a perverse view.'

By 1988, Central's export business had grown to the point where Jo and Morgan decided to set up a distribution and licensing arm in the US. They registered Central Station Records Inc. as a local company and installed Andrew Kelly as CEO in Los Angeles. 'Andrew was running the shop in Brisbane, and he wanted the opportunity to live in the States, so we set him up in LA at first, then we moved him to Atlanta which is the hub,' says Jo. 'We sold to American chains like Tower Records and other indies. We also manufactured a lot of vinyl and merchandise under licence in America. America was brilliant. The product was high quality. Everything sold out.'

Systems

While Morgan was out meeting people and dreaming up new schemes, Jo was busy in the office sharpening broad-brush ideas into simple, tidy systems. He sketched out a jargon-free standard contract for artists, and had it checked by a lawyer. The result was three pages of plain English compared with the typical twenty pages of legalese. 'The artist would refuse to sign something, because he couldn't understand phrases like "notwithstanding the above". So I changed all of that to say exactly what we meant. We signed lots of recording agreements during Central Station's history. The only time we had a dispute was with a complex contract formulated by a different lawyer – catchphrases, potholes everywhere. From that time on, I refused to sign those sort of agreements, only our simple one. Never had any problems since.'

Jo also jumped into the Mac world, after a friend told him that Steve Jobs's creation was the future of computing. 'It was a Mac Plus, that little one with no memory at all,' he says of his first computer. 'I hadn't realised that I needed the PC environment to run accounting and stock systems. But the Mac cost me about $6,000, almost enough to buy a house in those days! It was too expensive to change, so I stayed with the Mac environment, and did the accounts manually. Later, I bought a scanner and got into FreeHand software, and created a lot of flyers promoting the new store.'

Luckily, Microsoft Excel software eventually appeared on the Mac platform. As the business grew from four boxes of imports a week to twenty, Jo used the software to create a database for the shops to price incoming goods. He created an entry form for the key data – importation code, customs file number, freight rate and foreign exchange rate. 'Exchange rates fluctuated quite rapidly in those days. I had to price each shipment according to what I paid for it. So with the currency in there I could tell how much to sell it for.'

Jo also used this database capability for his marketing and grassroots political campaigning. 'I kept a database of politicians and changed it when elections came,' he says. 'I created the letters, Morgan rewrote them according to what they would like to read, and we mailed hundreds of letters every couple of weeks.'

But more of that later.

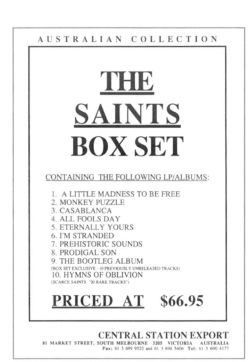

Central Station had success exporting Australian-made recordings. This flyer promoted the 1989 Australian-only limited-edition, 10-LP box set of recordings by iconic Brisbane band The Saints

8. The Dance Scene in the 80s

Creating music for dancing is nothing new. What *was* clearly new about the dance music that this book focuses on was the use of cutting-edge technology for both production and delivery. Disco and reggae musicians were early adopters of synthesisers and sound manipulation techniques like over-dubbing. During the 70s, both genres crossed over from niche clubland popularity into mainstream success. But after the Bee Gees' sugar-coated soundtrack for *Saturday Night Fever* in 1977 and Bob Marley's death in 1981, the excitement ebbed away for the masses. At the same time, a new generation of musicians was inspired to keep dance music alive and evolving in the underground. Hip hop bubbled up in New York, house in Chicago, and techno in Detroit. In southern Europe, Italo disco thrived. In northern Europe, Kraftwerk influenced everyone from Brian Eno to New Order with its futuristic electronic pop. At the commercial end of the spectrum, Madonna and Prince took electronica mainstream.

John Course puts it this way: 'A wave of music breaks through and then everyone starts playing that. I've been through a few waves. House music came out of the death of disco. The early house music producers (guys like Francois Kevorkian, Tony Humphries and Frankie Knuckles) were taking the disco sound and making it a little more electronic, introducing the drum machine and electronic elements. In the late 80s, the stuff you heard on a commercial level, as far as dance music went, were Depeche Mode, New Order, Erasure, and the Pet Shop Boys when they started out. And there was also Italo disco. In 87, 88, you had a lot of genres before house took over. Move forward four years and it's all house music, out of either America or the UK, with people like Yaz and

S'Express. The pop end of it became Rick Astley, and Mel and Kim, even Kylie Minogue, who were produced with very commercial house music backing.'

All of these influences came together in Ibiza. When four English DJs discovered ecstasy pills and Balearic beats on a holiday there and reinvented the feel-good formula back in post-Thatcher Britain, a revolution was unleashed on the world. The baby-boomers may have marched in the streets for social equality, but the ecstasy generation drove radical social change by choosing to dance together in their thousands, irrespective of race, gender, sexuality or social class.

'There has been no atmosphere like it since,' says Jon Wicks, a DJ who started his career in Canberra before moving to Sydney. 'Just the friendliness. I think it had a lot to do with the Berlin Wall coming down. We really felt like something was going on worldwide and this was a part of it somehow.'

The main population centres throughout Australasia all experienced a version of this revolution, but the scenes developed at different paces and adopted different styles. In the order of Central Station Records' presence, here is the story of seven cities in the 80s – the era of big hair, big beats and big change.

Melbourne

Melbourne is generally regarded as the live music capital of Australia, but its nightclub scene began to fire up in the late 70s, thanks to entrepreneurs like Brian Goldsmith and the city's liberal licensing laws. Each club had a different atmosphere and patronage.

The Underground, which Goldsmith opened in King Street in 1977, was the city's answer to Studio 54 in New York. It was *the* club for rich kids and visiting celebrities. Timmy Byrne, who now runs Kiss FM, was resident DJ there from 1983 until 1988 when he moved to another Goldsmith club, Redhead at Albert Park. 'It was early days then,' he says. 'The basis of what I played was dance-floor-friendly commercial music and then the stuff that I sourced from shops like Central Station and Mighty Music Machine, which was more underground and getting played at the gay clubs back then. Inflation up the road had a gay night on Wednesday and a New Romantic night on Monday. I got to know the DJs at Inflation, who were shopping at the same places. There was a bit of a fraternity going on.'

Kids like Ken Walker and Cameron Stirling, who'd grown up in

The Dance Scene in the 80s

Ken Walker DJing in 1984 (courtesy of Ken Walker)

rough neighbourhoods, either couldn't pass the Underground's strict door policy, or didn't want to. Then Madisons opened in Bourke Street with three levels – soul music on the ground floor, dance music on the first floor and funk and R&B on the top level. It was not only more inclusive; it was also the first club in Australia to bring in a DJ from overseas, Mario Gonzales from Los Angeles.

The visitor had a significant impact on locals in 1979. 'He opened the eyes for so many of us,' says Ken. 'We realised what we were missing out on and how little the record companies here actually cared about us, because he was being sent all the promos from America that we had absolutely no access to. Even he expressed frustration. He'd go into Central Station, and the stuff Jo was getting in was a month or six weeks behind what he was getting.'

Gonzales was crucial in helping Cameron Stirling's career. He visited Madeleines a few times when Cameron was playing there, and shared a few tricks of the trade. Shortly afterwards, Madeleines became Sheiks nightclub, a completely refurbished major venue. After a short stint working at Central Station at the beginning of the decade, Cameron's DJing career took off. 'I was working in big clubs in big times for those clubs,' he says in amazement. 'I did Sheiks from opening night, Madisons for three years (when that was still a *Billboard*-rated club, being one of the top fifty clubs in the world), Chasers, Underground ... But that all started with me working for Central. That's how I would look at it – a weird coincidence of events matched up with right place, right time and some degree of talent.'

Another popular club was the Chevron on St Kilda Road. The legendary Les Toth worked there (among many other venues) in the 80s. 'The Chevron was gi-normous,' he says. 'It was the biggest night in Melbourne and everyone wanted to be there. I had it hooked up with every record company. So if Jimmy Kirk from Simple Minds came down, they'd bring him down to me. Why? Because we didn't care how much they drank. Then the newspapers latched on. If they were trying to find someone in town, they'd go to the Chevron. I'd go home at six or seven in the morning, sleep until about one, go to Central on a Friday afternoon, spend three hours listening to music and chatting with other DJs, then off to work. It was a crazy whirlwind ride but worth every bit of it. I'd love to write a book, but I couldn't because I'd be shot.'

Although Les played dance music at nightclubs, he was better known for playing rock at pubs like the Ferntree Gully Hotel, and for supporting major mainstream acts like Midnight Oil, Cold Chisel and INXS. He witnessed the backlash from rock bands and fans as dance music began to encroach on their territory during the 80s. 'The pub scene was very healthy. Every little place on the corner had someone playing live. Then

'You gotta have a reputation or be a legend, and some of those guys are still the biggest,' says Les Toth of this photo. 'John Course, Ken Walker, Ivan Gough, just to name a few.' (Courtesy of Les Toth, the tall one at the back)

all of a sudden, the DJs moved in. In some cases that worked really well, because the pubs weren't really great rock pubs to start with. But the ones that *were* really did not want to hear DJs playing dance music. In the gay scene, it was uncool to talk on a microphone. They'd think you were a wally. Yet other gigs, if you didn't talk, you didn't get the place fired up. So it split up the DJs – rock DJs and full-on dance DJs.'

Of all Melbourne clubs in the 80s, the one with the strictest door policy and the coolest crowd was Razor, run by Gavin Campbell, who started DJing in 1983 and remains an important creative force in dance music today. While a student at Melbourne State College, he immersed himself in the St Kilda music scene, going to the Crystal Ball Room and little clubs run by friends. One of his flatmates – a music journalist called Craig N Pearce – had a huge record collection of soul, funk, R&B and avant garde European music. One day, Gavin suggested he and Craig start a club together. 'You've got the music and I know all these people,' he said.

So it was Pearce who actually opened the club and subsequently took on DJing, while Gavin helmed the door. 'What he was playing was very funky, very old school, the pure stuff that came out of The Factory. We attracted a very stylish crowd,' remembers Gavin. After only three months, however, Craig decided to move to Hong Kong. Having once subbed for him as DJ, Gavin saw an opportunity to move into the booth. Craig agreed to Gavin taking over from him on condition that he shut down first and then Gavin wait two weeks before reopening.

'I'm really glad he did that because it empowered me and gave me a real sense of ownership,' says Gavin. 'My debut as a legitimate DJ – because I don't count playing his records – was the opening night of my own club, Swelter. It was on Tuesday nights in the basement of a bar called Matilda's, in Queen Street in the city. We got the door takings and the venue took the bar. I played a lot of James Brown, 60s and 70s R&B, 80s soul, electro funk and club sounds, British new wave, post punk and eclectic pop genres, things like Elvis Presley's *Burning Love*, ABBA, ACDC, even rockabilly, whatever you could dance to really. More than fifty per cent was black funk and disco music, all of this wild shit that Jo had. Word of mouth back then was so strong, and the crowds poured in.'

Starting in 1986, Razor was Gavin's next club, held every Friday at the now-demolished Light Car Club in Queens Road. 'It was probably the most important club the country's ever had because we were quite radical and alternative, innovative and subversive all at once, with a lot

Gavin Campbell at a gig at The Underground nightclub in 1985 (Photo by Mark Schroeder, courtesy of Gavin Campbell)

of drugs and partying hard with a rock n roll lifestyle,' he says. 'All the famous underground and arthouse musicians would come – Hunters and Collectors, The Models and The Reels. At the same time, Melbourne's fashion scene took off and a lot of the new fashion designers began hanging out in clubs. Our crowd started to include fashion people, artists and socialites, along with the St Kilda grunge and music scene. Martin Grant worked at Razor and since then he has made a brilliant career in haute couture in Paris. Film and television types embraced Razor too, with people like Ben Mendelsohn, Greg Fleet, Tanya Hoddinott, Lewis Miller, Jacqueline Riva and Crusader Hillis all doing stints as part of our staff.'

Timmy Byrne credits Razor with being the first real crossover club, introducing straights to the underground music that had previously been restricted to gay clubs. At Redhead, he made his own crossover contribution, introducing acid house music to a mainstream audience in the late 80s. Gavin remembers how the arrival of ecstasy changed the club scene too: 'When ecstasy first came along in 88, 89, everyone was on a pill. They were great years and I know ecstasy had a lot to do with it. The club was fabulous already but to have a pill in you was quite a revelation.' A certain internationally famous pop star is rumoured to have taken her first pill at Razor. But Gavin, the ultimate name-dropper, insists we don't dob her in.

The Dance Scene in the 80s

The Hardware Club poster circa 1986

As cool as Razor was, especially with the fashion set, its claim to hosting the hippest crowd in Melbourne is challenged by supporters of the Hardware Club. Created by Paul Jackson and Jules Taylor, Hardware operated for several years in the mid 80s in a trade association building in Hardware Lane. Postings on the Hardware Club's Facebook page paint the picture: a dreamlike ambience, an arty crowd wearing black, black or black, and very hip music.

Morgan remembers it well: 'It was a crossover club, popular with gays and straights. It was very dingy and groovy, with Laminex-topped tables and beers for a dollar. The crowd was full of art college types, with groovy haircuts and nice clothes. Paul was the consummate DJ, very meticulous. He played really good quality funk and house music, absolutely leading-edge stuff, the latest. Paul would research his music, go through all the magazines. And, of course, he was in charge of Central Station's ordering and mail orders, so he knew what the latest releases were.'

Sydney

The story of Sydney's unique dance scene in the 80s really starts with the emergence of a strong, out-and-proud gay community in the mid-70s. The seminal club was Patchs on Oxford Street (later called DCM), and the most influential DJ was Lee Reiger.

In 1976, a fifteen-year-old kid from the suburbs by the name of Stephen Allkins walked into Patchs 'by accident', and couldn't believe his eyes or ears – the fashion, the music and the ferment of ideas. 'Gay people were just starting to revolt in Australia,' he says. 'In the 70s it was still illegal. So when you congregated at Patchs, it was a sign of strength of character. In the underground, no one checked IDs, nobody cared. There were lots of underage people, lots of forty-year-olds, but I'm seeing strong confident gay men, not people hiding in shadows. They were all free and loving, which needs a sense of self and caring about other things as well.'

The teenager would go on to become one of Australia's most celebrated and original DJs and producers. Now semi-retired and living on the NSW north coast, he pays homage to one of his biggest influences: 'In 1976, Lee Reiger was already part of record pools in the States and knew about all the New York clubs. On a Friday and Saturday, he'd do five-hour sets from ten until three and he would not play any top forty, only big and new stuff from overseas. So in one night I got this education that there was other music, the music I loved.'

Paul 'flex' Taylor also came under Lee Reiger's sway when he walked into Patchs in late 78. 'He was mixing records together, records that I had at home. I thought, "How does he do that? That's just brilliant – going from track to track so smoothly". So I introduced myself to him and he invited me to come up to the box, because it was the best place to learn.' At the time, Paul was DJing at The Zoo on William Street, just down the road from the Cross. Over the next few years, he worked at the craft until he became known as 'flex' for his turntable abilities. 'Practising became my everything,' he says. 'I wanted to put music together fluidly, smoothly, in an exciting way for people to dance to.'

In what Stephen Allkins describes as a 'perfect storm of fantasticness', a string of gay venues appeared on Oxford Street during the 80s, including the Exchange, Albury, Flinders and Midnight Shift. 'Everything just tweaked at once. The gay scene did have its progressive side, but it also had its totally commercial side. That's fine. You need the diversity. And it created a really strong scene. There were six or seven venues around Oxford Street that were all packed.'

As a DJ in this vibrant scene, Stephen stood out from the pack due to his varied taste. 'Anything you can dance to is my favourite – whether it's disco, funk, reggae – but that's so varied. In the 80s in particular there was all this in-between stuff that didn't quite fit anywhere. Back then it wasn't considered technically dance because it was too weird. Only twenty years later, *Go Bang* and others are considered dance classics. Because it was all happening in front of you, there was no guide. And the Tom Tom Club or Talking Heads, I'd go, "That's dance" but nobody

The Dance Scene in the 80s

From left: Reno Dal, Scott Pullen and Jac Vidgen at Ocean RATting at Bondi Pavilion in 1986. (Photo by William Yang, courtesy of Jac Vidgen)

else did that in Australia. I'd go, "Oh my god, listen to those rhythms". So for me, I was just buying what I liked and then shoving it into a set.'

In the early 80s, Jac Vidgen hired Ellis D Fogg to do the lights at one of his private parties. The famous lighting firm sent Reno Dal. After the job, Reno suggested charging guests at future parties to cover costs. Jac and his artist/designer boyfriend, Billy Yip, liked the idea and teamed up with Reno to form the legendary Recreational Arts Team (RAT). Their first event was held in October 1983.

'If you bought ten tickets, you'd get a free ticket,' says Jac. 'The purpose was clear – to get you to bring your tribe. Then the other thing was to make the party as interesting as possible, with varied visual and aural experiences. So we always had a bunch of DJs, different spaces, different décor, different types of performance. And the bigger we got, the more dramatic it could be.'

By the end of 1986, RAT was big enough to hire Luna Park for a New Year's Eve Party in partnership with the Triple J radio station. 'It was a fabulous venue, but it was quite complex and expensive to use,' he remembers. 'I guess we sold 3,000 tickets and we thought, "Wow, that's amazing."'

Then another good suggestion came Jac's way. Mark Taylor, who succeeded Reno as technical producer, suggested using the Hordern Pavilion (a venue within the Sydney Showground in Moore Park) for New Year's Eve in 1987. With the Rockmelons as the main drawcard, and

Maynard from Triple J also appearing, the event attracted 7,000 people. Bands played on a stage in the forecourt outside and a Tibetan flute player and magicians entertained people as they came inside to dance. Fireworks and a funfest added to the sense of celebration.

The team grew to include technical designer Wayne Gait-Smith, projection artists Tim and Mic Gruchy, and laser wiz Geoffrey Rose. Again, Mark Taylor came up with the idea for the next big step. 'Why

Top: Singer Deni Hines (fourth from left) appeared in a hair show at LaseRATrance in 1988. Above: Wayne Gait-Smith's famous plane lighting rig above the catwalk at Unite (with RAT and Dance Delirium) at the Hordern Pavilion in July 1989 (Photos by William Yang, courtesy of Jac Vidgen)

don't we get Grace Jones?' he suggested for the 1988 NYE party. Jac was sceptical at first, thinking that she wouldn't be interested, but he decided to shed any negative thinking, and made the call. To his surprise, the singer was indeed interested and RAT hit a new crowd record – 15,000.

'There was a bit of an issue about the contract,' Jac remembers. 'It was nobody's fault really, but it was a bit of a glitch that we had to sort out on the night ... which meant she went on at four a.m. instead of two a.m. It did look a bit scary for a moment. But she went on and it was a huge success. There had never been anything like it. Mardi Gras had never had overseas acts. *Ever*.'

Grace Jones at the 1988 Ratty New Year party (Photo by www.sonnyphotos.com, courtesy of Mark Alsop)

Another glitch marred the evening too. 'She didn't tell us that she would take her stylist on stage with her, so there would be no one in the dressing room during the show,' adds Jac. 'Some clever queen must have pulled the black plastic from the scaffolding, seen there was nobody in there and said, "Wow, look at those clothes". Then he must have climbed under the black plastic that was completely sealing the dressing room and stolen a patent leather coat that she'd worn during *Walking in the Rain*, her second number. Of course, as soon as she got off at the end of the concert, and she realised it had been stolen, she wanted to go straight up through the tunnel and trapdoor, and scream at the crowd.

I said, "You can't do that" and I had to get into the DJ box and make an announcement. I felt such an idiot. Everyone was just out of it and cheering.'

Subsequent RAT parties featured international artists such as Adeva, Boy George, Frankie Knuckles, The Prodigy, Graeme Park, Paul Oakenfold and Sasha. From inner-city bohemians – both hetero and LGBTI – the popularity of the parties spread to kids from the suburbs, as well as celebrities and celebrity photographers.

'RAT broke ground in the dance party scene because it bridged the gap between the gay world and the heterosexual world in relation to parties and dance music,' says Jac. 'Every promoter in Sydney jumped on the idea. "Oh, let's do a party." I think there were at least thirty parties at the Hordern the year after Grace Jones. British DJs were coming out and playing to 5,000 or 6,000 people. They had never done that before. We didn't come from a place where it was about the music. We came from a place where it was about creating an environment or environments that were really out there. Whether you took drugs or not, you would have a great time, because there was so much to see and do. And they were friendly.'

Meanwhile, clubs in the inner city had started playing English new wave electronic music in the early 80s. Stevie Bourk (aka Stevie B) was

Mark Alsop playing at Zoo, Hordern Pavilion, 1989

(Photo by Sonny Vandevelde, www.sonnyphotos.com, courtesy of Mark Alsop)

The Dance Scene in the 80s

only seventeen years old when he discovered the Tivoli on George Street in the city. He lied about his age when joining the Navy Reserve so that he could get an ID to get into the club. 'That's the sort of desperation I had as a kid to hear this music,' he says. 'I'm going back to the days of The Cure and New Order and that stuff was evolving into dance music. We all used to have studded belts and boots that had chains and buckles on them. And Mohawk haircuts. The look was punk but the music was a mixture of punk and dance. That four-by-four dance beat had started back then. The scene was sort of underground then too. There were maybe three, four, five clubs you could go to. And everyone else was playing rock and roll.'

Mark Alsop began DJing in 1984 because the gay clubs he frequented weren't playing enough of this new wave English music, particularly the Human League, Soft Cell, ABC, Thompson Twins and the like. A few years later, he was in the forefront of the dance explosion that hit Sydney in 1988. His first party, Renegade, was held in the Balmain area for a few thousand people. Shortly afterwards, he was playing to 6,000 plus people at the Hordern Pavilion. He was a regular at the Bacchanalia, Sweatbox, Zoo, Carnivale and RAT parties and is a font of information about this amazing era. 'The parties were drug-fuelled but I mean that nicely,' he says. 'Everyone was running around saying they loved each other and it was just a unifying, wonderful, happy experience.'

The combination of ecstasy, cutting-edge music and kick-arse lighting and sound was the common factor for dance parties around the world, but what made the Hordern so unforgettable for people was the extent of the theming. 'On occasion, Bacchanalia had car bodies suspended from the ceiling. Imagine it now!' says Mark in his typically bubbly way. 'One party was called Trash, and they themed it accordingly ... and it looked fantastic! There was also a Sweatbox party where they brought in industrial machines and they had little barricades around so you couldn't climb on them. These parties did so much theming that you'd walk in and go, "Whoa!" There was that surprise factor that really got the punters. The theming took you to another place. They really did put the effort in back then. On occasion you had to look twice upon entering the Hordern arena to check where you really were.'

Party-goers would put in effort too, dressing up in line with the theme. 'If you're having a party themed around the beach, everyone would turn up in their bathers. There would be lifeguards, divers, people dressed nautically, you name it,' Mark recalls. 'An industrial party meant ... you know how creative people are ... you had people in hard hats, bib and brace, little shorts and work boots. It was amazing to walk around the crowd and just look at how everyone had dressed. Sweatbox and RAT were very mixed. They weren't gay, they weren't straight, just happy people dancing the night away. Sweatbox in particular had the "in crowd". Almost everyone wore black. Unfortunately a lot of people remember the bad side of the Hordern – the fluoro! So many punters started wearing clothes that really shouldn't be bright pink, green and yellow. The women were the main offenders in this fashion "style".'

Of course, the Hordern fancy-dress style took a leaf out of the Sydney LGBTI Mardi Gras book. 'Mardi Gras created a sensation years before the Hordern,' says Mark. 'You always dressed to impress at Mardi Gras, and then when their annual Sleaze Ball came around, everyone *undressed* to impress.'

The 'official' story is that noise complaints from nearby residents killed the Hordern parties, but Mark believes there was also a natural use-by date. 'At the end of the Hordern era, the crowds were changing. A lot of the people who were there at the beginning didn't attend so much, and then you would find more people coming in from the suburbs because they'd heard about this great big phenomenon that was going on every week. The party dynamic started to change. People also started burning out. How many years can someone go out most Saturdays on ecstasy and not burn out? Those attending the parties in this state also started to notice that the drugs were changing and weren't as potent as they used to be. So I'd say that those factors are why it ended up fizzling out. It was special, it was new, it was fabulous, but after a couple of years you'd go, "That's not so new any more". Everyone had done it.'

Many early Gen-Xers wax lyrical about how much fun they had in these halcyon days, but was there a greater social significance to the 80s dance music scene?

For Stephen Allkins, clubbing began as an outlet for social activists and became a force for change in the mainstream: 'By the 70s, even though the summer of love had died off, the sixties had created an entire generation of thinkers, doers and strong-willed people who tended to be gays, women, and black and Latino people who were on the outside. These people went to clubs. That became their outlet. It was so energising and fun and vibrant. You could talk politics, do drugs, have sex. It was a breeding ground of positivity. I don't think people realize how much disco helped the political change, as much or more than rock and roll. It wasn't meant to be anything more than entertainment, but it *was*.'

Paul 'flex' Taylor believes that the arrival of ecstasy removed the musical divide between minorities and the mainstream: 'In the early 80s, the music culture was divided into ethnic minorities, gays and straights. And let me tell you, straight boys didn't know how to dance. Gay boys weren't much better, but they could shake their booty and weren't afraid to. But the boys who could dance? They were the Italians and the Greeks who were going to ethnic clubs in the suburbs. It wasn't until ecstasy hit in 87 that all of these different strands got together. It was the drug culture that taught white boys how to dance, how to loosen up, and brought people together. Drug culture was a very big part of breaking down stereotypes and bringing people onto the same page musically and mentally.'

Adelaide

In the 80s, Adelaide was all about quality rather than quantity. Simon Lewicki (aka Groove Terminator) – most famous for his Chili Hi Fly track *Is It Love?*, the No. 1 US *Billboard* club smash of 2001 – played house music at the Metro in the Richmond hotel on Rundle Mall. So too did Carmelo Biamchetti (aka DJ HMC and Late Night Tuff Guy), who was among the first DJs in Australia to champion Chicago house and Detroit techno (and who later put Australia on the world's techno map with his *6AM* and *Marauder* tracks). Across the road, George Vagas played punk, new wave and later acid house at Le Rox in Light Square.

'In the early days there were only three or four DJs and if one of us was sick, there was no one else to sub for them. The club had to close for the night,' remembers Simon Lewicki. 'In the late 80s, early 90s, after Central opened, we developed a very good DJ and dance culture in Adelaide, and Tony Caraccia was instrumental in getting the groove.'

From 1986 to 1990, former punk musician George Vagas ran Le Rox, a large-capacity venue that was the 'grittier, grimy street-type' alternative to the upmarket Metro. He played The Cure, New Order and other new wave material, until he discovered acid house in London in 1988. One of the cast members of the *Starlight Express* musical that he'd met through Le Rox took him to Shoom, the now-legendary, then-secretive club run by Danny Rampling. Danny's wife, Jenny, guarded the door fiercely. 'If she didn't know you, she wouldn't let you in,' recalls George. 'I went there with Bobby and she thought I was an undercover cop or something.'

Luckily, Danny came upstairs and intervened: 'Yeah, he's all right.

Let him in'. And for the next three weeks George kept coming back to Shoom, falling ever deeper in love with the music and culture. So he bought two crates of vinyl from Black Market Records and returned to Paris, where his girlfriend was studying, excited to play his haul at the French Kiss, a gig he'd lined up. He laughs remembering the occasion. 'They were into Madonna and all that sort of thing, and then I come on with this acid house, and I just cleared the dance floor! The promoter said, "What are you doing? I thought you were a top DJ from Australia? This music is no good for here". And then I got another night there and I put on *Kiss* by Prince, and I got the crowd back. Yeah, it was funny.'

Adelaide wasn't ready for the new sound either. Le Rox would regularly attract 2,000 on a Saturday night, but within six weeks of his return to playing there, George had whittled the crowd down to 500. 'I kept playing this pioneering underground sound because I'd been to London and seen it all, but no one here initially appreciated it. So I had to start playing all the alternative stuff again. Then ecstasy arrived in Australia and the whole thing turned around.'

Brisbane

Paul 'flex' Taylor DJd in Sydney, Melbourne and Surfers Paradise throughout the 80s. In the middle of the decade, he also managed Brisbane's first dance music store for eighteen months. But he couldn't make a go of it. 'Brisbane just wasn't ready for a dance music scene,' he says. 'The DJs in Brisbane were really commercial and played a lot of rock in the discotheques, or just Italo disco. If you had anything else that had a funk edge or a techy edge, they wouldn't touch it. We'd get all of these records in, put them on the shelves, and they'd sit there. DJs would say, "Dude, I love the record but I won't be able to use it".'

By the late 80s, when Central Station opened a store in the Valley, things had changed. Jonce Dimovski, who moved from Melbourne to kick-start Central's presence in the city, discovered that BrisVegas was ready to party. His first club was at the Waterloo Hotel in Newstead, near the Valley. 'It was one of the roughest pubs in Brisbane. No one had dared to go there, but I thought I'd do an R&B night on a Friday. So I hired the place and Jo couldn't believe how we were taking thousands of dollars. We packed it in.'

With 'the best R&B collection for a white man' and a personal friendship with Chaka Khan, Jonce had chosen this genre for his core stock, attracting professional basketball players from the Brisbane Bullets into the store. Knowing that the sport was very popular in the city at the time, Jonce cultivated connections and made sure that team members were present at the opening night of the new club. He also hired some of the most popular figures in the local nightclub scene to greet people and mingle, believing that they would bring in the crowds. The strategy worked. Called Deco-Tech, the club drew in 2,500 people on one memorable night when Jonce managed to put the word out to a visiting US navy ship. He then added a techno night at the Waterloo on Wednesdays, a monthly techno party at a club in the Myer Centre in Edward Street, and a dark techno night on Saturdays at Tunnel on the Gold Coast. He always hired the most popular DJs in town. 'I got Betty from Le Freak, Mark from Tunnel, and Angus from The Beat,' he says.

Canberra

Jon Wicks hosted a Sunday night album show on 2SSS FM, a full-power community radio station in Canberra. When he took the night off one time in 1989, his replacement played club music. The response was so enthusiastic that Jon decided to change format and renamed his show *D-Mix*. The result plugged into the 'second summer of love' phenomenon sweeping the world. Many of the records he played came from Central Station Records. 'Quite often, one of the guys came back from Melbourne

Dancing at the Canberra Theatre Centre in 1992, one of a series of Elevation parties (courtesy of Jon Wicks)

with a bunch of records just before the show started on a Sunday night,' he says. After three months of being harassed by listeners, he and show colleagues decided to throw on a club night. 'Back then, there was nothing for dancing really. We used to call the clubs "meat markets". That's why I wasn't into the club scene until I discovered underground dance music. We decided we had to do something. It was so exciting.'

Within two weeks of opening on Wednesday nights at Club Asmara, Voodoo had to find a bigger new venue. That was Smokeys, a little suburban club in Braddon in the central part of Canberra. 'We took them over on Wednesday nights,' says Jon. 'It was three times the size, but within three weeks there were people lined up around the corner.' A few months later, the event moved to Jaggers. The main focus was on hip hop, followed by hip house and acid house.

From top: Roger 'Ramjet' Close, Chris 'Kooljack' Ripoll, and Jon 'DJW' Wicks presenting the D-MIX radio show, Canberra 1989 (Photo by Roger Close, courtesy of Jon Wicks)

From the age of fifteen in the late 80s, Danny Corvini got into the events that DJ duo Jon Wicks and Roger Ramjet organised in Canberra. 'We were sneaking into these very early acid house and hip house parties. "Exclusive" is not the right word, but you were either in it or you weren't. For a lot of us who were gay, it was the first time in our lives when we could step into this scene where everyone was pretty cool and welcoming.'

Perth

Born in 1947, Colin Bridges is the veteran among the DJs interviewed for this book, reminding us that our modern electronic form of dance music comes from a long tradition of 'music that you dance to'. His parents loved to dance and the labels on their old 78 records would indicate what style the music was intended for – two-step, foxtrot, cha-cha and so on. In the early 60s, he and brother Ron would play records on a battery-operated record player when on family camping holidays up and down the coast of New South Wales. 'This record player would become the mainstay of the camping grounds,' he says. 'There was always a weather shed, so when it was dark, after the fishing excursions and that, they'd all come back to the tents for the cook-up and after that would be the party time. All us kids would be playing these seven-inch records on this portable Chrysler.'

Colin grew up in Sydney and travelled around Australia several times before eventually settling in Perth at the end of the 70s. He and his Cairns-based brother became big mail-order customers of Central Station, after getting hooked on club music and twelve-inch singles. 'They became our gods,' he says. 'I used to ring up Central. Then later on, they would send me a box of records and say, "Take what you want Col and send the rest back". I said, "I'm keeping it all". To send something back was sacrilege. It might grow on me.'

Eventually, the brothers built up such impressive collections that they decided to make use of them via community radio. In November 1985, Colin began hosting a five-hour dance music program (*Beats Per Minute*) on 6UVS FM 92.1 (now called RTR FM), the first FM community public broadcaster in Perth, based at the University of Western Australia. In 1989, his show was nominated for an award in the inaugural *Dance Music Report* awards to be presented in New York. Talking to Jo or Morgan (he can't remember which) on one of his regular ordering calls, he said he'd love to go but couldn't afford to. 'They were going as well to these awards and said they'd pay for my return airfare,' recalls Colin. 'My brother said he was coming too, so we had a five-week tour of America. We flew over to LA and spent a week there because we had a lot of contacts. And when we got on the plane to go to New York, I said, "There's a guy with a suitcase that's got Central Station stickers on it". When the flight was in the air, we went up to this fellow and it was Morgan! That's where we met.'

Thanks to this generosity, Colin was able to collect his award for 'Best Hi-NRG dance music radio program in the world' from the magazine's chief editor at Monster nightclub in Greenwich Village. Many years later, Colin is still doing the red-eye shift from one until six o'clock on Friday mornings.

Auckland

Sam Hill played hip-hop, funk and electro in mid 80s Auckland. With only a handful of DJs on the scene at the time, he got plenty of bookings. One of his first paid gigs was at The Box. Another top Auckland club was DTM (Don't Tell Mum), where a lot of Aussie DJs played as well as locals. It was a crossover period, he says, when anything danceable worked – from *The Message* (Grandmaster Flash) to *Pump Up the Volume* (Marrs).

Then acid house hit in the latter end of the decade. Sam was importing dance singles for Sounds record store and recalls ordering fifty copies of *French Kiss* by Lil' Louis on the strength of a distributor's review. In that deadpan Kiwi style that makes *Flight of the Conchords* so hilarious, he describes what happened when the massive UK club hit arrived in store. 'It would go for eleven minutes and there wouldn't be a single lyric. And in the middle there might be a breakdown with three minutes of sexual noises. And you'd play it for people and they'd say, "You're having a laugh. There's no way I can play this. I play things like Rick Astley". Most of these tracks ended up in sale bins, just because people couldn't get their heads around it.'

The tipping point came with catchier, more vocal songs like *Show Me Love* by Robin S, which worked on the dance floor. Because DJs needed other 'housey stuff' to mix with these tracks, the genre soon took off.

9. The Commercial Battlefront (1989-92)

In October 1987, stockmarkets around the world slumped. Australia's index fared worse than most, dropping by forty per cent compared with the global average of twenty-five per cent. Celebrity entrepreneurs such as Christopher Skase and Alan Bond were caught with massive loans they couldn't repay, putting their lenders in jeopardy. Many financial institutions went to the wall, including the State Bank of Victoria and the Pyramid Building Society. By July 1990, Australia was officially in a severe recession. Home loan interest rates peaked at 17 per cent in 1989 and the unemployment rate reached an all-time high of 11.1 per cent in 1992.

In the midst of the downturn – in October 1988 – Lionel Bowen (who had replaced Gareth Evans as Attorney General four years before) announced the Copyright Law Review Committee's recommendations regarding parallel importation. The Committee unanimously agreed that people should be able to import non-pirated copyright material if it wasn't available in Australia within a reasonable time frame and it was identified as an import via the packaging. The Committee also argued that outlaws like Central Station and Monash Records should not be whacked with criminal proceedings, only civil ones.

But it was all very vague. Some major recording companies swiftly shot off letters to Jo to make everything crystal clear. The missives were full of sentences beginning with 'you will not be entitled' and 'you will not be permitted'. Essentially the message was: 'Hands off everything on this list. Keep clear of top-forty chart material for two months.' Not in those words, of course – but in many more of lawyerly brutality.

More determined than ever to stand up to the bullies, the Central Station team began writing to politicians, protesting about the majors' behaviour, and urging them to support amending the copyright legislation. More on that in the next chapter. For now let's focus on the commercial battleground.

Remember the sticker agreement with RCA? In December 1988, lawyers acting for BMG (as RCA was then called after merger and acquisition activity at the parent level) wrote a nasty letter to Central Station about finding two imported CDs in the 340 Flinders Street store. No prior approval, they said, had been sought or given to import *Silhouette* (Kenny G) and *Direct* (Vangelis). The usual undertakings and client costs were demanded.

Morgan's style is stamped all over Jo's response. The letter acknowledged 'an administrative oversight' in relation to the CDs and proposed paying a royalty fee for the items 'inadvertently imported'. The tone is conciliatory but firm. All the same, there's a sting in the tail: '…we are increasingly concentrating on our own product plus the importation of product from independent labels overseas.'

In other words, the big six companies didn't matter as much to Central Station any more. Brave words. All the same, Morgan the harmoniser tried to recast the relationship with the majors from antagonism to collaboration. In April 1989, for instance, he met with John Rossiter, a senior manager at BMG. He said that Central Station wanted to set up an export account with BMG. He also raised the idea of BMG making custom pressings of deleted dance classics for Central. Morgan was even open to signing a general pressing and distribution agreement with BMG for the Central Station label.

When BMG rebuffed Morgan's offer of collaboration, he turned to EMI, proposing similar avenues. Discussions hummed along nicely for a while. EMI's managing director, Brian Harris, showed enough good faith to suggest a way around the big stumbling block – pay EMI a royalty for all imports of labels it controlled. Morgan was keen to nut out an agreement that would serve as a model for the industry and clear the air for wider discussions with EMI. All of a sudden, though, the veil came down. Harris abruptly stopped responding to Morgan's calls and letters.

Despite the political heat being turned up on them, the majors decided to flex their collective muscle in the marketplace more aggressively than ever. Within weeks of each other, they wrote to all record retailers, demanding their agreement to new trading terms – including suspension of supply for any retailer who imported infringing product. Later, the majors tried to force Jo and fellow members of the

The Commercial Battlefront (1989-1992)

Australian Recordsellers Association to sign onerous 'import agreements'. Refusing to be bowed by this collective thuggery, Jo continued to do what he'd always done – to import records that customers specifically ordered from him and which were unlikely to be released in Australia.

Retaliation was swift. In June 1989, EMI and Virgin Records closed their trading accounts with Central Station. The next month, CBS, WEA and BMG followed suit. Jo complained to the Trade Practices Commission, but it would be a full six months before any action would be taken (ultimately to no avail). Morgan was later told that the MD of one of the majors had advised his lawyers to destroy Central Station Records 'no matter the cost'. In Morgan's words: 'He hated the prospect of some upstart small business intruding on his turf. This was the defining motivation of the battle over parallel imports of music.'

The situation was dire for Central. For three months, Polygram and Festival Records were the only majors prepared to supply the stores. The others had declared all-out war. Not content with simply choking Central, they wanted to kills its baby too – the label. Other record storeowners told Jo they had been pressured to stop stocking Central Station product. Then Myer and Brashs refused to stock Central Station product too. The timing couldn't have been worse. Lisa Edwards was

Promotional material for the ill-fated Lisa Edwards tour

about to do a promotional tour, coinciding with the release of her single, *It's Our Love*. Advance publicity had gone well, with appearances on *The Midday Show*, *Hey Hey It's Saturday*, and *Countdown*. But, without the support of national record chains such as Myer and Brashs, Jo and Morgan knew the economics did not stack up – the tour and single release were cancelled.

The majors even shut down Central's export accounts, prompting Morgan to ditch his conciliatory tone and take to writing filthy letters. In September 1989, he targeted Denis Handlin, managing director of CBS Records, threatening to unleash a public relations campaign (in Japan as well as Australia) if Central's export account was not reinstated. Within a few weeks of this stinging letter, Central Station and CBS reached an agreement of sorts about imports.

To survive the majors' embargo, Central Station bought some must-stock local product from friendly independent retailers, even if it meant making zilch on sales. They also ramped up imports. But they badly needed another source of cash to stay afloat. Enter Emilio Palumbo.

'Because we were such a unique shop, I thought there was an opportunity to bring more clothes into the stores,' he says. 'Back then, rap was huge. And anything a rapper was wearing – like a cap or runners – the kids wanted. I spent something like $50,000 on Fila runners. and I

Emilio Palumbo at 340 Flinders Street (with Wes McDonald in the background)

remember my brother ringing the night I did the deal and saying, "Are you sure this is going to work?", and I said, "Trust me. It will work". And we could have sold twice over! In fact, we were selling more merchandise than records. Which was good. Some of the staff weren't behind it, because they thought we should only sell records. But I said, "If we want to survive these hard times, we've got to get behind it".'

Jo acknowledges how important Emilio's initiative was to rescuing Central Station. 'I realised that my brother had other skills. He loved cars and he loved design. Still does. He came up with the idea of buying T-shirts from a local company, and printing pictures of cars on them. Suddenly he was selling more T-shirts than records! Then we started sending them to all of our stores. I said to him, "You've done something I couldn't do". I was extremely happy. He brought in some cash to save the business. We had to evolve.'

If the majors were out to drive Central Station into bankruptcy – as Jo believed they were – they must have felt very frustrated by this stage. Did they strike back in petty ways? Morgan believes so. 'Our export line was thriving,' he says. 'The Victorian Government had set up these awards to recognise export success. In 1990, we applied for one in the category of new exporters, and were told that we had won so make sure to turn up to the gala night. Then one day we got a letter saying that they'd changed their mind. We got in touch with them and were told that they had been pressured to reconsider the award. It was obvious that the majors had intervened in the process.'

Although Jo was indeed amassing enemies, he was also finding powerful allies. Around this time, he got word from reliable sources that many Labor Party insiders and some Liberals were fully determined to change the copyright law in line with the PSA recommendations. These 'guardian angels' gave him a sense of protection and confidence to continue importing, because he risked only civil proceedings. In return, however, he was expected to gather hard evidence of the multinationals acting collusively and abusing their market power. He was sworn to secrecy on the details, and took the promise so seriously that he didn't even share the story with Morgan. But he was emboldened by the signal of support and plotted a survival plan. If the local majors wouldn't supply Central Station, then Central would ramp up imports and merchandise.

Jo remembers his reaction this way: 'So I imported everything and put Madonna and George Benson up on the wall. Instead of $28.95, I priced them at $20. Sold the lot in one week. The majors kept suing

Attending their first MIDEM conference in France, Morgan shakes hands with Australia's Trade Commissioner while Jo (at right) looks on

me. Their reps used to come in and shout, "This belongs to us. You must stop". Lots of bad energy spilled out of me. Whatever I made, and whatever I could do, went into the fight. I kept all the writs on the one big spike, and I'd have five, six, seven altogether at one time. I waited the full course of the law. I just wanted to know how far they would go. Everyone else was married and had children. They were too exposed financially. I was the only one who could fight, and all the court cases kept adjourning.'

No company was more incensed by Central's survival plan than Warner. When Jo started importing everything he wanted from the company's catalogue, bypassing the local operation altogether, Warner responded with more court action. First, they initiated proceedings against Central Station over a Madonna import. Then they claimed that Jo had imported some 400 titles in infringement of Warner's rights.

Jo's next move bordered on reckless. Nick Dunshea remembers the event clearly. He was working in the Central Station warehouse when Jo decided to pull all Warner product out of the shops as a protest against the barrage of litigation. 'My memory is that I suggested selling the stock off cheap ... putting big posters on the racks and getting rid of it all. Call it a "Warner" sale,' he says. Jo jumped at Nick's idea. One of his hip hop customers was an artist who had worked on the graffiti wall at the City Square store. Jo paid him to produce giant banners. He also made a flyer to explain the rationale for the sale and ordered a huge print run.

The Commercial Battlefront (1989-1992)

Staffers were expected to put one of these into each bag of goods sold.

James Fraser was working in the Prahran store at the time. 'We had these huge black and white signs put up for the now infamous "Fuck Warner" sale. All the Warner label product was racked at the front of the store, and the prices were slashed to get the stock out of the store asap. At the time, we were all a bit panicky ... Where it would all end? Would we have to close? What would happen to our jobs? In retrospect, though, it's quite hilarious, and typical of Jo's "take no prisoners attitude". You have to love that part of his persona. He was never afraid to stand up to the majors, and the DJs were completely supportive. They were onside, because they knew the game. They knew how bad the local record companies were.'

The campaign got a bit of traction on television news and in the street press, especially *3D World*, and Jo continued to promote his side of the story in Central Station's best-seller charts. Although Morgan had not been keen on the idea of a 'Fuck Warner' sale at the outset, he later came to see it as a good gimmick that raised Central Station's profile and ultimately led to a breakthrough in relations with Warner. In the meantime, though, it caused more headaches. Warner's lawyers latched on to the wording in the flyer. Somehow, Jo had incriminated himself,

One of the thousands of flyers Jo had printed for his 'Fuck Warner' campaign

admitting for the first time that he had knowingly imported their material.

'I didn't get my lawyer to check it because I wanted to save money,' says Jo. 'Before that, there had been no hard evidence whatsoever. It was implied ... hearsay. They had documents, but they couldn't prove anything. The courts kept throwing the cases out. They needed more substantial evidence to nail me, and stupidly I gave it to them.'

Jo's solicitor, Sue Dowler, was pessimistic about his chances in the Federal Court case about to be heard. So was his barrister. 'You can't win this one,' he said. 'You've admitted. They've got you.'

When all seemed lost, a couple of helpers appeared. Not quite fully fledged guardian angels – more of the apprentice type – two university law students came to visit. 'We've been studying your case at the Federal Court, and we see that tomorrow morning you might lose,' they said. 'We're passing on some advice about how you should fight. You are entitled to ask the judge for the original contract that Madonna signed with Warner Music to make sure that it covers the Australian territories that they imply you've infringed. You don't want a copy of it – you want the "mother", the actual original master. That contains an encryption of who owns the copyright to the recording. That is your protection.'

Armed with this idea, Jo went to court the next day. He recalls what happened: 'The place was full of wigs acting for the other side – lots of them, twenty, thirty – with trolleys full of documents. And there were executives from record companies other than Warner too. Everyone had come to see me destroyed. This was to be the day of my crucifixion. I looked at the judge sitting there with his white hair, looking like a saint, with his powerful hands and gentle manner. Our legal team requested the original contract with Warner Music, to verify the rights they alleged we were infringing. And then they asked for the "mother", this all-important master for the pressing of vinyl. You should have seen the other side. They all went white. The room fell silent. Before that, there had been joy, with everyone thinking, "Hooray. We've got him". The judge gave them a few seconds. Then he said, "How much time does the party need to fulfill the request?" or something like that. Basically, they didn't answer. They just turned their backs and walked off.'

In a better economic climate, Central Station might have been able to tough out the majors' bully tactics, but the recession of the early 90s nearly wiped them out. The business employed around sixty people across its retail and distribution operations. Spooked by highly leveraged

The Commercial Battlefront (1989-1992)

clients with falling asset values, Central Station's bank demanded a huge injection of money to reduce debt on the South Melbourne warehouse. 'I told them that would sink the business. You'll lose everything, guys,' says Jo. 'But they insisted. So I refinanced with ANZ, who were very good. But I learned my lesson, and I've stopped borrowing money ever since.'

However, the biggest blow came in mid 1990, when Brashs returned all of its Central Station Records stock. The representative who gave Jo the bad news initially blamed his own company's financial problems – discretionary spending on music had plummeted – but later said that a major recording company had offered Brashs a generous discount if they would stop supporting the Central Station label.

The now-defunct retail chain was a big player at the time (commanding a large portion of record sales nationally), and Jo couldn't come up with the cash to refund them. This was his absolute low point. Not only was he facing mounting legal bills, but the economic conditions were dire. 'It was just hell,' he recalls. 'Cash flow was terrible. We were losing money. We were bleeding. It got to the point where I almost brought in an administrator. I was just going to get out.'

One day, feeling sick with worry, he took a deep breath, meditated for an hour, and recognised that the only way the business had a chance of surviving was for him to shut down the distribution network immediately. For reasons as mysterious to himself as others, he donned a Japanese headband for the painful task of sacking twelve people. 'One by one, I had to tell them that they didn't have a job any more. Everyone was shocked, and some people started crying. We had some great employees, so losing them felt like our future was in jeopardy as well as theirs.'

Nick Dunshea was one of those shocked employees. He'd been working in the Central Station distribution centre for eighteen months, and was excited about a potential promotion: 'I'd seen a memo to Jo in Morgan's out-tray, suggesting that they should get me more involved in the recording side, something like "Maybe Nick should be involved more in helping us find product". When Morgan got me in to say, "We're going to have to let you go," I couldn't believe it. I hadn't seen it coming. It was my first job.'

Luckily for Nick, he was soon offered a role at Shock Records, an indie rock distribution company that bought a lot of vinyl from Central Station to export. 'In my last week, I told Andrew McGee and Frank Falvo to make sure they picked up their export order by Friday, because I wasn't going to be around after that. They asked me to bring the order out to them. Then they told me that they wanted to get more into this dance stuff. They knew that the dance boom was about to happen. "Maybe you should come and work with us," they said. I had the intention of just working through until January when I would finally start a university course. I hadn't really decided what, probably marketing. But I ended up staying at Shock for sixteen and a half years! Then I left Shock to start Liberator which is now ten years old, so I've really only had three jobs in my life. I also never got to study.'

After the horror downsizing, only two people remained in the office – Pam Verity and Jo's sister Leonie, both in the accounts section. Leonie demanded to know why Jo was sacking her colleagues. He told her that the business couldn't afford to continue paying them. Indignantly, she offered to join the exodus and Jo accepted her resignation. 'That's how hard I had to be,' he remembers. 'We cut back a lot of costs, but Central Station Records still made a loss. The bank was getting upset but I said, "Everybody's making a loss. Behave. This is all temporary. The government's got to go."'

After closing down the distribution function, Jo made a deal with Polygram to distribute for the label. (That arrangement stayed in place until 1995, when Shock Records took over distributing for Central in Australia, and BMG did likewise in New Zealand.)

But the tough times took all the puff out of Central's plans, and the label went by the wayside as other priorities took over. 'Our A&R had an

An example of the release sheets for Central Station titles after Polygram began handling distribution

inclination towards pop, and that was the wrong direction,' says Morgan. 'So apart from a few minor hits, the label petered out. We had to put stuff out in all the formats – vinyl, cassette tapes – and distribute them ourselves. That was a big chore. With one thing and another – the legal action and logistical issues – we just let it die.'

Feeling depleted, Morgan applied for a job at Westpac and moved back to Sydney. Jo remembers: 'I told him that he'd better get a job in finance to help him understand numbers. But Morgan went into a bank writing bloody letters and speeches, not learning numbers! He still doesn't understand money. But he's very good at PR and people. I try not to give him anything that he can fuck up.'

Morgan remembers his return to Sydney and a plum Westpac job somewhat differently. Apart from needing a psychological break and a solid income stream, he believed that Sydney was the true power centre for dance music. 'I loved the time we spent in Melbourne, but our problems had emerged there and we were sort of stuck on a sandbar,' he says. 'Besides, I've always loved the glamour and bullshit of Sydney.'

'I've got to give it to Jo,' he adds. 'He wouldn't give up. I didn't want to either, but I just had to step back for a minute. I still kept working on the label and the political fight. I remember slipping out from Westpac one lunchtime and going over to EMI on the North Shore to have a meeting with the guy who'd replaced Brian Harris. I remember him saying, "Every time I go into your shops and see EMI product that you've imported, I feel like my wife's been raped". I was shocked at the analogy. That's how personally he took the fight. In any case, I struck up a relationship with him, and persuaded him to reopen our account, so we got them back on board. Jo wasn't keen on that.'

Although Central Station's head office officially moved to Sydney in 1990, for a while it effectively floated between Australia's two biggest cities. Morgan was in Sydney, juggling a full-time corporate job and a part-time Central role liaising with financial journalists he'd cultivated through Westpac. Jo continued living and working at the now-empty South Melbourne warehouse. Emilio rented the ground floor from him for his motor repair business.

'Closing down the distribution system and even the label itself broke my heart,' says Jo. 'All the computers were shut down. There was a lot of leftover stock. And Pam Verity and I worked upstairs alone in this huge warehouse, taking care of accounting and administration and everything else while we waited for the economy to pick up.'

May 1992 was a hugely stressful month. Warner launched yet another legal action against Central Station Records, this time for importing records and CDs by Prince. Lawyers acting for Warner demanded a huge sum to settle the dispute. In that same month, vandals attacked two of the Melbourne stores – 340 Flinders Street and Metal for Melbourne in Banana Alley. Roll-down screens were bent, windows were broken, and vomit and urine were found at the entrances. Jo notified the police, initially suspecting late-night hooligans. Then the vandalism at 340 Flinders Street took a more serious turn. Somebody opened the fire hydrants on the building's rooftop car park. The roof flooded and collapsed. Water infiltrated the side of Central Station's flagship store,

Crime in the music industry

Phil Tripp is an American expat who now lives in Coffs Harbour. He met Jo and Morgan through his long-standing role as publisher of the 'AustralAsian Music Industry Directory'. 'My thing is about the business of music, not the art of it. But I did a lot to free up the music industry in Australia and that endeared me to people like Morgan and Jo,' he says.

As a freelance journalist, Phil specialised in writing articles about criminality in the music industry. One of his trophy stories was about the head of Warner (Paul Turner) being 'wrapped up in a multi-million embezzlement scandal'. Although Warner's chief bean counter was fingered as the main culprit, Tripp argued that Turner should be investigated because he was the boss. Following the story's publication, Turner threatened defamation action. Tripp countered by letting him know that he had evidence of Turner co-signing the cheques involved, and that he would use this information as part of his defence. No defamation suit eventuated, but Phil Tripp subsequently took a series of late-night calls from someone making serious and 'graphic' death threats against him.

He tells many other stories about the seamy side of the music industry. Although there were 'many brilliant people', the industry was beset with drug problems, corruption and legal double-dealing, he says.

Morgan remembers Phil's support and sage advice with great fondness: 'Phil was a huge supporter when we were at our lowest ebb. He knew where all the bodies were buried in the stinking music industry and was prepared to share his knowledge. Phil is a hero of the Australian music industry. He channeled so much energy into it over the years.'

Photo by Lisa Treen, courtesy of Phil Tripp

The Commercial Battlefront (1989-1992)

flooding the place. Staff mopped up and repaired what they could. But the culprit was not finished with them – two further incidents occurred.

'I realised that my holiday was over,' says Jo. 'The store was completely degraded. The police had no leads. The landlord refused to improve security and the insurance company refused to pay. I took the landlord to court many times and ended up losing and having to pay his costs. It was a disaster. Fittings, stock and image had been destroyed. I'd given personal guarantees on the lease, so I couldn't get out. Our cheap repairs made the shop look tacky. Trade dropped by half, cutting the income that was sustaining the group.'

It was a sad time. With the flagship store in the doldrums, morale dropped at the other Melbourne stores too. Jo started wondering whether someone had authorised the destruction of his store. 'They must have taken time to study the building. There was a car park on top so it was easy to access.'

The 340 Flinders Street store in its heyday

Meanwhile, Jo tried to bring an end to the Warner dispute by sending an anonymous letter to Paul Turner's ultimate bosses in the US. After listing criticisms of Turner ranging from 'inebriation at a nationally televised awards function' to 'frivolous litigation against record sellers', the letter stated, 'Warner Brothers in Australia deserves better and you would be well advised to review his position before he is able to wreak further damage'.

Two weeks later, Jo's assistant called out, 'Hey, there's a long distance call for you.'

'My energy was so grrrr I could have killed the Pope,' remembers Jo.

'Do you think you're David?' asked an American voice on the phone.

Twigging immediately that he was talking to someone from Warner, Jo replied, 'In that case, you must be Goliath".

When the stranger laughed, Jo knew that he had some leverage.

'I know you have this "Fuck Warner Music" flyer going around. Have many do you have of them?'

'I printed 100,000. I'm very angry with your group.'

'What do we have to do to get you to stop that campaign?'

'Well I have a court case in Melbourne and another in Sydney. I want you to withdraw them immediately.'

'OK, agreed.'

'And I expect compensation for my legal costs. I've spent over $75,000 so far and that doesn't count my time, my energy, my youth.'

'Understood. But I can't give you money – I'll give you some promotional goods. Enough to make you happy.'

'Whatever you can give me. Just as a token of friendship, and that will be the end of the story.'

By this stage, the Warner executive must have known that Madonna had refused to supply the 'mother'. He must have also known that Jo's campaign was hurting Warner's sales in Australia – its market share had dropped substantially. Importantly, he must have also known that the PSA had released its report after the sound recordings inquiry, recommending the removal of the import restrictions from the copyright act.

Jo castigates himself now for not realising just how much leverage he might have had during that phone call with the Goliath from Warner Brothers in America. But he certainly was aware of his promise to the guardian angels. So he actively engaged with a couple of major recording companies to nut out the terms of his surrender: 'I said, "I give up. I've had enough of this. I'll do whatever you want me to do. I'll sign an

The Commercial Battlefront (1989-1992)

agreement". They were very friendly and courteous actually. I went to one guy's office, had a cup of tea, and he said, "We're going to start stamps. So every record you sell will have a sticker on it saying you've paid a dollar royalty". And he gave me a big reel of stickers for free just to make me happy. But I didn't give a fuck about money. I just wanted to get the law changed so I could get on with my life. It had become this thing I just had to finish. I would die before I gave up. And it was killing me health-wise. If you're happy, your body performs. If you're not happy, you get a lot of trouble.'

As soon as the contracts were signed, Jo gave them to the Attorney General's department. Despite all of the anger he had built up over the years, he still felt a pang of guilt about doing the dirty on his opponents, especially the ones who acknowledged that he was actually promoting their product through his loyal DJ following. 'It was a headache for them,' he says. 'They had the government on their shoulders, the PSA, the Federal courts. They got fined, penalised. I heard the rumours. I took a low key. I didn't want to be seen to be behind that. My intention was not to be what I've become. I wanted a small business and happy ever after. They forced me to grow the business. I needed to get to the point when I wasn't dependent on them any more.'

For Morgan, the turning point in the battle occurred when they hired senior barrister Leslie Glick. 'He gave us hope,' he says. 'There are some lawyers who seem able to get to the nub of an issue and to see a way through. He laid it all out and gave us a chance to survive, which turned things around in our minds. So we could put the legal battle to one side and continue our political battle. Cost a fortune, of course. Hundreds of thousands of dollars. How do you afford that sort of money?'

Having been poor as a child, Jo knew how to survive on very little. He would go to South Melbourne Market near closing time when stallholders slashed prices. 'We managed to buy enough fruit and vegetables to last us the whole week and also give some away to my family in Glen Waverley, where we used to go every Sunday to have lunch,' he recalls.

What's more, working long hours wiped out most of the opportunity or inclination to spend money. 'I can remember when we were in Market Street we would finish on a Friday night at nine or ten o'clock,' says Morgan. 'We'd hear all the party kids outside. Somebody would ring us and say, "Come down to Inflation. It's a great night", and we'd look at each other and knew we were too fucked. We couldn't do it.'

One of the key aspects of Glick's strategy was to protect Central Station's main assets from legal action by restructuring the company. So Jo set up several separate businesses – one owning the trademarks, another responsible for ordering, and yet another responsible for sales.

'Leslie Glick was very personable,' says Jo. 'One day we were in court in Melbourne. It was Warner Music against me and I really thought my head would be chopped. Late in the afternoon, when our case was due to be heard, the judge suddenly put everything else aside to hear an urgent matter. Leslie Glick grabbed me and told me to run. I thought it was a fire. "Don't ask any questions," he told me. "Just run." Outside, he explained that my case would be adjourned for about eight months. "How do you feel?" he asked. "Like surfing," I said. Because I knew I had some breathing time to fight the copyright law.'

Blitzing the media to gain support for his commercial and political battles, Giuseppe Palumbo also raised his own profile.

In October 1992, gay magazine *Outrage* published a piece by Stephen Nicholls. The next month, *Personal Success* magazine ran a feature page story on Central Station entitled *Dancing in the Dark*. Naturally, Jo took advantage of these opportunities to hammer away at his bugbear.

Interestingly, two things that happened in the aftermath of this chapter's events do appear to vindicate Jo's belief in 'the energy'. First, Paul Turner resigned in June 1992. Secondly, after a long-running case, two major companies were fined more than $2 million in 2003 for threatening retailers over CD imports.

10. The Political Battlefront (1989-92)

> 'I would be playing the new Kylie Minogue single weeks ahead of all the major stations because I was getting import copies. I was very much on the side of the parallel importers, because I always thought that this whole territories thing with copyright was merely there to help large companies. A global release schedule is something they should have got on board with decades ago. If they had, maybe we would still have a music industry. It's a classic example – if you hang on to something too tightly, eventually someone will take it from you.'
> **Maynard**

As well as doing battle with their commercial tormentors, Jo and Morgan took up arms on the political front. In October 1989, Jo wrote to the Attorney General, Lionel Bowen, protesting about the majors' refusing to supply him. He said that he'd developed handshake agreements with Warner, CBS and EMI that allowed Central Station to import non bread-and-butter lines, but that this 'uneasy truce' had recently broken down. 'There is no doubt in my mind that the companies are acting collectively in breach of trade practices law, but under the guise of the Copyright Act, to put my company out of business,' wrote Jo. 'The reason is clear; I have been at the forefront of a campaign to change the Copyright Act.'

While the Hawke Government debated what to do with the Copyright Law Review Committee's recommendations, the Opposition came out in support of change. So Jo wrote to the Opposition Leader, Andrew Peacock, asking for his help in persuading Lionel Bowen to change the law. He also lobbied customers, collecting 5,000 signatures on a petition.

Morgan took up the pen to Lionel Bowen again in November 1989, complaining about vexatious litigation: 'WEA Records Australia have taken an action against my company in the Federal Court of Australia for importing seventeen copies of a Debbie Gibson record, 'Out of the Blue', and twenty copies of her record, 'Shake Your Love' ... The major record companies continue to harass us with this frivolous type of legal action, where the cost of the legal proceedings far outweighs the quantum of damages sought.'

Jo's badgering of the Trade Practices Commission finally delivered action in January 1990, when the TPC announced an investigation into allegations that the major recording companies were squeezing small record importers and retailers out of business by refusing to supply them. Unfortunately, nothing came of this process. Jo met with TPC representatives in his office in South Melbourne. 'They told me they couldn't help me, because copyright law prevailed over trade practices laws.'

Fortunately, however, a true champion did emerge for Central Station's cause – the powerful and high-profile chief of the Prices Surveillance Authority (PSA), Professor Allan Fels. Not long after he had been appointed chairman in 1989, the PSA had raised concerns about book prices – having found that they were, unlike all other product categories in Australia, impervious to fluctuations in the exchange rate. So the Government had asked the PSA to conduct a formal inquiry into the issue. What the PSA found was that prohibiting parallel imports delivered a bad deal for Australian book consumers – not just in terms of higher prices, but also the timely availability of titles. Because of concerns raised about a similar situation for music consumers, the Hawke Government then gave the go-ahead for the PSA to conduct a follow-up inquiry into the price of sound recordings.

The major recording companies were not happy with this turn of events, lobbying Cabinet and challenging the process through the Federal Court. They demanded legal representation, the right to cross-examine witnesses, and access to confidential information during the inquiry. But Cabinet held firm on its resolve, and the majors eventually withdrew their legal challenge.

The PSA held public hearings in Sydney and in Melbourne throughout 1990, and announced its findings in December of that year. Under the heading, 'PSA Finds Record Prices Excessive: Recommends Structural Reforms/Removal of Import Restrictions', the release ran to twenty-three pages, including graphs and background material.

The Political Battlefront (1989-1992)

Print media reports tended to give the bulk of column inches to comments from Professor Fels. His figures showed that CD prices were relatively higher in Australia compared with elsewhere in the world, and that the music industry enjoyed a much higher profitability than other sectors. Beyond that, journalists tended to look to the Australian Record Industry Association (ARIA) for the opposing case, and to consumer and union groups for the supporting view.

The majors spent a lot of money trying to hold on to their monopoly, and they paraded some big stars to support the cause. John Farnham, Peter Garrett, Kate Ceberano and Boom Crash Opera all lobbied Canberra. Television footage of them attacking the proposed changes made Cabinet members nervous.

> **RECOMMENDATIONS OF THE PRICES SURVEILLANCE AUTHORITY FOLLOWING THE SOUND RECORDINGS INQUIRY**
>
> Dec – 1989
>
> 1. After considering the possible consequences of allowing parallel imports of records, the Authority is convinced that such structural reform is the logical and preferable policy solution to the problem of high prices. It is therefore recommended that sections 37, 38, 102 and 103 of the Copyright Act be repealed in relation to parallel imports from countries providing comparable levels of protection over the reproduction of musical works and sound recordings.

When the PSA released the findings of its inquiry into sound recordings, Jo and Morgan photocopied this excerpt and used it in their grassroots political campaign

Of course, the digital revolution had already begun, and the majors would soon face much bigger threats than from specialist record importers like Central Station. Napster, iTunes, YouTube and MySpace were just around the corner. From the comfort of our current internet-enabled, instant-gratification world, the battle to break the majors' monopoly on imports may seem quaint and irrelevant. At the time, though, it was a life-and-death matter for Jo and Morgan. While the dance world was partying hard and exploring new genres, they stayed behind after class writing endless lines about copyright law and CD prices. 'I used to jam the fax machine at the Attorney General's department by sending so many faxes, one after the other,' says Jo. 'They would call me and ask me to stop. I would say, "This copyright law is killing me. Fix it!" I used to go to Canberra and pace the corridors. I wasn't a businessman any more. I was a politician with nothing to lose.'

Hearing this comment at a dinner party that Jo and Morgan had thrown in Sydney in May 2016, Mark Vick shook his head in disbelief:

'So this was 91, 92? For me, the buying public, that was the peak of things. The music, the parties, the clubs. You don't even imagine what's going on behind the scenes.'

Early in that action behind the scenes, Clyde Holding invited Jo to his office in Port Melbourne. Having showered his local MP (and the Minister for Aboriginal Affairs) with letters over the years, Jo was excited to get the chance to finally meet him. Unfortunately, he was also anxious and over-prepared. Clyde Holding sat down in a big chair and invited Jo to sit opposite him, across a big wooden desk. Jo opened a Central Station carry basket full of vinyl, and spread records on the table. Holding's attention was drawn to Lisa Edwards first, and then to Ruth Campbell's very gay *This Is It* cover. He asked questions about Lisa.

'We've spent $20,000 promoting this record in London,' explained Jo, trying the PR path before launching into his complaints.

'What are you doing about the copyright law?' he asked eventually.

'We're reviewing it,' came the reply.

Whipping out his spreadsheets, Jo delivered what he thought would be a killer argument: 'Do you know that these companies are transferring anticipated profits by royalty transfers and interest payments on loans? So they export all their profits and minimise their tax in Australia?'

'We, the Labor Party, are aware of some of those activities.'

'But this is what the copyright law allows them to do. How can we compete? I'm working just to fight the law.'

By Jo's recollection, Holding said that the Labor Party couldn't be seen to oppose powerful interests, especially with an election coming up. 'I was so sad,' he recalls. 'I was there, full of life and hope, and this guy was telling me he couldn't do anything because the Labor Party needed media support.'

From sadness, though, Jo's mood soon switched to anger.

'Hey, if you don't wake up, you're going to lose the next election,' he told Holding. 'Labor people expect you to support small businesses, not big ones.'

When Holding repeated that he couldn't do anything about the matter, Jo turned up the heat. 'I've lost faith in you and the Labor Government, and you will lose the next election,' he shouted. 'I'm going to see Peter Costello after this.'

Then, angrily, he shook the desk and some of the contents fell onto the senior MP's lap. Not surprisingly, Holding told him to get out.

'As I was leaving, he wanted to have his last say,' recalls Jo. 'I said

The Political Battlefront (1989-1992)

there was still hope for the Labor Party to change its ways. "You people have to understand what we need to do in this country is to make a living and employ people. You have to change the law to help us. Don't sit with the multinationals. Expose them.'"

Holding slammed the door on Jo as he stood in the doorway. But Jo was wearing Blundstone shoes with metal toes, and he put one foot out to protect himself. The door bounced back on Holding's face and smacked him on the nose.

'This was my entry into Australian politics,' says Jo matter-of-factly, as if the whole sorry episode were inevitable. He was a jumpy young bull in an antiquated political china shop – looking for strong decisions and solid action where only dancing games and weasel words were on offer.

Whether you're amused or appalled by this incident, you'll have to admit that Jo made an impression. Shortly afterwards, Clyde Holding sent a letter inviting him to a meeting in Canberra.

Peter Snow and other independent record storeowners were also invited. 'We had become a threat because we were making the news,' Peter remembers. 'There were decent shops – like Red Eye in Sydney, Dada in Perth, and Readings in Melbourne – who had joined the cause. We had academics on our side. My customers included Barry Jones, Bob Carr, and Eddie Maguire. They'd come into the store I had in Collins Street next to the Kino. So it started to become a bit of a movement. We were invited to Canberra to meet people who supported our cause. But when we got to the meeting room in Parliament House, every seat was taken by the multinationals and their lawyers. So we all had to stand around as if we weren't important.'

Offering his trusty spreadsheet, Jo tried to make the case for the little guys.

'This is how much the multinationals are controlling the market,' he announced, showing their market share figures.

But the lawyers and politicians kept grilling Jo about his imports – trying to trap him into admitting illegal activity – rather than listening to his accusations of market bullying. So Jo stormed out of the room. One of the assistants followed him.

'What's happening?' she asked.

'I really hate those leeches. They're screwing us, and taking all the money out of the music business,' Jo told her. 'Look at them – wearing their velour suits and $300 shoes. They are my enemies. They want to stab me in the palace of the emperor.'

As hard as the record sellers worked to get their points across, they were no match for people like Peter Garrett. Peter Snow recalls buttonholing Midnight Oil's lead singer about his opposition to the PSA's recommendations, asking, 'Why aren't you allowing your CDs to come in from America so people can buy them for $10 instead of $30? These people you sing about – the oppressed and under-privileged?'

Garrett brushed off his question with, 'You don't understand copyright'.

Back then, Peter Snow didn't hold back in his response: 'Well, I do understand that you work for the other side. Your records are on the Sony CBS label, so you're just the lackey of the multinationals.'

Nor has he softened his view over time: 'The reality is that most artists don't make money, and the big companies screwed them. They'd say, "Here's $100,000 advance on sale against your next album". But, if you didn't sell enough, you'd end up owing the company.'

Gil Matthews, another independent record store-owner (and former drummer with Billy Thorpe and the Aztecs), also took on Garrett when he released *The Flipside to Peter Garrett* statement in August 1991.

As debate raged, Allan Fels continued to take a high profile on the issue, understanding the importance of breaking down complex economic arguments into digestible chunks for the public arena. On 15 August 1991, for example, *The Sydney Morning Herald* published his article, *Little pain and huge gains from lower record prices*, which countered the pop stars' views. On the same day, *The Australian* published the Paddy McGuiness article *Just for the record, consumers have their rights too*. The Musicians Union weighed into the argument as well. The secretary of the Union's Victorian branch, Maurice Stead, was quoted in a *Financial Review* article (*Rock stars off key, say musicians*) by Mark Davis on 23 August 1991.

Thanks to his mastery of Office Works, Jo merged form letters with politicians' addresses to confetti Canberra and beyond with letters about Central Station's plight at the hands of the majors. When someone suggested his efforts would have more sway if coming from an interest group rather than an individual business, he and Morgan invented a character called Ms Karen James who wrote on behalf of the Australian Record Sellers Association, the once-vigorous but now largely defunct group of independent record storeowners. (Incidentally, when Jo and Morgan revived the group, they chose to split the original word 'Recordsellers' in two, so the initials changed from ARA to ARSA – their little in-joke.)

The Political Battlefront (1989-1992)

For years, this fictitious Karen James bombarded Canberra with letters, and a surprising number of political heavyweights replied. On one occasion, she enclosed a copy of Stefan Dennis's single on the Central Station label, and many even commented that the record was not to their taste! Hilarious. In August 1991, Karen James also managed to have a letter published in the *Financial Review* before morphing into Kevin James for a letter-writing blitz. Neither Jo nor Morgan can explain this sudden gender switch.

Jo sent multiple letters and faxes under his own name too. He was a serial pest, determined to keep the issue alive in Canberra. But he was not exactly 'on message' as far as the PSA was concerned. One day, he was advised to switch tactics, because the only way to win the Senate's support for changing the copyright law was to hammer home the benefits for consumers rather than small businesses. 'If parallel importation is allowed, CD prices will drop,' he was told. 'That's the message.'

'I'd wanted to argue technicalities – the copyright and trade practices laws were in conflict,' says Jo. 'But from then on we focused on cheaper prices.'

Jo poured a huge amount of time and energy into lobbying. 'Of course, there was a risk that the government wouldn't change the law and all our court penalties would add up,' he says. 'But I thought I had nothing to lose. The customers supported me. They saw me on TV or in the papers, and they heard me on the radio. Plus I had pamphlets in the shops urging people to write to their local MPs. I had massive customer support. Thank you to them. It warmed my heart. The Attorney General's department complained to me that they were getting a lot of letters and would I please stop doing whatever I was doing. I said, "I won't stop until you change the law. It's unjust. You know that".'

Amid the high-profile debate, Professor Fels was rewarded with an extra job – heading a newly strengthened Trade Practices Commission, as well as the PSA. (The two bodies would be amalgamated into the Australian Competition and Consumer Commission in 1995.) But there was no reward in terms of legislative action for many years to come. The ALP's internal ructions saw to that. Bear with us. The story is complicated. When the PSA made its recommendations on sound recordings in December 1990, Bob Hawke was Prime Minister, Paul Keating was Treasurer and Michael Duffy was Attorney General. By the time Cabinet considered the matter in October 1991, John Kerin was Treasurer and Paul Keating was stewing on the back benches after losing round one of his tussle with Hawke for the top job. In the midst of their own internal strife and a celebrity campaign against change, the Hawke Government got cold feet as Senator Graham Richardson tried to drum up support for an alternative plan (maintaining the monopoly, but with industry-wide price surveillance).

While Cabinet dithered, the Australian Democrats party showed signs of resisting the proposed changes. In September 1991, Jo and fellow campaigners Peter Snow and Gil Matthews met Democrats Senator Sid Spindler to make their case.

'He wanted to see us in his office in Melbourne,' remembers Jo. 'He didn't like me, and didn't give me a chance to express myself. And he was sitting there as if to say, "I've got the power and let's see how much I can get out of you". I felt uneasy. So I started teasing him. I said, "You know what? It's only a matter of time before Peter Garrett and John Farnham become extinct. Your party will have the same fate unless you get into progressive thinking". His secretary tried to get me out. I said, "Just let me finish. You have to understand that the copyright law is restricting a lot of Australians in developing their own businesses. Hundreds of them have been destroyed by the big players". He asked me to leave. So I said, "Goodbye. You are a spent force! You've lost your hope. You've got no idea where this country is going and you still want to be a senator!" Peter and Gil stayed on and had a little chat.'

Despite increasing pressure from pro-change voices – ranging from academics and senior journalists to the mysterious Kevin James – Cabinet deferred a decision on the PSA recommendations yet again. Speaking at the National Press Club in October 1991, Allan Fels expressed disappointment at the ongoing delay.

Meanwhile, Jo issued a memo to all Central Station staff. 'Sell, Get Some Cash,' it said. 'Our Government adjourned the decision to amend the Copyright Act until next week. Let us hope we do not have world war No. 1058 before that.'

Well, in December 1992, a war did break out. Paul Keating moved against Bob Hawke again and grabbed the leadership. John Dawkins became the new Treasurer.

Another six months passed before Cabinet finally made a decision on changing Australia's copyright law. In June 1992, Treasurer John Dawkins and Attorney General Michael Duffy issued a joint press statement: 'The Federal Government has decided to open up the Australian market to imported records of foreign performers in two years time.'

The Political Battlefront (1989-1992)

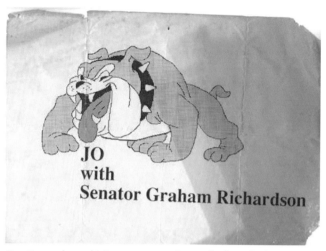

How Morgan depicted Jo's response to Graham Richardson's back-room dealings during Cabinet deliberations on the PSA inquiry into sound recordings

Parallel imports would be allowed, but only for non-pirated copies of recordings from the US, EEC and NZ released after 1 July 1994. Although Professor Fels welcomed the decision, he said that the two-year delay was unnecessary.

Jo was approached by ABC radio to comment on the decision. Morgan advised him against participating. From Sydney, he faxed a note to Jo in Melbourne: 'I've thought about it and don't see any value at all in you going on radio tomorrow. It's a shame but it would not sit well with getting agreement with Warner. Get ABC Radio to say that you "declined to comment as you are negotiating a long-standing dispute with Warner over copyright" on Friday ... You must learn to live with the industry now.'

Disregarding the advice, Jo was on air at seven o'clock on the morning of 11 June 1992.

'What's your response to the government postponing the changes?' the interviewer asked him.

'Well, I would advise everyone to hold off buying any more CDs until 1994, because they'll be cheaper then.'

When the interviewer didn't respond immediately, Jo ploughed on.

'The whole thing is idiotic. We need the changes now. Over the next two years, there will be a lot of changes in the music retailing business, and we won't be able to hold on. People will give up and die or diversify.'

Later on that morning, Professor Fels called Jo. 'I was shaking, wondering what I'd said,' Jo remembers. 'But he told me that I'd done a brilliant job, and that the Government was reconsidering the decision because of what I'd said. I was so relieved that something had come across, but the Government still postponed the changes.'

To this day, Jo's blood boils at the mention of Paul Keating's name. 'He betrayed the Australian public,' he says. 'He knew he had to change the copyright law because the digital age was coming. But there was a lot of pressure from John Farnham and Peter Garrett. The multinationals manipulated them to support protection on the basis that it helped Australian artists. In fact, the multinationals would promote the imported product first and not worry about the Australian artists, except for token gestures. Peter Garrett's band, Midnight Oil, was distributed by Sony, so there was a conflict of interest. John Farnham was distributed by EMI, so a conflict of interest again. These people were backing the multinationals against hundreds of little businesses who were struggling to survive and being burdened by litigation many times a year!'

Feeling let down by the Keating Government, Jo and Morgan looked to the Opposition for action. On the same day that Jo had urged radio listeners to stop buying CDs until 1994, the Shadow Treasurer, Peter Costello, had issued a media release headed, 'No need for delay on cheaper records'. So Morgan promptly lined up a meeting.

'He doesn't understand how copyright law affects the market,' Morgan told Jo. 'He's more interested in GST.'

So Jo prepared himself thoroughly before heading to Costello's office. Another independent record seller had been lined up to go with him, but failed to materialise.

'Where's your colleague?' Costello asked.

'I don't know,' Jo replied. 'The multinationals probably bought him off. I started this political fight with many friends, but they've dropped away one by one – either too afraid of the multinationals or prepared to do a deal with them.'

Jo then launched into his spiel. After listening intently for a long time, Costello stretched and yawned.

'Now I understand what you're saying, and the first thing I'll do when I get into government is make the changes you've recommended.'

Showing Jo out, Costello put his arm around his shoulder and said, 'Thank you, Giuseppe. I wish there were more people like you in this country. Would you like to join me on Sunday in the electorate? To promote the Liberal Party in your jurisdiction?'

Jo felt overwhelmed by the unexpected comment. 'I thought I'd bored the fuck out of him,' he says.

But he was happy to accept the unexpected invitation. 'I was there first thing in the morning. Seven o'clock. In St Kilda, trying to unseat Clyde Holding.'

Despite Jo's best efforts, however, Clyde Holding kept his seat and Keating led the ALP to victory at the March 1993 election.

The copyright amendment bill was put on the back burner.

Notes Jo made ahead of his 3LO interview after the Keating Government announced a two-year delay in allowing parallel importation

Advertisement for the Oxford Street Store

11. The Reboot (1992-2000)

> 'They were the first label I recognised as releasing Australian electronic music. That was kind of rare in the early days. I guess I had that cultural cringe or bias, where I always thought that stuff coming from the US, Europe or the UK was the good stuff. I think Central Station releasing local music helped change that. Having those big stores, they enabled a whole range of artists to get exposure. It was incredibly important.'
> **Kid Kenobi**

While the proposed copyright law changes languished in the political wilderness, Jo and Morgan had plenty to occupy them in the Central Station business. Dance music was taking off in a big way.

When the rave scene hit Sydney, promoters approached Jo about selling party tickets at the original Pitt Street store in return for a booking fee. 'A lot of British boys came to Australia and started these parties,' he recalls. 'We just sold the tickets, but it was very important because people often bought vinyl, or a shirt and cap, at the same time. Mostly we were the only outlet. It was a scary time for me because protecting the cash wasn't easy. We used to have security guards in the shop and to escort us to the bank.' When he worked at Pitt Street, a young Nik Fish remembers people almost dissolving into tears when tickets had run out. 'Central became a real place to go, to get your music, your dance party tickets. We were a one-stop party shop,' he says.

In 1990, George Vagas and his girlfriend packed their bags and moved from Adelaide to the big smoke (Sydney) to carve new careers. Soon after arriving, George threw a rave party (Astrology) at 46 Oxford

Street, convincing the real estate agent that he wanted to hire the place for a modest night with friends watching the FA Cup final on a big screen. Two Central Station employees happened to come to that rave and later praised the site to Jo and Morgan. So George claims credit for Central's move to the cavernous space that became its most spectacular store. Not long afterwards, George went to this Oxford Street shop and noticed that the big room to the left was only being used for storage. With an impressive background in retail fashion in Adelaide as well as DJing, he approached Jo with the idea of selling streetwear in the underused space. Jo said he'd think about it.

As luck would have it, Morgan had recently scored some redundancy money after a Westpac restructure. When George later formally pitched the Flipside concept – streetwear, accessories, hardcore music and dance party tickets – Morgan decided to invest that money in the new venture. The name was as much about skateboard slang ('catch ya on da flipside') as it was about the reverse side of a vinyl record.

George knew exactly what his target market wanted to wear. Initially, he focused on the main labels favoured by skaters: Vans, Etnies,

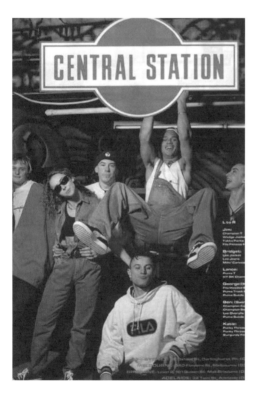

Central Station advertisement with (clockwise from left) Jim Turbafield, Bridget O'Sullivan, two unidentified men, Cait O'Sullivan and George Vagas

Spitfire, Alien Workshop, Airwalk, Real, Blind, Girl and so on. He also brought in stock that was hot with the ravers: Puma, Adidas, Nike, Levis, Calvin Klein, Ralph Lauren, baggy jeans and big, bright, oversized T-shirts. When the business started to grow very rapidly, George was sent overseas to check out new sources. 'They sent me to a fashion expo in Las Vegas called Magic, which was a massive international fashion buyers' thing every year, with all the new and freshest streetwear labels coming out. Then I went to New York, Holland, Belgium, Italy and Germany, meeting all the underground record distributors as well making contact with all the infamous international producer/DJs. I brought in a heap of new labels, like Third Rail, Crazy Life, Pornstar, Neighborhood, X-Large and Freshjive, as well as all the international rave/dance music record labels' T-shirts, baseball caps, bomber jackets and other merchandise which had never been to Australia before.'

George created and managed the Flipside concept store from 1991 to 1996. He built its success by offering 'the bizarre, the weird, the colourful, the fluoro, the cutting edge'. The 'money-makers' among his clientele – the DJs, promoters and club owners – were very particular,

Advertisement for Flipside at the Adelaide store

wanting one-off samples of the latest stuff, but they served as walking billboards for new labels so George was happy to oblige. Clothing, he says, helped Central stay ahead of the pack, because it broadened the store's appeal. 'Probably eighty per cent of Central Station customers were gay when I moved in. I brought in the straight skater and raver element with Flipside. It became bigger and better with that style of mash-up of clientele. There was no segregation after that, musically or culturally.'

Another important character in the story is Alan Thompson, a graphic designer who did a lot of work for the stores. 'He was a fantastic designer,' says Jo. 'I used to give him an idea of what I wanted, and he would make recommendations and produce visuals. We thank him for his creativity and getting our image right in the market.'

While legislative change was still many years away, Central Station did experience some relief from legal pressures after the 1993 election. Word got to Jo that Paul Keating was telling the multinationals to stop suing him. 'Just leave that man and his business alone, because he squeals too much,' was the way the new PM reportedly put it. With Professor Fels now in charge of the Trade Practices Commission, Central Station also finally saw some action on its complaints about the majors' refusing supply. But the country was still wallowing in the recession that Paul Keating said we had to have, and unemployed kids couldn't afford records. So DJs' mix tapes appeared on the market.

'Those mix tapes were recordings from Dutch, Italian, UK producers – all very underground and not commercial,' says Trent Rackus, a rave DJ who shopped at Oxford Street in the 90s and worked there from 2000 to 2007. 'The tapes would walk out of the door. Some of them became iconic. DJs back in the day – Jumping Jack, Pee Wee Ferris, Nik Fish, Phil Smart, Abel, Ming D, Sugar Ray and Robin Knight – would put them together. Sometimes you'd be at a rave and it would get shut down and you'd move to a park down the road. Someone would open the boot of the car, and they'd be playing a mix tape and there would be a hundred people dancing to the boot of a car. Even today there are forums on Facebook. "Has anyone seen this?" Then someone will upload a file and everyone goes "Shit!" All of these things are etched in people's memories and they were all bought at Central Station Records.'

Simon Lewicki saw what was happening in Sydney and decided to follow suit in Adelaide, producing separate CDs for hip hop, trance, hardcore and house. 'The dance culture lived on these mix tapes,' he says. 'There was no dance on radio back then. I did one of the first mix CDs, *House 5*, and I still have at least five requests a week on my Facebook page asking about that CD.'

Although selling tickets, clothing and mix tapes kept Central afloat during the early 90s recession, the pioneering retailers were no longer alone in the dance music market. 'As the music became more popular, more distributors evolved and started importing,' says Jo. 'The market became extremely competitive.' Retail chains like HMV, Sanity, JB Hi-Fi and Virgin also muscled into the space, and a host of independent copycat shops sprang up on Oxford Street.

In his new role at Shock Records, Nick Dunshea could read the runes. 'From Central Station's point of view, I wasn't a dance-only kind of guy. But I understood dance when a lot of people didn't understand it at all. When I saw that the dance boom was starting to happen, I said to Jo, "Look you've got these five stores. You're seeing these singles come in before anyone else does. Why don't you get the label up and running again? You've got the perfect avenue to jump on things before everyone else. Shock can do your distribution. It seems like a no-brainer".'

Jo remembers his initial response being along the lines of: 'Oh, fuck off, I've had enough of this business. I'm going to get out. Australia is too

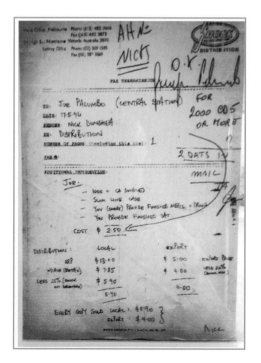

The 1994 agreement-by-fax between Shock and Central Station Records (courtesy of Nick Dunshea)

hard. Politicians are stupid. You can't develop business here.'

Morgan, however, saw the logic in Nick's suggestion: 'The retail operation wasn't that profitable. It was OK, but there was more margin in selling your own product. We had accessories, record bags and merchandise. And when I left Westpac, I put my retrenchment money into Flipside clothing. Rebooting our label was the next logical step.'

A deal was done with minimum fuss, as Nick Dunshea recalls: 'The only paperwork that existed between Central Station and Shock was a fax that I'd sent Jo. It was very rudimentary. We'll sell it for X dollars, we'll keep X as our fee, you get the rest, minus the cost of manufacturing. That's the deal. And he just faxed it back with "OK, Jo." Everything else from there was negotiated verbally. There were changes to the distribution rates and the way payments were made, but there was never a formal document that stipulated how the business would run. A number of years after, I found that original fax and I photocopied and framed it for them.'

The reinvigorated Central Station label was a great success. One of the early hits was *Here's Johnny* by Hocus Pocus, which spent five weeks at number one in the national charts in 1995. 'We had that one in the shop for a couple of years,' says Jo. 'It kept selling. All these Lebanese, Greek and Italian women from Bankstown and Parramatta used to come in and buy it, not just the inner-city DJs. Women have more intuition for these things. I thought I'd better license and release it. So I got on the phone and made a deal.'

'By memory, Paul Holden found that track and really hammered it,' adds Morgan. 'And it took off. Paul had been in the gay scene, but crossed over into the straight rave scene and *Here's Johnny* was a rave product that crossed over into mainstream success.'

So how did Central manage to take a two-year-old Italian underground hardcore rave track and make it a mainstream hit? For one thing, the timing was spot on. Rave parties were attracting huge crowds right across the country, and influential people were awake to the trend. 'A good friend of ours, Gary Dunstan produced *Video Hits* on Channel Ten,' says Jo. 'He liked our songs and knew where the market was going, so he asked us to create a video for *Here's Johnny* and gave it plenty of exposure on his show.'

'For the video, we linked up with a woman at Nightlife Videos, a Brisbane-based business that distributed video clips to second-tier club venues,' adds Morgan. 'She made a basic computer-generated video and

The Reboot (1992-2000)

Celebrating the chart success of 'Here's Johnny' (Hocus Pocus) and 'Total Eclipse of the Heart '(Nicki French), from left: Andrew McGee, unidentified person, David Williams, Nick Dunshea, Jo Palumbo and Morgan Williams

only asked us to pay for the Beta master. So that was a stroke of luck.'

In 2014, Cameron Adams, the national music writer for News Corp Australia Network included the song in 'The Sh-tlist: the worst No. 1 hits in Australian chart history', comparing *Here's Johnny* to a migraine headache. It's certainly aggressively repetitive – 'bam, bam, bam wit'you' being the extent of the lyrics apart from the Jack Nicholson voice sample from *The Shining* – but it's also very catchy and upbeat.

Another 1995 hit for Central was the Nicki French dance remake of the Bonnie Tyler song *Total Eclipse of the Heart*, which peaked at number two. 'James Fraser spotted that in the Sydney store,' remembers Morgan. 'It was from Kylie Minogue's stable, PWL. Jo came to me one night and said, "Let's try to pick this up". I'd met Mike Stock from PWL, so I called him directly and did the deal. Our releases were very diverse. They were anything from techno and hardcore, to more melodic stuff.'

The third in this early set of hits was Nick Skitz's 1996 techno trance remix of *The X-Files Theme Song*. This time, John Ferris was the DJ who championed the track and Gary Dunstan who produced the video. 'Because Channel Ten was broadcasting *X Files*, the TV series, and Gary

Dunstan said he'd like to do the video for us, using original footage,' remembers Jo. 'No one could have dreamed about such luck. I thought I would have to pay $5,000 for a video and the song might not sell. So I said, "Sure, go ahead". Even better, because he made the video, Gary kept playing it. It reached third or fourth in the charts.'

As manager of the Oxford Street shop, Tim McGee had been instrumental in picking and promoting the early hits. He had started shopping at Central Station in the late 80s. 'I used to buy records off Nik Fish,' he laughs. 'That was pretty funny. And Sugar Ray was working there at the time.' As a DJ and party promoter, Tim got to know Jo and Morgan through using Flipside's ticket-selling service for the parties he threw. He must have impressed them, because they asked him to come on board, first as store manager and later in the A&R role.

'Because we had such success with the first two records, it was back on in a big way,' Tim says. 'It was a pretty amazing time. I remember my first day and three pallets of hardcore tunes rocked in from Holland. And I was sitting there and I couldn't believe how much stock there was for a start. And Biz-E was the guy who looked after all the hardcore and I was just there going, "Why would you possibly need to import this many records in one go? This must be two or three months worth of stock." And he goes, "Dude, I totally said the same thing when I first came here. Give me three days". And he sold ninety per cent of it in three days. There was just this amazing thirst for these records and there weren't many other places you could get them.'

Tim decided to create five sub-labels to deal with various genres: Tinted (house), Bang On! (trance/hard house), Dinky (NRG and all Australian artists), Central Cuts (commercial dance) and the Hardwax label (R&B/2-step).

Central Station's chart success ruffled a few feathers in the industry. Jo remembers hearing from an insider that the managing director of one of the multinationals had abused his staff for not performing. 'How can those poofters be doing so well in the charts?' he'd shouted.

There were two main reasons for Central Station being able to read the dance market so well in the 90s – staff knowledge and store intel at the micro level, plus long-standing connections at the macro level. One story, related by Simon Lewicki, aka Groove Terminator, at a dinner party in Sydney highlights how both aspects inter-played. Tony Caraccia, Central Station's Adelaide store manager, gave the label a boost, for example, when he signed up one of Adelaide's top DJs and producers.

The Reboot (1992-2000)

From left: Nick Dunshea, Tim McGee, Aaron Sines, Jimmy Olsze and Morgan Williams at a MIDEM trade fair

'Obviously there was the record store part of Central, but the label part of it was super important for me,' recalls Simon. 'I made a house record with this girl who becomes my girlfriend and Tony put it out. The band was called Devotion and the record was called *Gotta Make My Love Work*. It was complete rip-off of this old Turntable Orchestra record. Just before I left Adelaide, Tony put out another record of mine, which was a more underground house twelve-inch, and that is a club anthem to this day. Then I moved to Sydney and later signed with Virgin Records.'

In Sydney, Simon Lewicki lived in a one-bedroom apartment in Elizabeth Bay, where Tim McGee ended up sleeping on the couch for six months. 'Jo was super angry,' laughs Simon. 'He'd tell Tim, "Stop living with that Groove Terminator" because he was coming in late every day. We'd go out, have a laugh, end up at a club and come home at five in the morning. Then Tim's got to wake up to go to work at Central.'

Simon had one track that didn't fit on the album he was producing for Virgin, so he decided to offer that to Tim McGee. 'He thought it was pretty good and gave me the money. Fifteen hundred bucks on the side was a lot at the time. Two months rent. Fucking awesome. Then two months later, Ministry of Sound buys the record.'

Morgan laughs. 'Yes, we sold them Simon's record — Chili Hi Fly, *Is It Love?* — which was the hottest dance track at the time. Simon got his cut, of course.' That track became a number one US *Billboard* club smash in 2001.

But Tim didn't just wait until artists approached him. He also kept an eye out for talent and wasn't afraid to muscle in on other labels' territory. Rebecca Poulsen (aka BeXta) moved from Brisbane to Sydney at the end of 1998 and got her first DJ residency at Plastic. The next year, she began touring nationally. After Tim called her about releasing her music under the Central Station label, her first *Mixology* compilation came out in 2000. 'They were pretty open with creative ideas and concepts,' she says. 'I was a bit of a creative control freak I guess. It's a bit of give and take, but it worked really well. They gave me the guidance I needed.' After her relationship with Sony wound up, she released some original tracks through Central, including under the name of 'Unconscious Collective' with Ben Suthers.

'BeXta did a lot of CDs for us and they were extremely popular in Australia and overseas,' says Jo. 'She is a remarkable DJ and I admire her work.'

Central relied heavily on staff input to select material, says James Fraser: 'Eighty per cent of the time the staff were really on the ball. Many were DJs themselves. This meant they knew what was working in the clubs straight up. It was the perfect formula for success. One example was Deuce's *On the Bible*. I could see this track working on the floor from day one, so in conjunction with Central Station Records and my own label VMA, we licensed Deuce's *On the Bible* from London Records, a subsidiary of the major label Polygram. We ended up getting the license because Polygram in Australia passed on it. The track went top twenty in Australia. That pissed off Polygram no end. They couldn't break their own records in Australia because they had never employed the right staff with an ear for dance music. They were at least two to three years behind the game. That was one of the defining strengths of Central – Jo and Morgan had employed the right people from day one. We could see what was going to work, we could pick hits, and that fed up the system very quickly. There weren't multiple levels of management with pitfalls along the way. It was pretty much straight to Jo in Melbourne. He was quick to react and would take us on our word.'

Wes McDonald recalls how staff played a part in finding *Forever Young*, a huge 1994 happy hardcore hit from German techno project Interactive. 'Jo always hired people from the subcultures so there was a woman DJ called Jade who worked for him as well, maybe in the distribution area, and she always played that kind of music out. She was bubbly and had quite a strong following. She probably put us on to that track. They sampled the vocals from Alphaville's song, which was a bit of an alternative hit in about 1982, and sped it up to sound like chipmunks. Then laid a new backing track behind it. It was quite a new genre then.'

Although Central cultivated a lot of homegrown talent, the labels' mainstay remained licensing material from elsewhere. 'We went overseas regularly,' says Jo. 'We'd visit all the places where the music was coming from – Germany, Manchester, London, Milan, New York, Chicago, Miami, Los Angeles and then back to Sydney or Melbourne. We'd also go to different places like Brazil, trying to pick up some samba or other beat. We had a lot of black material. Morgan was very good at knowing all the DJs and labels. That's the fundamental stuff, where there's energy, and the multinationals didn't know how to deal with it. But I was capable of saying, "Take them all. Give them four hundred bucks each, put them on a contract, release the vinyl, one thousand pieces, export them. Are we done?" Japan used to buy a hundred pieces, England bought 250, Germany bought 250 and Australia got the rest. By the time we finished with that, the record had sold out. Some of those artists became so popular that multinationals bought them over. Paid a million bucks for them! But my game wasn't about big numbers. Medium hits are the bread and butter. So you always focus on them and the big hits are a bonus.'

'I remember going to Pop Komm in Cologne one year and going to a Paul van Dyk gig and meeting him. He was the world's number one DJ at the time,' adds Morgan. 'Another year, we saw James Brown at MIDEM, a big trade fair held in Cannes every January. We had the best times in New York where Tom Silverman from Tommy Boy Records would pick us up in his limo and we'd go out to the Limelight. Around about Easter there was another big event in Miami. You'd go around and talk to indie labels and go to gigs. We took Simon Lewicki with us to Miami one year, and it just blew his mind – all the parties we went to and the hobnobbing. It was all about cementing relationships.'

Simon's memories are less glamorous. 'Tim and I would be going over there for our first conference and I was landing two or three days ahead of him. He put me on to some friends to hook up with. I ring them from the airport and they say, "Just come and stay in our lounge room". There were people coming all day and all night. I was only twenty-six or twenty-seven.'

To Jo, the secret of Central Station's success was not hobnobbing but fast follow-through. 'I was the first guy to go to MIDEM with a cheque book and settle a deal on the spot,' he says. 'When you make a verbal deal with these independent producers, the next thing is someone else pops in and gives them more – because the contracts are usually done back home. So I said I'm not going to have this. I got a pro forma. Two pages. "Sign here. Here's the cheque." So I got photographed for *Billboard* as the first person to hand over money at MIDEM. That's why we started to make inroads overseas.'

The Central Station label reached far and wide: Austria, the Czech Republic, Denmark, Finland, France, Germany, Greece, Hungary, Ireland, Italy, Macedonia, Netherlands, Norway, Poland, Portugal, Slovenia, South Africa, Spain, Sweden, Switzerland, the UK, USA and Turkey. Even throughout South East Asia and South America.

This success transformed the business. While the stores continued to carry vinyl for the DJs, they devoted more and more floor space to CDs for the general population as digital technology entered the picture. Compilation CDs were particularly successful. Mark Vick remembers *Dance Mega Mix Hits* as one of the first techno rave compilations. 'That had all those things on it like *Black is Black* by the Jungle Brothers, *Heylom Halib* by Capella, *Jack to the Sound of the Underground* by Hithouse – and I remember seeing the TV ads some times in 1990 when I was only about fourteen years old.'

The biggest selling compilations by far, though, were the ones done in conjunction with community radio stations Wild FM in Sydney and Brisbane, Free FM in Sydney, Hitz FM and Joy FM in Melbourne and Fresh FM in Adelaide. (See chapter 14.)

Meanwhile, Shawn Yates took control of Flipside when George Vagas left to set up his own clothing store. Shawn started Central's own clothing line, and eventually established a stand-alone clothing business, Flipside Distribution, becoming an equity business partner with Jo and Morgan and running the Carhartt franchise, a hugely successful business to this day.

12. The Heyday of the Stores

'They were the pioneers who really busted dance music open. Other people got records but they didn't know how to sell them. If you went to another store and asked, "What's the hottest song?" they'd say, "Oh I don't know. There's the shit over there. Go through it". It was like *Pick a Box* and hopefully you'd pick one that was good. But at Central Station, you'd say I'm looking for some upbeat stuff, about 124 ... or 160 when the hardcore techno stuff came along. There was so much music. But they were the only ones who had a good idea of what was going on.'
Les Toth

'I think most people would agree it was the best time of their lives. We learned an awful lot from Jo. He was a very hard taskmaster, but you soon developed a very good work ethic, and that stuck with you for life.'
James Fraser

The stores were not just the face of Central Station – they were the senses, heart and soul. Locations were handpicked for their street cred, with an underground vibe considered essential. The whole experience – from the look and the product lines to the staff culture – was based on the model that had been created in Melbourne and refined in Sydney. But each store did its own ordering and marketing, so there was plenty of scope to run with the local scene.

As well as the major locations mentioned in this chapter, Central

Station also had a presence in Darwin, Newcastle, the Gold Coast, Auckland and Canberra. Jo and Morgan travelled extensively to keep in touch, spreading ideas and sorting out issues, including the occasional outburst of sibling rivalry. Sydney was accused of cherry-picking from other stores' orders, so Jo introduced a system. He asked record wholesalers overseas to colour-code when packing each store's orders. When the overall shipment arrived, the boxes could be forwarded straight to each city. 'There was no cheating then. They got what they ordered,' he says.

But the stores generally played nicely together – swapping intel on new suppliers and over-stocks, for example. In the early days, there were no computers, so you couldn't just click a button to see what other stores were doing. Staff kept in touch by telephone and the odd interstate visit.

Everyone laughs when they think back to how primitive the process of sourcing new music was. Staff would stay in late to call suppliers and listen to tracks over international phone lines. Stevie Bourk remembers the Thursday night ritual when he was vinyl manager at Oxford Street: 'I'd have a call from Amsterdam, the UK, Germany. If a track came out on Thursday, I would get it played to me over the phone and I'd get the order on Monday ... heaps of vinyl in every week, from different countries ... listening to it all, trying to get ahead of other shops. There may have been five or six shops around. Everyone was very competitive.'

Each store had its own vibrant social network. 'DJs would meet other DJs and pass on their demos through Central Station,' says Jim Kontogiannis. 'And they hosted this thing where promoters would promote their parties. I can think of countless friends I've met through Central Station.' Flying around, Jo and Morgan connected the networks together and left staff reeling in the wake of their latest round of stories and ideas. It was very obvious when they were in store. Especially Jo.

Emailing from his current base in the US, Andrew Kelly (Brisbane store manager in the early 90s) tells a particularly illuminating story: 'Jo had many unique ways to motivate us as employees, and one of the most feared was his impromptu visit. He would come up the escalator to the store in the Valley, wearing a wry smile, and the blood would rush out of your face, because you were never adequately prepared. He would immediately find glaring problems that we had not noticed, with an uncanny way of putting a dollar value on each of these issues. His pet peeves were clutter and dead stock. After the inevitable criticisms and chastisements, he would educate us on how to do things better and run a more efficient business. One such education was to create sale bags – ten random records for $10 all taped up, so you couldn't look inside until after you'd bought the bag. In preparation for one of his visits, I decided we had more dead stock and sale bags than he would like to see, so I took matters into my own hands. During a massive cleanup, I tossed out a bunch of dead stock along with old faxes, takeaway food bags and other rubbish. Thinking I was finally well prepared for his visit, I awaited his arrival anxiously. (He never wanted anyone to pick him up from the airport, preferring to appear unannounced.) Next thing I knew, he came in through the back entrance (where the dumpsters were located) carrying the very records I had thrown out earlier in the day! He was wearing his trademark piercing look, with one eyebrow raised, and the blood rushed out of my whole body.'

Melbourne

Central Station moved around a lot in Melbourne, but the city incarnations were all a short walk away from Flinders Street Station, while the suburban locations were all in the vicinity of the Chapel Street/Commercial Road intersection in Prahran. Hatched in the early 80s, Jo's overall plan was for Chapel Street to concentrate on DJs while the City Square stores reached out to the masses. In reality, the demarcation was not quite so stark.

Les Toth – definitely an elite customer – favoured the Chapel Street store, where Kris Prpa (aka Ms Krystal Pussy Cha Cha) was manager, ably supported by fellow DJs Guy Uppiah, Maurie Guarnaccia and Greg

Kris Prpa at the Chapel Street store in the 90s

Molinaro. 'I walked in there and instantly hit it with this chick who was running it,' recalls Les. 'Everyone was scared of her because she didn't show much emotion – they didn't know whether she was friendly or not. And I didn't give a shit because I was getting my records and she was good. I was buying ten or fifteen records a week. It was the only place you could go to get looked after.'

'Kris Prpa was an exceptional manager with an ear for a certain type of sound,' says Jo. 'Chapel Street was one of the most preferred stores in Australia. DJs loved the atmosphere.'

Another elite customer, Kevin Attwood, has fond memories of the 'riff raff' location. 'When Jo was in the store in City Square, he would ring me up when a new shipment was coming in, and I'd come down from work at night, and we'd lock the doors and start playing the records. Jo would be running around, dancing and singing while I'm playing Lime's *Babe We're Gonna Love Tonight*, and the Boys Town Gang's *Can't Take My Eyes off You* – all these songs that were huge hits. I used to go there with the express intention to get half a dozen records that no one else in Melbourne had. I'd get first access and play them at Pokies that Sunday night. It was like a party.'

What made the City Square era so remarkable was the way Central embraced multiple new music streams. Originally there were two stores on the outside, a narrow one offering new dance releases (usually disco), and a much larger one (known as the 'alternative' shop) offering synth

Billy Andriopoulus behind the counter at the City Square store in the 80s (courtesy of Billy Andriopoulos)

pop, New Romantic and back catalogue dance items. Later, the 'narrow' store was devoted to items on sale, while the dance shop moved to a much bigger location further inside City Square, with a checkered dance floor, serving counter, video screens, and racks of twelve-inches and CDs all around.

Wes McDonald began working at City Square in 1985. Sometimes he worked in the alternative shop with Vivien Rogers. 'Vivien was an amazing woman to work with – very stern but also caring and straight-talking,' he says. On other days he worked in the disco shop. 'The customers were kids – mid to late teens – and they'd come in after school in their uniforms,' he remembers. 'They'd want to hang around and listen to everything. It was almost like an underage nightclub. I remember lots of girls having a dance, not so many guys. It was a good testing ground for the music. If you were playing something they liked and they danced, then you'd put on something new. If they kept dancing, that was a good indication that the song would sell. A lot of those kids are now local DJs in Melbourne who are still playing after twenty or thirty years.'

Singer, songwriter and producer Peter Wilson is a case in point. He was just twelve years old when he visited the City Square store for the first time, spending all of his pocket-money savings on twelve-inch singles by Shannon, Carol Lynn Townes, Sinitta, The Flirts, Hotline and Divine. 'I remember the black-and-white checkered dance floor, and a row of turntables for people to listen to their prospective purchases. There was even a small selection of a new product called CDs. This is where I bought my first ever CD ... *Bobby O And His Banana Republic*.'

Jim Kontogiannis, later a DJ, also shopped at City Square while still at school. 'It was our wagging destination,' he says. 'I remember lots of peachy leather couches out in that big bit before the store, and lots of peach Laminex inside. I remember wandering around looking at import records and going, "Oh, I really want that". It was so much nicer than the Australian equivalent. You had full-picture sleeves. Aussie ones just had flimsy vinyl in budget cardboard sleeves. One of the things that kept Central Station retail going a long time was obsessed fans who needed to have the British twelve-inch and the German CD singles. There was nowhere else to get them but at Central Station.'

While Central had serious square metres at City Square, the full impact didn't come together until the move to 340 Flinders Street in 1989. Jonce Dimovski had joined Central Station in 1988 as a part-time assistant accountant while studying for his second degree (in recreation). Within a few weeks, he'd started begging to have a go at retail. One Sunday, Jo handed him the keys to the new 340 Flinders Street store, and left him to it. Sink or swim. Jonce had trouble opening the door and couldn't find the safe, but by the end of the day, he'd beaten the Sunday sales record. Before long, he was working for Emilio Palumbo full-time. After a stint in Brisbane, he eventually became manager of 340 Flinders Street when Emilio left Central and went back to being a motor mechanic.

Left: Jonce Dimvoski at 340 Flinders Street in the 90s with an unidentified colleague

Below: Interior of the 340 Flinders Street store in Melbourne circa 1989

The Heyday of the Stores

'I turned that shop into a goldmine,' claims Jonce. For him, it was all about 'really powerful customer service'. He allocated a personal locker to every DJ spending more than $400 a week. When shipments came in, he would then drop records into the lockers according to each DJ's taste. 'They never had to rush or worry about missing out on a new release,' he says. 'There was a little bit of competition to get a locker. I even had mobile DJs spending enough to get a locker.'

Jonce is proud of the way he helped DJs' careers. He was instrumental in getting John Course his first interstate gig, for example, and in Anthony Pappa getting his first ever gig. At the same time, he happily catered for the teenagers who would go crazy for Take That memorabilia. One day he decided to give them a treat, featuring the band's new video in the store. 'We darkened the shop, played the video, and raffled hampers of Take That merchandise,' he recalls. 'All of a sudden, I had hundreds of these teenagers. It was like a nightclub. They couldn't believe it. We were selling Take That dolls for $20 or $30. They used to go nuts.'

In 1992, Jim Kontogiannis started working at 340 Flinders Street. 'It was much bigger and they skipped the peach for black and white tiles,' he says of the difference with City Square. 'It was a record buyer's paradise, because they had such a big back catalogue of vinyl and these sacred booths in the back corner for the VIP DJs. If they flashed their card, they got to listen in a private booth with headphones. And there were these big DJ booths in the middle with video screens. Guest DJs played there occasionally.'

Dancers inside 340 Flinders Street, circa 1989

Sydney

People remember loud music, echoing floorboards, and so many records stacked everywhere that 375 Pitt Street looked like a second-hand store. They loved the vibe. Once you clicked into the DJ community, it was a fun and friendly place.

'Walk in there and the sound would hit you like a piece of wood. Bang, bang, bang!' remembers Mark Vick. 'It wasn't only a record store; it was a meeting place. We were seeing friends at parties on the weekend, and then you'd see them during the week at the record store, chatting about where we were going next weekend, and about the latest tunes and obscure imports that we'd just snapped up'

On Tuesdays when shipments arrived from London, DJs would run down the stairs shouting, 'Open the boxes! What's in them?' Long lines formed to check out the new stock. Jo weighed the booty to save time. 'We didn't even check the labels. That's about a hundred kilos, a thousand records. No worries. And we used to throw the records all out on the floor.'

DJs would be on their knees going through vinyl for hours, making their picks from their knowledge of artists and labels. 'That was the fun of it,' says Mark. 'You'd be taking a gamble with some of those things.'

Flyer promoting the opening of the Pitt Street store in 1987

The Heyday of the Stores

Jo is full of praise for Paul Jackson who was the manager at Pitt Street from day one and then ran the shop at Oxford Street until his untimely death. 'He was very knowledgeable, extremely friendly to customers and attentive to details,' says Jo. 'Everyone respected him. He had an amazing ear for sound, and was very influential in new music. He did a fantastic job and was a wonderful person. We miss him very much, and are so sad that he never witnessed the later success of the label and the business.'

In 1989, Central Station lured Mark Alsop from Disco City to help Paul with shipments at the Pitt Street store. Mark laughs when recalling 'the punters' coming in to search for records they'd heard on the dance floor. Sometimes, they would remember enough for him to twig that they wanted *Theme from S'Express*, for example. Other times, it would be hard work: 'My favourite is, "We heard this track and it was brilliant and it had the word *love* in it". And you'd say, "Oh, that's a really good one. I wonder what that could be." That information would nail it down to possibly only ninety per cent of the current tunes! Generally we'd pick up five or six records to play for them. Sometimes you'd hit it on the head and sometimes you wouldn't. But I would say to people that I knew, "Just get my attention, wave your hand in the air like you're holding a pen, and I'll write it down. And when I see you next in the club, I'll give you the list," so that way some of the punters would just come in to the store with the list, and I'd fulfill the records that they wanted. I actually had small note pads made with the Central Station logo that we gave to DJs who didn't mind writing down a track or two and handing it to the punter. Others would write requests down, depending on whether you entertained such folly, but that was certainly not the idea behind it!'

Nik Fish spent a year between 1989 and 1990 working at Pitt Street. 'I was one of the youngest people they'd ever employed,' he says. 'I was still eighteen. I think they gave me a break because I was a young kid excited about music. It was funny because I had never been exposed to the gay scene -- being the era it was. There were people working in the business who were as camp and queer as anyone could be. It was eye-opening for a very straight boy. They were so open and flamboyant.'

Having been warned about the 'crazy man Italian' in charge, he came to a different conclusion when he finally met Jo Palumbo. 'He tapped his forehead with three fingers, came behind the counter and said, "I have this third eye. I know what happens here when I'm in Melbourne". And I'm looking around, thinking, "Have you got hidden cameras I don't know about?" He was very dramatic, talking at me, laying down his modus operandi. Then you saw his shoulders drop, like he'd been putting on a performance, and he became more neutral and normal, and he put his arm around me and said, "Anyway, good to have you working here". And I saw this guy with this reputation as a mad professor was really just a normal guy who liked to be expressive.'

James Fraser started managing the Pitt Street store in 1991. 'By the time I got to Sydney, the rave scene had started,' he says. 'It was like a clubbing festival. You had DJs like Abel, Nik Fish and Sugar Ray who were either running their own parties or establishing their reputation and sound. It was a very English scene – there were a lot of backpackers who had been through the UK summer-of-love phenomenon. They'd come to the store and buy records they'd heard at the weekly raves. Techno had really started to evolve, as well as the UK house scene, and at the same juncture you had the hip hop/rap scene starting to take hold in western Sydney. You would have an abundance of suburban white kids coming into the store on the weekend looking for NWA, Public Enemy and Ice Cube albums. In some ways, I found it ironic that you had mainly Caucasian Australians buying hip hop and gangsta rap records, when groups like Public Enemy were writing politically charged lyrics advocating the concerns of the African-American community. In retrospect, I think it was more about a connection to a music style that was completely different from what their parents had listened to.'

Jo's regular presence at Pitt Street made a deep impression on many early customers. 'I remember shopping there since I was seventeen, going back to 1987,' says Stevie Bourk, a later employee. 'Jo used to serve me. I lived at Marylands out in the west, and I used to catch a train in when I got paid as an apprentice sheet metal worker, and I'd spend everything on records. I still remember the way Jo served people – the excitement in his voice – that guy knew how to sell records.'

Andrew Parkes (aka DJ Andrew James) was another teenaged shopper. When he started DJing in 1992, he went by the name of DJ Hype after the Public Enemy song, *Don't Believe the Hype*. At the time, he was really into US rap. Later he discovered that someone in the UK was using the same name, so he decided to change persona, using his own first and second names. He made the switch just in time, before his career took off in earnest. But the change wasn't just about avoiding a WTF moment if his namesake ever came to Australia – Andrew had fallen for a new genre after a visit to the Pitt Street store. 'About the

The Heyday of the Stores

second time I went in was when Inner City released *Big Fun*, Kevin Saunderson's first big hit,' he remembers. 'I bought that and it changed everything. I got into acid house and a lot of music from the UK, and I thought James had an English sound to it.'

By 1992, Central Station had outgrown its crypt-like location in Pitt Street and opened a new store at 46 Oxford Street, a huge basement space with a more industrial feel. 'It was the perfect location,' says Jo. 'When we moved in, the area was dead. Within a few months, it was full of clothing, music, banking and takeaway food.'

One side of the new store was the main music-selling area, offering CDs and vinyl. The other side was soon devoted to Flipside. Roaming around, Jo could hear people phoning friends to meet them there, so he put in seating for customers to sit around and talk.

Having left Central to concentrate on his DJ career, Nik Fish became a customer at the new location. 'If you were into hip hop, you could buy your T-shirts there. If you were into raves, you could buy your raver pants and fluoro stuff. It became more than just a place where the big-name DJ walked in and was handed vinyl on a silver platter, which is what it was like at the old Pitt Street store,' he recalls. 'At Oxford Street, it was all on for young and old. And the volume increased. The store contributed to the aspiring DJ having access to the music.'

Central's famous neon sign at 46 Oxford Street

Music Wars

Philip Bell, a Kiwi DJ, has really fond memories of visiting the store when touring Australia. 'I remember going into the hip hop section and it was just pumping in there. Those were the great days. We all interacted in the clubs, but it's a different beast from buying records that made us happy. I think Central Station Oxford Street is the greatest record store Australasia has ever had.'

Stevie Bourk remembers 'a busy store with a lot of staff': 'They probably had four or five women in the clothing section, two or three guys in the hip hop and R&B section, two or three people in the CD section, one or two working out the back, four or five in the vinyl section.' Stevie had started collecting records as soon as he'd got an apprenticeship. 'Whatever money I had went to records and clothes. That was life. Music first, clothes second.' By age seventeen, he had been

Flipside at Oxford Street

The Heyday of the Stores

DJing on Thursday nights at DCM, the Oxford Street club that replaced Patchs. Not wanting to make a career of it, though, he had finished one apprenticeship as a sheet metal worker, and had then done another as a chef. Busy as he'd been in 1996, he'd decided to approach Jo about working one night a week at the Oxford Street store. Over the next few years, he'd progressed from one night a week to two, and had then become vinyl manager. 'It was a really cool place to work. My job was to listen to and buy music. Dream job. There's nothing better than going to work doing what you love to do.'

Trent Rackus 'slipped into' the rave scene while still at school. On Saturday mornings he would buy records at Central Station before heading to a mate's house to practise playing on his turntables. He got his own second-hand kit in 1994 when he was nineteen. 'I was desperate to get them,' he says. 'A lot of people had got into it and then went, "Nah, this is not for me". So I bought a couple of decks, a mixer and a couple of crates of records off this guy for $1,200 – something ridiculous, probably that much worth in vinyl – and from there I was hooked!'

In the mid 90s, he got work as a mobile DJ, playing at friends' parties in the back yards of waterfront mansions at Cronulla. Then the club work started coming in. By 1999, he'd given up his day job to DJ

Pictured outside Flipside at the Oxford Street store in October 1996, from left: Kate Dubauskas, Luke Spellbound, Paul Elstak, George Vagas (courtesy of George Vagas)

full time. As a familiar face around Central Station, he jumped at the chance to work in the vinyl section when an opening came up in 2000. His job was to order progressive and techno while Stevie Bourk handled the more commercial material.

'It was pre-internet, so you'd get a phone call from England on a Thursday night, with some geezer playing you tunes down the phone and giving you the up-sell on all the records,' he says. 'Or they'd fax through their order lists, and you'd have to look through, then take a punt based on who made the record and what label. We were really pumping out the records in those days. You'd be doing 500, 600 records in a day. On a Thursday, you'd be absolutely hammering it. People coming in and buying twenty, thirty records at a time. No day went slowly, that's for sure.'

Not all customers were DJs. 'You'd have people come down from the Central Coast, or Canberra,' says Trent. 'I've got a guy who works for me today and he talks about the trips up from Canberra on a Saturday to go record shopping – spending $500 on records and then driving back home, the whole time shaking with excitement about playing these new tunes. People would tell you that they'd just flown in from Adelaide. Central was the biggest record store in the southern hemisphere. We had that volume of customers to allow us to really cater for a big market. It was always a destination for people from interstate to source tunes they couldn't get at home.'

'On a Saturday, people would go there to meet. They'd hang out for frickin' hours. There are probably people who have met there and married. It was just one of those places. People would come there to get their rave tickets. Music was blaring. It felt like a party. It was a cool place to go. It had such a soul to it. It was phenomenal. Talk to anyone from that era and they will have multiple stories to tell you about it. As soon as you went in, you really felt a connection to the music, the people. It was like going to church. People used to plan their day around going to Central Station Records. You didn't realise it at the time, but it's such an integral part of who we are and how we got here.'

Adelaide

A mobile DJ who discovered Central Station Records on a weekend visit to Melbourne, Tony Caraccia based his sets on records he bought there. Get him started on his passion for music, and it's hard to stop him. He lobbied Morgan to open a store in his hometown of Adelaide, and then ran the operation throughout its entire presence, initially as employee

The Heyday of the Stores

The store in Twin Street, Adelaide

and later as owner. He also instigated the Perth store.

The original Adelaide store opened in Gays Arcade in 1989, with DJ Groove Terminator playing at the launch. Within a few weeks, Tony had to move to a larger space in the arcade, two levels up. After two years, the store again outgrew its quarters and moved to Twin Street. Noise complaints forced the next move to Rundle Street, Adelaide's main precinct for bars, clubs, cafes and fashion stores. Tony felt like 'a kid in a chocolate factory'. He had the perfect job, listening to music all day and 'educating' Adelaide about exciting new music.

The Rundle Street store expanded into clothing, with Mark Christie sourcing stock from Flipside in Sydney. 'We catered for different fashion from street to club. We were one of the first importers of Diesel when that came out,' says Tony.

In the mid 90s, Tony set up the South Australian Dance Music Awards. 'The awards recognised all the hard work to promote the music, whether by a DJ, a club owner or a promoter,' he says. 'We set up the categories and nominees, advertised it through media and got the punters to vote. Then we announced winners on the night. We had about 120 people for the first awards night. For the last one, we had 600. It was a big reunion for everyone in the industry.'

For Jo, Tony's biggest triumph was pulling off a story in a special supplement produced by *DJ Magazine*. The famous British monthly was visiting Australia to review the local dance scene. By luck or intel, the magazine visited the Adelaide store, interviewed Tony, and took the photo that became the iconic image for Central Station. 'They loved the concept of the store and the range of music we had,' says Tony. 'They also loved Gina, a beautiful African American who worked for us in the clothing department. We were selling mirror balls, and they put a picture of her with one of them in the article on our store. That was a big honour.'

In contrast to some Central Station stores that focused overwhelmingly on DJs and aficionados, the Adelaide store embraced

On the right in this spread from 'South – Club Life Down Under' in 'DJ Magazine' is the iconic image for Central Station, taken of an Adelaide store employee (Gina) with one of the mirror balls the local store sold. A profile of Simon Lewicki (aka Groove Terminator) is on the left hand side. (Reproduced with the permission of 'DJ Magazine')

The Heyday of the Stores

Pictured in the Adelaide store (from left): Diana Elstak, Tony Caraccia, Jenny Yeeles and DJs Angus Sanders and Paul Elstak (courtesy of DJ George Vagas)

the punters. 'The music brought everyone together, and that was what I loved about it,' says Tony. 'Straight, gay, black, white, street kids, lawyers, judges, police officers, accountants. We had all walks of life coming through the door.'

At the outset, there were only a handful of DJs in the city. Tony allocated a pigeonhole in the store to every one of them. 'If they were promoting the music in venues – like HMC and Groove Terminator, DJ Brendan, Philip Hardy, George Lelos and GTB, just to name a few – they obviously loved the music and played it to three or four hundred people each. That's a thousand-plus potential customers hearing music they don't hear anywhere else. That's how we started getting the punters in, buying the CDs etcetera.'

Brisbane

The first Brisbane store opened in November 1989 in Fortitude Valley, immediately northeast of the CBD. Jonce Dimovski, who'd earned the 'king salesman' tag in Melbourne, was given the task of getting the store up and running. 'Because the Valley was so rough in those days, there was only Central Station, the Bank of Melbourne and an optometrist. Every other shop had closed down,' he recalls. 'They didn't expect much of Brisbane. But in no time, the shop was doing great business.'

After ten months, Jonce returned to Melbourne and Andrew Kelly

Poster for the nightclub that Central Station's Brisbane store ran at the Waterloo Hotel in Newstead

took over. Andrew had been around from the very beginning, having heard about Central's plan to open in Brisbane during a call to Melbourne as a mail-order customer and budding DJ. 'When Jonce arrived here, my friends and I helped out as unpaid employees, opening boxes and stocking the shelves so we could ensure that no one else got to touch the records before we did,' he remembers. After spending every spare hour hanging around the store, he'd been offered a part-time job. But he had no expectations of landing the manager's role when Jonce left.

'In that era, Central Station was very much the pinnacle of cool, so many people would have taken this role for little or no pay,' he says. Feeling that his good friends and colleagues, Remo and Milton, were more likely to be anointed, he was ultra-nervous when interviewed by Emilio Palumbo and later Jo himself. 'Much to everyone's surprise, including my own, I was given the job and instantly became a workaholic.'

As manager, Andrew recognised that he could no longer focus exclusively on the funk, soul and R&B that he was so passionate about: 'To grow sales, I needed to understand dance music, merchandising, promotion, and all the other areas Central was involved in. So I brought in Angus Galloway for his hip hop prowess, Edwin Morrow for his knowledge of dance and house music, and Sonia Basille to build relationships with some of the more commercial DJs.'

The Heyday of the Stores

Andrew continued running Deco-Tech (with Remo as DJ), introducing singing and dancing contests to maintain interest, but an ugly incident one night ultimately led to the club's demise. 'It was probably the competitiveness mixed with alcohol that caused the mêlée,' he says. 'Beer bottles were thrown as well as punches. People were already a little on edge about coming to the "seedy" Valley, so this incident proved to be the death knell. Our crowds thinned considerably. We upgraded the club and relaunched, but we were never able to put the genie back in the bottle.'

After lobbying Jo, Andrew finally got the go-ahead to move to the city – on the onerous condition that there would be no disruption to opening times and no cost.

'Our new location was on the second floor of a building right on the Queen Street Mall in the CBD,' Andrew remembers. 'The landlord insisted that we only use the fire entrance at the rear to move everything in. So from late on Saturday until the early hours of Sunday morning, we carried boxes of heavy records and CDs up three flights of stairs from the basement. The chiropractors downstairs quickly grew to despise their noisy new neighbours. We could manage their complaints pretty well by keeping the door and windows closed. But when we started offering paint can nozzles as part of our hip hop merchandise, a few small tags appeared on the whitewashed walls of the staircase, and the complaints increased. We tried painting the staircases every Friday night after we closed, but we wound up having to employ a bouncer to guard the area.'

Harry Katsanevas started working part-time around 1993 when he was still at university. Jo offered him a job, he says, because he was so often at the store buying music. Later, after Andrew moved to the US to run Central's office there, Harry became manager. His early experience of the store stayed with him, and he tried to make it a more welcoming, less cliquey place. 'Everyone used to go to shop there, but for me it was quite an intimidating space,' he says. 'So, the first couple of times, it was walk-in, walk-out for me. It felt like I shouldn't be there. But I *wanted* to be a part of it. Then, after a while of buying things, I started to make friends with everyone. The whole record thing was like a cult scene. When you were in it, you knew everyone, and it was a big community.'

'We did a lot of cross-promotions with party promoters,' he adds. 'We used to have stalls at a party called *Adventure* – just showing a presence. Then when certain fads came through – like the hardcore fad and there was a *Thunderdome* series – we were the only one who had it. Your friends would say, "Oh, you have to go to Central Station to get it". There was no social media back then, so it was all word-of-mouth.'

His favourite memories are of Sundays in the store after big parties: 'You'd have the store full of people who'd been out the night before in a happy state and then come in straight from the party. Then just having all the big-name DJs come in. Back then, they were doing it for the love, whereas nowadays they're doing it for the fame.'

Matt Nugent started working with Harry in 2000, ordering US house music. Soon afterwards, the store moved to a larger space in Elizabeth Street and introduced the Flipside clothing line. When Harry left to run a nightclub, Matt became manager and the store broadened its customer base, thanks to the clothing and a bigger CD range. The store even stocked 'lifestyle stuff' for café, bar and restaurant owners looking for chill-out music to play in their venues. DJs would drive from as far afield as the Gold Coast – Craig Roberts (aka Tran-C) being a case in point.

Perth

Adelaide's Tony Caraccia was the driving force behind the expansion to Perth. While visiting family in the city, he saw a big hole in the local market and persuaded Central Station to fill it. A relative, Rudy James, was enlisted to find the right site. At the time, Rudy was studying architecture by day and serving drinks by night at Pinocchios in Murray Street. In September 1996, he managed to find Tony a basement store in one of the main shopping arcades in the Murray Street Mall, Carillon Arcade. 'It was pretty grungy, with link-mesh fences and old wooden and steel gates,' recalls Rudy. 'It was the look they were going for.' To underline the point, three street artists were paid to design and paint murals in the foyer and throughout the store.

Patrick Cronin was appointed manager, and two others from the Adelaide store (Andrew Meredith and Anthony Dutton) came over to get things going. Rudy was hired to help out part-time, and a local woman was brought in to run the Flipside department. The team worked through the summer break to open in February 1996. The store was an instant success. 'Everyone loved it,' says Rudy. 'The one thing we were missing here in Perth was imported American hip hop CDs. We only ever got the censored versions before Central started ordering the explicit ones from the States. So we had a very good hip hop section on CD, as well as a few dance titles as well.'

13. The Dance Scene in the 90s

> 'I remember standing in Central Station in Pitt St. Nik Fish who worked there said, "This'll be big" and handed me a twelve-inch called *Groove Is In The Heart*.'
> **John Wall**

Central Station's recovery in the 90s was based on good timing as much as good judgement. As well as the growing popularity of nightclubs, a new market emerged for dance music – the rave scene – which flourished despite (or perhaps because of) the severe recession. Dancing to futuristic music in surreal, loved-up environments was a great way of forgetting exam results, McJobs, or summer-of-love dreams dashed by Tiananmen Square. But it was all over by 1996, thanks to police cracking down on illegal locations and illicit substances. New clubs appeared to fill the vacuum, but many people feel something had been lost and a lull descended on the scene until the late 90s.

DJ Nik Fish, who hosted a pioneering rave show on 2SER for seven years in the 90s, says peaks and troughs occur in any scene. 'Like the Hordern Pavilion. In 87, it was fantastic. In 88, it was peaking. In 89, it was going places. But suddenly it went too often and too mainstream, and forces shut it down,' he says. 'Well the rave scene was similar. So much happened in 91, 92, 93. Then people were starting to grow up. If you were eighteen and going to these things, you did them for a year or two and you're twenty and you decide you've had enough. You've taken too many drugs, given too much time to it. People get married, get careers. Then you get new eighteen-year-olds coming through. They want a different music style. Then new producers came along. Ever since the late 80s, there seems to be a cycle for three or four years and then it changes.'

Gavin Campbell playing at Red Raw warehouse party, Docklands, 1994 (Photo by Robin Dallimore, courtesy of Gavin Campbell)

Melbourne

In the 90s, Gavin Campbell branched out into promotion and recording. As well as the glamorous Razor club, he ran underground events, including Savage, Uranus, Temple and Tasty. In 1994, police raided Tasty (in the Commerce Club in Flinders Street). From the early hours of the morning, 463 patrons (mainly LGBTI) were detained for seven hours and strip-searched for all to see. The incident resulted in a front-page story in *The Age* and a successful class action against Victoria Police. Meanwhile, as a member of Filthy Lucre, Gavin had achieved international success with a dance remix of Yothu Yindi's *Treaty*. 'That was the biggest talking point of my career because it was the first time an Aboriginal band had been on the charts in Australia, let alone internationally,' he says.

John Course also made a mark with an independent dance label (Vicious Vinyl) in the 90s. Growing up in Frankston, on the southeastern fringe of Melbourne, he'd developed a fascination with hip hop and break dance. A scene in the movie *Beat Street* – with a DJ playing in a basement – had made a deep impression on him. 'Wow, this is cool,' he'd thought. He started buying imports at a local record store. One day, when he was playing just for himself, another local teenager, Andy Van, happened to walk by, and was intrigued enough to make connection. Already DJing,

Andy invited John to drop by one evening. Only seventeen, John was underage when he went into his first nightclub.

Soon the new friends were travelling into Melbourne to watch the break dancing crews outside Central's City Square store in the mid 80s. When they both landed gigs in the city, they spent most of their pay shopping at Central, building up their collections. 'The first residency I got where I could play seriously cool music was The Drinkers Club, which was at a venue on Greville Street called ID and later Boutique,' he says. 'That was a Tuesday night in 1988, playing new house and hip hop, the very early days of the house movement. A lot of industry people were going because the big clubs were all shut on a Tuesday. So it was an opportunity to showcase to the movers and shakers of some heavyweight clubs. And it's probably out of that club that I ended up DJing at Chevron and Chasers. Tuesday at the Chevron used to do 1,500 people. The club I DJd at did a 150 to 200 people on the same night. But it was a very cool, music-driven night, so it was great.'

Around this time, John and Andy bought some equipment and set up a little studio in a Frankston shed, where they took samples and produced remixes. In 1992, they set up their own label, Vicious Vinyl, and started releasing music of their own and other DJ producers. In 1999-2000, the label had a big hit with *Don't Call Me Baby* by Madison Avenue (a duo consisting of Andy Van and Cheyne Coates), which reached number two in Australia and number one in New Zealand, the UK and USA.

Melbourne's early rave scene may not have been as high profile as Sydney's, but it's just as fondly remembered. Jim Kontogiannis played at many clubs and raves during the 90s without ever having a set genre: 'I played housey stuff, but nothing too epic, sort of slow. I liked to mix it up with old hip hop records.' He remembers warehouse parties at Global Village in Footscray, along with events at lots of 'weird venues' such as car parks and rooftops. Most people wore the sort of clothes that Central Station offered. 'At one stage, you could buy those big fluoro rave pants,' he recalls. 'But among the Central Station clientele, there were always those chin-stroking DJ types who were more into streetwear.'

Like most DJs, Jim went to see every big name touring Australia. When DJ Derrick Carter from Chicago first played in Melbourne in the mid 90s, the venue was only small (Carousel on Albert Park Lake) - odd considering that the man would now command crowds of 20,000. Jim was so excited that he fell out of a friend's car on arrival and ended up with grass stains on his pants.

Although that particular event started early one Sunday evening, Melbourne nightlife was generally much later. 'When I was playing for Gavin at Savage, my usual set time was five until seven in the morning,' he says. 'Sometimes if we had to go out earlier, it was a long night. Otherwise I would get up at four o'clock and go to work. It was open to nine or ten in the morning. Melbourne's nightclub laws were, and are still, quite relaxed in comparison to Sydney.'

Janette Pitruzzello (aka DJ JNETT) also got her start in the 90s, inspired by fellow Central Station staffers like Jim. Back in Melbourne after living in London for three and half years, she'd felt rather disoriented until she'd figured out that Central was her best chance of reconnecting. She had happened to call the store at 340 Flinders Street and the manager Jonce Dimvoski had instinctively given her a job, despite her being an unknown. 'They had long lists of people who wanted to work there, but he obviously connected with my energy,' she says.

When Janette's new DJ friends asked her to fill in one night, she found her calling. From that first gig at the Lounge in 1994, she went on to a co-residency (with Paul Main) at the revamped Prince of Wales hotel while also hosting the ABC's *Recovery* show. 'Sometimes I would literally go from my gig to the ABC studios and do live television,' she recalls. 'That was just bizarre.'

Sydney

While still at high school in 1987, Nik Vatoff (aka Nik Fish) was sneaking over the fence to Hordern Pavilion parties, catching the DJ bug. At home, he would listen to a radio show on 2SER called *Madhouse*, with Jo Ormston and Guy Perriman playing house music for two hours from eleven o'clock on a Monday night. When they held competitions, Nik called in so often that he became known as 'Nik from Manly'. On one occasion when he was about seventeen years old, he won tickets to a RAT party and, unbeknown to this parents, went along with his best mate, Pat Davern (who later became Grinspoon's lead guitarist).

Standing near the bar, Nik recognised voices nearby.

'Mate, I know those voices,' he told Pat.

Then it clicked.

'Are you Jo and Guy?' he asked the twenty-something radio hosts he'd been ringing all year. 'I'm Nik from Manly.'

'Oh my god!' said Jo Ormston, grabbing his cheeks. 'Look at you. You're so young. You shouldn't be here.'

The Dance Scene in the 90s

Nik told her his story – about how crazy he was for radio that he'd been mocking up radio shows since he was twelve years old, using the tape-to-tape recorder and microphone his grandfather had given him.

'We do programs to help people get into radio,' the 2SER announcer told him. Over the next few months, she took Nik under her wing and trained him up on the community radio station. She also introduced him to Central Station's Pitt Street store, so that he could borrow records for his new Wednesday night show. Not long afterwards, Paul Jackson gave Nik a job there.

After the Hordern Pavilion era, many news clubs opened to cater for the dance explosion. 'The people that were going to parties at the Hordern were forced to decide which club scene they'd go to,' he says. 'There was Base in the city, a huge underground warehouse space near Circular Quay that used to be called Jamieson Street. Pee Wee Ferris became a resident there. Then there was Ziggurat in Kings Cross, which was a small, dark and dingy venue. There was a lot of choice.'

Nik's big break came from promoter Sean Finlay who was running a night at Kinselas at Taylor Square. 'I want to push new blood,' he told Nik. 'I'm trying to find fresh talent. This is the 90s now. You seem to be into your hip hop. I might be able to offer you a gig if you're willing to work.' So Nik ended up playing a five-hour set of hip hop on Saturday nights in the middle bar of Kinselas, while Groove Terminator played house upstairs.

But shortly after turning nineteen, Nik discovered rave music while visiting his former 2SER mentor in London. When he came back, he got the opportunity to take over a Monday afternoon hip hop slot on 2SER and changed the genre overnight. 'I renamed my show *Musiquarium*, which is the title of a Stevie Wonder album. I liked it because it alluded to fish,' he says. 'The show lost all the hip hoppers, but ravey people were ringing up and saying, "I can't believe we're hearing this. This is what they play at parties". The show was ahead of its time. It was very unusual to play dance music on radio in the early 90s.'

Through the show, Nik met promoters and was booked to play at the warehouse parties that sprang up as an alternative to the clubbing scene. Former Central employee Wes McDonald describes the prevailing mood: 'The very nature was, "Let's get back to where it's less organised. We want to get away from the club culture and have our own society".'

In 1990, DJ George Vagas moved from Adelaide to Sydney, bringing the three crates of records he'd bought in London. He knew no one in town but soon attracted attention by setting up his turntables and amplifier at the Bondi skate ramp. 'I got my first nightclub gigs at Spagos, Kinselas, Fishbox, Bentley Bar, Ziggurat, Bondi Hotel, Mars and so on by talking to the owners and promoters of clubs. The rave promoters could recognise the acid house and techno, so that's when I got my first plays at early raves in 1991, thanks to the promoter of Eden, and Malcolm and Michelle of Deep Joy promotions.'

Back then, he says, English promoters and DJs had sewn up all the illegal warehouse parties. So he decided to hold 'Ravers Playground' recovery parties at the Graffiti Hall of Fame, a wholesale meatworks owned by Tony Spanos. On Botany Road in Alexandria, it was surrounded by fifteen-metre-high walls full of graffiti. 'It was Australia's first outdoor rave recovery,' says George. 'When the Pommie promoters would finish their warehouse parties at five in the morning, I'd open up, featuring no-name DJs back then. In the coming years, they became some of the biggest promoters and DJs in the next generation of the Sydney rave scene. I'm proud to say I gave residencies every Sunday to DJs like Nik Fish, Biz E, Abel, Jumping Jack, Nick TT, Wizard, DB and Techno Terrorists. The Graffiti Hall of Fame later became *the* rave venue you would go to when your party was closed down or cancelled.'

Mark Dynamix was one of those English expats who had the rave

Day raving at the Graffiti Hall of Fame in the 90s (courtesy of 'I Partied in Sydney in the '90s')

The Dance Scene in the 90s

Events run by George Vagas as an international touring agent, from top: DJ Nightraver and the Dyewiness Dancers at Darlinghurst Gaol, Sydney in 1994; Ultrasonic (featuring Mallorca Lee and David Forbes) at St Paul's, Adelaide; and Charlie Lownoise & Mental Theo outside Flipside at Oxford Street with the poster for their appearance at Itchy & Scratchy, 1994 (all images courtesy of DJ George Vagas)

scene sewn up according to George. At just fourteen, he'd persuaded his favourite radio station, 2RDJ FM, to give him work experience. He'd started out answering the telephone and ended up on air shortly after turning fifteen in 1990. He came to the attention of rave promoters through his show, *Tuesday Night Rave*, and rose to fame playing at raves in Sydney and interstate, following his taste from one sub-genre to another. 'I was involved in one scene in particular in the early 90s, but my music intake was and still is wide and varied, and as the club scene took off in the late 90s, I went where my music tastes wanted to go. So for me, it was acid house and hip house in 1988 and that lasted until about 1992. From 92 to 94, there was a lot of Italian house and rave music, and then from 94 to 96, you started having all the early trance records from Germany, so it got a bit faster in tempo. And all of these sub-genres would wave in and out of raves and the clubs.'

Katie M Little (aka Plus One) chose her DJ name 'to take the piss a bit – it was such a boys' scene and I didn't want to be the plus-one on the door list'. After leaving school, she discovered rave music in London and built her life in the 90s around it. Then-boyfriend, now-husband Tim Poulton (aka Mach V) started promoting parties (Jurassic, Itchy and Scratchy, Star Wars) as well as doing a Friday club night (Speed Racer)

Mark Dynamix showing promise as a DJ at just three years old (Photo by Nola Vick, courtesy of Mark Vick)

in Kings Cross. Katie often did the lighting, and teamed up with Tim to start a business designing rave flyers. 'It was brand new and we would go shopping for records at Central Station,' she remembers. 'We'd go into one of the little booths under the stairs. Most of that early stuff was Italian that we used to play on full speed. And other stuff being imported from Rotterdam, lots of Dutch happy hard music. And then English breakbeat started coming in. It was really fun. Crazy days.'

Back then, the couple lived in a warehouse in the Haymarket area and used a huge vacant allotment behind the Agincourt Hotel for many of their parties. Coming from a theatrical family (her mother is former TV personality Jeanne Little), Katie is a natural storyteller. 'The worst thing was worrying that the cops would shut us down,' she says.

Left: A very young Katie M Little (Plus One) with her celebrity mother, Jeanne Little

Below: The 'insanely cool scaffolding set up for Star Wars Rave' – an event run by Plus One and Mach V with a huge mirror ball above and speaker stacks at the four corners

(both courtesy of Katie M Little)

'Thousands of people jammed full. No safety things. DJs and people dancing off their chops while on scaffolding towers that would be swaying from side to side. Cables running along the ground through puddles of water. Looking back, I don't know why there weren't people dying all over the place.'

There was a strong connection with Central Station. Often George Vagas (from Flipside) would DJ at the events, and Jo and Morgan would come along. The scene was very tribal, with everyone getting right into the look and the moves. 'Mum, who did everything over the top, made my bell-bottom trousers way bigger than everyone else's,' she says. 'I'm a small person anyway, but I used to wear tiny, tight, minute T-shirts and then bell-bottom trousers that went right down to the ground in the mud when you were dancing. And I'd be wearing my Vans sneakers – because I was a skateboarder as well. Breakbeat especially had a real style. You could dance to it, going from side to side on the offbeat and syncopation. The house DJs were like, "Oh, we're too cool for all of that". But it *was* really cool. And I remember George's girlfriend, Bridget, and her sister, Caitie. They'd be right down the front dancing, going bananas, like an aerobics workout. And you would dance straight for hours and hours.'

But Katie's favourite memory is of doing the lighting for a Sven Väth gig. 'I really love lighting. I thought it was just as powerful as the music in setting the mood and building stuff up. When the track went totally nuts, you could throw in a strobe light,' she says. 'Sven Väth was DJing on the scaffolding beside me in front of a packed crowd who were all so into the music. A few punters had climbed up onto the speakers and the scaffolding, and it was all bouncing up and down, like we were on a train. It gives me chills even thinking about it. It was so much fun.'

Mikel Goodman is another rave entrepreneur and flyer designer of the era. From 1988 and throughout the 90s, he progressed through Italian style, hard dance, UK hardcore and freeform at nightclubs and stadiums around Australia, including in Sydney, Canberra, Brisbane, Adelaide, Perth and Cairns. But he didn't limit himself to DJing. From 1991 to 1995, he promoted rave parties around Sydney. With names like Space Cadet, Outer Space, Inner Space, and Noddy Has a Party, these events were 'all underground stuff, ring on the night to find the location'. Illicit though they were, Mikel's parties were not slapdash. Space Cadet One, for instance, was held in a film studio in Alexandria. 'The DJ booth was on a scissor lift, which lifted the DJ up twenty feet while smoke machines went off. Very space-like,' he recalls. 'In 1992, it was

The Dance Scene in the 90s

DJ Fenix (on left) at a 2004 gig, System 6, one of Brisbane's most influential and longest running event series (courtesy of Mikel Goodman)

voted best party in *JRA* magazine, ahead of huge events like Prodigy and Tribal.' From warehouses in the early days, Mikel moved to bigger, more formal venues (such as Olympic Park, the Tennis Centre and Macquarie University) as the rave scene exploded. Then he turned to designing flyers for other promoters, including Powerhouse events like Utopia and Godspeed. 'I was doing so many parties that my previous designer just couldn't keep up,' he says. 'Then other promoters saw my designs and it just worked out from there.'

In the early 90s, Jon Wicks moved from Canberra to Sydney, after being hired to advise on sound systems for early Sydney rave parties in Alexandria and Waterloo. 'They were very experimental and the mood was fantastic,' he says. By the mid 90s, he too was organising events of his own, but felt that the scene had lost something: 'The feeling back in the late 80s was "Everybody's in this together". But by 94, it had become "What are you going to do to entertain us?" It was a big change in attitude.'

As the dance scene became more popular, the process of fragmentation accelerated. New genres appeared, with many swelling from niche to major popularity – as Jesse Desenberg discovered. At age nineteen, he became Kid Kenobi for his first gig, choosing the name for its hip hop vibe. Because his kind of music was still very much on the fringe in the early 90s, he teamed up with friends to promote parties so that they could all get the chance to play. The parties were called Green

& Jazzy and the main venue was the Burdekin hotel on Oxford Street. 'At that time, house and rave were the predominant sounds and we were doing drum n base and early breakbeat, hip hop and old school rave,' he says. 'I was always interested in the black end of dance music. Dad was in reggae bands, and I used to listen to hip hop when I was younger. Then I got into raves.'

Around 1996, police cracked down on the illegal parties and the scene died away. Rave DJs started putting on nights in clubs. Nik Fish, for example, began doing a regular Friday night at Sublime in Pitt Street, Sydney. 'The rave scene went a bit happy hardcore, with 180 bpms and kids wearing candy bracelets and jumping up and down like Energiser bunnies, chewing their faces off and sucking dummies. Ravers who were in their mid-twenties by then were wondering, "What's all this going on?" I rolled with the times and played a bit of that for a while, but I decided I didn't love it and I got more into German hard trance – sort of the tempo of happy hardcore but a bit darker, moodier.'

Mark Dynamix began a regular night at Sublime in 1997. 'That's when I started playing more house music rather than the faster stuff,' he says. 'I'm talking progressive house, progressive trance and also some funky house as well. Because I played a lot of different styles and genres, I'd get booked for a wide variety of gigs. It doesn't happen so much with DJs these days. They tend to be pigeonholed by the agents or promoters, or even by themselves or their audiences ... but I feel things are changing and DJs are being allowed to express themselves over a range of genres without sacrificing one genre for the other.'

By 1998, happy hardcore had reached its peak. 'It got to the point of crossing over – songs getting on to the top forty – and it was very visible at street level, especially on Oxford Street,' says Wes McDonald. 'It was like 1988 came back again ten years later with the smiley face and all that stuff. Central Station licensed a few big tracks like Charly Lownoise & Mental Theo's *Wonderful Days* that became top forty hits as well.'

All this action excited a new generation of dance music lovers. In Sydney's inner west, an underground dance scene was thriving – with the Equinox dance parties in Five Dock, which catered for the under-18s, figuring among the more notable events. 'It was a very rich, vibrant scene awash with European dance music,' says Jim 'JimmyZ' Hirst of Wild FM music directing fame. 'The style of music was melodic, energetic, fun, uplifting and euphoric. The early 90s were a bit of a dark time, especially for this demographic of youth who had new-migrant parents

The Dance Scene in the 90s

Central Station in Adelaide sold tickets for this 90s event

and were barely represented in the broader culture, so it was an exciting opportunity to connect with them and to showcase what a rich music scene they had.'

Adelaide

By the 90s, Adelaide's dance scene was pumping. 'It was fantastic, a big family,' says Tony Caraccia, Central Station's store manager. 'All the clubs, the promoters, us, and a magazine called *The Core*. It was a niche but close-knit community. Everyone respected each other and were in it for the music.'

The Metro Nightclub was at the helm of clubbing, offering cutting-edge underground house, while Le Rox catered for the ravers. But, in the early 90s, Synagogue opened up with a more progressive focus. Hip hop was also big at this time. 'It was great for us because we were catering for them all – the house, the techno heads, drum n base, the rave heads, the hardcore heads, the hip hop,' says Tony.

Independent record labels also sprang up. Cam Biamchetti (aka HMC) and Damien Donato founded Juice Records, Australia's first techno label. When HMC produced some tracks that didn't fit into the

DJ JoSH (courtesy of Jo Altman)

Juice catalogue, he teamed up with Theo Bambakis to launch Dirty House Records. 'Dirty House and Juice went on to produce music that attracted the world market for those genres, so Adelaide was renowned as the techno/house capital in the southern hemisphere back in the mid 90s,' says Tony.

Jo Altman (aka DJ JoSH) considers herself lucky that she learned her craft in Adelaide. 'If you can please people in Adelaide, you can please them anywhere in the world,' she says. 'And we were very underground. We were playing techno way before every other State in Australia. We were playing house before every other State. It was just amazing.' Laughing, she adds, 'I'm the people's DJ. I'm like Princess Di! That came naturally because I'm such a music appreciator and I understood what it did for people and I grew up at such a lucky time – there weren't many female DJs around. I was at the forefront.'

Using money from her paper run, DJ JoSH had started collecting records as a young child. Music had been a passion and an escape. The next stage had been sneaking into underground clubs in the early 80s, when she'd been only seventeen. 'I went from 5KA radio music and *Countdown* to discovering these nightclubs with sounds I hadn't heard before, and it was just amazing,' she says. The Toucan Two had been a standout venue for her: 'They used to play a lot of Gothic music like The Cure, and The Smiths, and then Dead or Alive and all that electronic music that was coming through.'

After a couple of years she'd moved on to playing, with her first resident gig at the Mars Bar, Adelaide's longest-running gay venue. For the next eleven years, she'd stuck to playing in the gay scene, including at Beans Bar, The Ed Castle, the Mars Bar, and Magoos.

In 1995, John Pike booked her for her first straight gig – supporting Dead or Alive at Heaven nightclub. HMC then hired her to play in 'the lick room' at his Dirty House 'Intercourse' party at St Paul's. There she was 'discovered' by the top brass at other nightclubs such as Q Club, Cargo, Synagogue and Planet. 'All of a sudden I was this young girl in leather garb getting booked for all of these gigs, so I hit the straight market pretty hard,' she remembers. 'I became sort of the "it" girl because I was a female DJ with the name Josh and I was banging out beats that no one had heard of before.'

'I couldn't tell you what my genre is,' she continues. 'I started off in the gay scene so it was very gay-orientated music – Hi NRG euro – and because I was buying records from Central Station it was very Italian house. Piano, vocals about love lost, be gay and happy, *Everybody's Free* and that sort of stuff, very uplifting. Then I discovered trance out of Hi NRG euro pop, and I was probably more widely known from 1995 right through until the peak of my career in 2005 as a trance DJ.'

Brisbane

In the early part of the decade, Italian house was the major driving force in Brisbane's dance scene, says Harry Katsanevas. The main venues he patronised were The Beat and The Tube, both in the Valley. But by the end of the 90s, Brisbane had become more orientated towards UK hard house, according to Matt Nugent: 'Whereas Sydney got into that Hi NRG DCM kind of sound, and also the hard trance that people like Nik Fish were pushing, Brisbane was more oriented to the sounds that Tony de Vit made popular at Trade nightclub, and that Edwin and Jen-E played at The Beat after Angus left.'

Angus Galloway (aka DJ Angus, DJ Bribe), Edwin Morrow (aka DJ Edwin), Jenny Juckel (aka Jen-E), and Tracy Brennan (aka DJ Miss Tracy) all worked for Central at some stage. 'Angus was one of the most gifted DJs I've ever witnessed – eccentric but brilliant,' says Andrew Kelly, a former Brisbane store manager. 'We enticed him to work for us to give some credibility to our hip hop offerings. He didn't really need the job, but he became a surprisingly reliable and valuable member of the Central Station community. He definitely brought the street cred of which I had none. His father had built him his own flat below the family house in St Lucia. He had a full-on DJ studio set-up there, where he and his friends would perfect their mixing skills all day.'

Matt backs up this view: 'Angus is probably the most important DJ in Queensland from the beginning of the 90s to the 2000s, even from the 80s. He was a hip hop DJ, turned rave DJ. Sadly not with us any more. But you have to give him a mention as one of the pioneering DJs. Edwin, Jen-E and Barking Boy adopted that sound and influenced a whole bunch of kids to play that music.'

Bobbie Bright, Angus's mother, recalls how working at Central Station had a major impact on her son: 'Morgan once told me with much laughter how this kid turned up on the doorstep of Central Station Records when it was in the Valley. He must have been about eighteen or nineteen. Angus said, "I want a job. You've got to give me a job". Angus was always someone who was a bit difficult to get out of bed – a typical teenager – but the minute he got that job, he was out of the house like a rocket. He was absolutely devoted to it.'

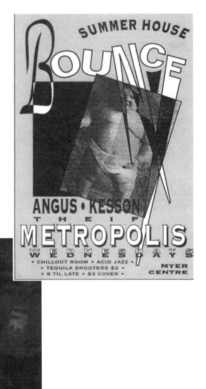

Right: Poster for a Brisbane event

Below: Bobbie Bright, mother of DJ Angus (and an activist in women and disability sectors) with a painting of her late son by Zorbs (courtesy of Bobbie Bright)

The Dance Scene in the 90s

Morgan recalls: 'Angus was such a charismatic personality and DJ. He lit up a room with his DJ prowess. He was a huge asset to our new store in Brisbane.'

Such a cult following remains for Angus that filmmaker Simon Walshe was able to crowd-fund his documentary *Flow* (due for release in 2017). 'The story from my point of view is about him as an artist, the events that led up to him becoming one of the best DJs in the country and why people continue to love him so much. He was quite a theatrical guy – an accomplished juggler, fire breather and unicyclist who became a street performer. He had quite an obsessive nature about him, and that's what led him into being a DJ because it was such a detailed art form and it took a long time to master.'

Central staffers mourn another memorable character. 'Edwin is sadly no longer with us either,' says Matt Nugent. 'He was the main resident down at The Beat nightclub. He was definitely a tastemaker. He played there for twenty years or something ridiculous, and he used to put on parties called Adrenalin that were raves as well. He looked like a Goth. He was always dressed all in black, with super-pale-white skin and long, black hair. But he played Hi NRG hard house stuff. Another super important one who used to play The Beat with Edwin was Jen-E. She was the first popular female DJ in Queensland. But she also used to play raves in Sydney and Melbourne and make mix CDs.'

In 1993, Edwin gave a young BeXta Poulsen her first gig, performing at one of his Adrenalin parties. At the time, BeXta was studying at the Conservatorium of Music in Brisbane, aiming for the only degree then available in music and music technology. There were just seven people in her year, and a few in the course were in pioneering dance music band Vision Four 5. When they introduced her to the early rave scene in Brisbane, she knew exactly what direction she wanted to take. 'From that point, there wasn't a question any more,' she says. 'It was an instant falling in love with dance music.' But BeXta wanted to produce the music, not just play it. She took cassette recordings of her tracks into Central Station, and bugged Edwin to listen. Eventually, he gave her a chance. 'There weren't many females around at the time either, so that was setting me apart a little bit,' she says.

BeXta was only nineteen when she jumped in at the deep end, playing her own music at the 3,000-capacity Roxy (now called the Arena) for her first gig. Friends danced on stage with her, establishing her trademark theatrical style. She says that Brisbane was a little behind

BeXta (centre) with dancers and Bexta cam in 1998, after finishing shooting the 'Make It Phunkee' video clip. Photo taken at Sega World in Sydney, where BeXta was working part time as an audio visual technician. (courtesy of BeXta)

Sydney in the rave phenomenon. 'Occasionally, they'd put events on at the showground. Actually, there were a few raves out in fields and things, but it was very legalised compared with the early Sydney days when you'd call a number and get directions. I don't think they needed to go underground to have a good event. There were people organising parties at venues that had enough capacity – three or four thousand.' The clubs were the mainstay of the scene in Brisbane, she says. People would regularly go to smaller ones like The Beat or The Tube unless a big event was being held at The Site or The Roxy.

In the early nineties, there was a lot of ecstasy in Brisbane clubs and raves, says Matt Nugent. Then speed began permateing the UK hard house scene at the end of the 90s. But alcohol was what DJ Edwin was well known for favouring. Matt recalls: 'Edwin would come into the shop on Friday nights dressed in his all-black gear ready to go to work. He'd also bring in a brown paper bag with a bottle of Scotch in it and he'd ask, "Can you look after my set-maker for me?" So we'd put that under the counter while he listened to records and we'd have a chat.'

Canberra

Before moving to Sydney in the early 90s, Jon Wicks had a regular club night called Canberra House Authority at Heaven nightclub. He remembers going to a lot of warehouse parties, but says forest parties were big too. 'There were a series of parties put on by Clan Analogue called Panopticon after the circular French prison invention. They were held in the pine forests around Canberra, always within view of Black Mountain tower, which can be seen from many kilometres away. They were never commercial ventures. It was just a bunch of people going out and having fun. They were really good times.'

Perth

Rudy James was 'as green as' when he started working at Central Station in late 1995, but he quickly made friends among DJs and mapped out the scene. 'The main clubs were Limbo and Aqua, both in Northbridge, and another one that was just opening, Krush,' he says. 'There were probably four main DJs in the underground scene – Dave Jackson, Miggy, Darryn Briais and JJ. Most of it was US house.'

Rudy caught the mixing bug by the end of his first year at Central and began DJing at the Aqua Café with Dave Jackson, downstairs from the nightclub. 'I was playing chilled US house, a bit of down tempo stuff,' he says. He also became resident DJ on Thursday nights at a club called DC (Dual Control) and on Wednesday nights at The Globe. From mid 1997, he started DJing at raves organised by the city's biggest party promoter, Delirium. He also supported international artists being toured by Ministry of Sound and Renaissance. A career highlight was playing at a New Year's Eve party in Indonesia in 1998. The opportunity came about when a radio presenter heard him DJing at Aqua Café, and decided that this was the sound he wanted for his rave party. 'I had no passport. I had never been outside the country,' says Rudy. 'I played at a beach party at an area called Charita which is west of Jakarta. They flew me over and back. Amazing experience.'

'All the people I know now I've met through nightclubs and working in the store,' he says. 'I loved everything about the store – the people I met, the friendships I made there, and the passion people shared about the music. I even met my wife there twenty years ago.'

Barely into his teens, Ken Lockhart (aka DJ Kenny L) got his start playing at the Roller Drome in Balcatta where he learned to mix with the seven-inch singles on hand. 'They didn't have cross-faders in the early 90s, just the channels up and down,' he says. 'I learned to mix by tapping my feet, and fading one track in over the other in the last bar or two. As I did that more and more, no matter what the music was, I found certain tracks complemented others well. That got me more interested in

DJing, and that's all I've done all my life.'

While still working at the roller-skating rink, Ken landed his first paid nightclub gig – at James Street in Northbridge. He was just sixteen. As the rave scene hit Perth, he went on to play happy hardcore at warehouse parties (held in industrial suburbs such as Belmont, Osborne Park and Welshpool) as well as at established venues in and around the city. When authorities clamped down on issues such as fire exits and evacuation plans, promoters moved to function venues and indoor sports centres. 'You had boxing promoters who turned their gym in Northbridge into an underaged rave club called Elevation,' Ken recalls. 'Then some of the promoters would hold an event in an indoor cricket centre and use catering companies who could get a temporary liquor licence. It generated a whole VIP thing where you'd pay a bit more for a ticket and you were able to gain access to the licensed area. At the same time, lots more clubs popped up, in places like Northbridge and Fremantle. Somewhere in there was the beginning of the festival scene. At first they were like the raves. It was a slow transition from illegal to legal. All the dodgy underworld promoters were washed away by the legal parties.'

Auckland

Auckland had its share of warehouse parties in the late 80s and early 90s. Sam Hill would be booked to play in 'pretty random' locations, but the crowds numbered in the hundreds rather than thousands. Police would sometimes raid events, hold people for a few hours and then let them go, more concerned about noise and illicit substances than break-ins. 'Up until that point, it was all very down-tempo R&B and a bit of fruity disco, and it was all very organised,' remembers Sam. 'Then all of a sudden people are dancing in warehouses and fields, and there was no bar system set up. Why are these people here?'

Unlike Australia, New Zealand had no import restrictions for records and no license stranglehold for radio, so it could plug into new music quite quickly, despite its small population. Sam Hill worked at a store called Sounds, where Grant Kearney was his boss. Together they handled the dance music imports, astounding the fifty-year-old storeowner with the way tracks like *Jack to the Sound of the Underground* outsold greatest hits albums of baby-boomer favourites like the Eagles. 'There was a fruitful period when we were selling everything we were getting in and we couldn't keep up the stock,' he says. 'We were selling some of those really good, more crossover tunes for $25 a twelve-inch single.'

When Sounds went into receivership, Sam and Grant decided to open their own store, Bassline Records, in O'Connell Street. 'At the time, we were just young and naïve,' says Sam. 'It worked, and we did well out of it. But I look back now, and I think, "How did I get the balls to sign a four-year lease on a business and we're only going to sell twelve-inch dance vinyl?" We introduced other things like mix tapes and T-shirts and that all propped up the business.'

For a while, they continued to source all of their stock from UK distributors, but in the latter half of the 90s, when Central Station began licensing tracks for Australia and New Zealand, it became cheaper, easier and faster to deal with them for certain tracks. Sometimes they would cross the ditch to raid the warehouse. 'You guys in Australia have a different market to us,' he points out. 'We have a very large, urban R&B, drum n base, hip hop market, as well as the house thing. We were doing both, but at that point Central Station was more into the house, Hi NRG, the early trance. And we were finding things in the warehouse that were dead in the water in the Australian market. There were titles where I'd go, "I just sold my last copy of this to a collector for a lot of money", and they've got fifty of them sitting on the floor for a dollar each!'

The markets may have been different, but DJs' desperation to be the first to get their hands on new music was not. 'It's funny how that side of things has gone out the window now,' says Sam. 'With the internet, you can get anything you want any time. Back then, it came down to which DJs were in the know, or willing to stand around in the rain and cold waiting for it. We'd open the store at nine o'clock and there would be five or six people waiting to get in. "I heard there's a shipment coming in this morning. I thought I'd come in early and hang out." You'd end up talking about music.'

Sam doesn't recall a lot of hugging going on in Auckland during the ecstasy era. 'From my memories, I felt that more people were on acid than on pills, for a long, long time. It felt more like people were wasted than on a buzz. They would be mugging out on the dance floor and being a bit anti-social. Then the whole rave scene kicked in – where you're playing gabber and hardcore. Because there were limited DJs, and we owned the store, it wouldn't be rare for Grant and me to grab twenty gabber records and do a gabber set. You might get paid 500 bucks each, and then these records would be 200 bucks, because we're paying cost price. By default, we'd end up doing these different genres because we owned the store and had the music.'

Philip Bell (aka DJ Sir-Vere) believes that The Brain parties organized by Sam Hill and Grant Kearney in the 90s changed the New Zealand market. 'That was the really tipping point for rave culture,' he says. 'I'm a firm believer that the kids and streets dictate what popular culture is. You can't tell kids, "This is hot" and that was the cool thing about Central Station. They would just say, "We're going to bang it out and see what happens."'

In the late 90s, Philip took over from Grant Kearney as assistant A&R at BMG Records, inheriting Central Station as a label. Morgan would call him about a single he thought would work in his old stomping ground and send over samples to consider. Unlike Australia, the key to breaking a tune in New Zealand has always been radio, because the population is not big enough to support super-clubs and massive festivals. If Philip liked what Morgan sent, he would focus on securing airplay. 'New Zealand radio frequencies are deregulated,' he says. 'So you have a lot more small groups listening to smaller radio stations with a real tastemaker thing going on ... He was handpicking things and sending them through to me and we had a ball. Because when we got it right, we really smashed it ... True popularity is things that make you happy. And there's no doubt that was a lot on the Central Station catalogue that was happy music.'

Lemon Tree by Fool's Garden was a particularly big hit for the label in New Zealand.

Promotional item for one of Central Station's biggest hits in New Zealand

14. The Dance Media

Since time immemorial, tribes have had their mark-makers, storytellers and message-senders. The dance music tribe is no different, and Central Station was a major supporter of the dance media across Australasia.

Press

Adelaide had *The Core*, a fortnightly youth magazine covering music, clubs, DJs and fashion. Brisbane had *The Scene*. Central Station sponsored these and other street press publications such as *On the Street*, *Rip It Up* and *Onion Club Culture Magazine*. But the biggest association of all was with *3D World*. Nicole Fossati was hired as a staff writer in 1994 because she didn't wear her customary Adidas trainers for the interview (she'd just washed them). The newly appointed editor wanted to move *3D* away from the dance scene and was ruling out anyone looking like a raver. In 'accidental disguise', Nicole slipped through the net and soon took over the top job after an outcry from readers about her predecessor's direction.

In Nicole's time at the helm (1994-1997), the magazine was printed in black and white on cheap porous paper, with occasional spot colour. It was stocked in record stores, music stores, takeaway joints, fashion stores, cafes and some newsagents throughout Sydney, Newcastle and Wollongong. Central Station was not only one of the biggest advertisers, but employees also contributed weekly columns. 'There were three to five Central Station contributors discussing new imports, new trends, great finds, and thoughts on their chosen genres,' says Nicole. 'They were at the coalface and they were the experts.'

Not long after Nicole became editor, she had to deal with a nasty slanging match in print that erupted between a Central staffer and hardcore DJ called Torquemada, and another contributor. Nicole warned them both to knock it off, or she'd pull their columns. When Torq persisted, she decided to contact Tim McGee, then store manager at Oxford Street, to enlist his help in reining him in. Tim didn't return her calls. Worse still, when one of Nicole's sales reps, Jade Harley, prompted him in the store, she was given short shrift.

'She came back to me with the reluctant message that I could stick the magazine up my arse,' recalls Nicole. 'Next minute I was in my car on the way to Central, primed to give this Tim McGee character a piece of my mind. I was told by a staffer he wasn't in his office, and she didn't know where he was. Not a problem, I'd wait. And I sat in his office and waited, and waited ... and waited. He eventually entered looking like thunder, but before he could have a crack at me, I launched at him. "Stick the magazine up my arse?" I think was my opening sentence, likely followed by "Who the fuck do you think you are?" God bless him, he sat there like a stunned schoolboy for my five-minute tirade of grievances against him, his staff, jeopardising a business relationship and blah de bloody blah blah. I only stopped because he'd given up trying to interject and instead raised his hand. He'd just been talking with Torq about toeing the line. He'd gone on to warn all staff about their behaviour in regards to the magazine. Problem solved. He apologised about the mag-up-the-arse comment. We both had to laugh. Jade had just got him at a bad time. I was totally diffused. We chatted for a while,

Nicole Fossati with Canadian VJ Gordon Blunt (aka G.I. Blunt) around 1999 (courtesy of Nicole Fossati)

The Dance Media

shared challenges in our respective roles, and ended up being surprised by the other. I wasn't the bitch he'd heard about. He wasn't the asshole I'd heard about. We ended up dating for about three years.'

Nicole's successor, Danny Corvini, was co-editor of *3D* from 1996 to 1999. 'It was the era when dance music had just become really big in Australia,' he says. 'In the late 80s and early 90s, it was still quite an underground thing. But things crossed over into the mainstream in the mid 90s, so it was a really big scene in Sydney, but not so commercial as it is today with EDM festivals. By about 94, the first sense of commercialism started creeping into the rave scene and it took probably

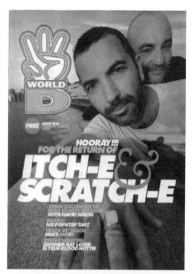

Left: Front cover of '3D World' featuring Itch-e & Scratch-e (Paul Mac and Andy Rantzen) in 2010. (Reproduced with the permission of Street Press Australia P/L)

Below: Danny Corvini (centre, behind woman in cap) with friends at the Romper Stomper rave in Canberra in 1994 (courtesy of 'I Partied in Sydney in the '90s')

the rest of the decade to become complete. While the scene existed under the radar for a long time without too many incidents, the big parties at Homebush gave the authorities a grip on it. Things started splintering off. My group of friends dipped out of the rave scene to go to house music parties, which were a smaller and older crowd, and were held at smaller venues in Sydney – up on the rooftop at Flight Soho, Club 77 and so on. In the second half of the 90s, Sydney started getting purpose-built dance clubs. Sublime opened on Pitt Street and The Globe opened on the corner of Park and Elizabeth Streets. Chinese Laundry became a really cool kind of dance club. And Home opened at Darling Harbour. It mirrored what was happening in the UK when the illegal scene started moving into the clubs. There were probably more people DJing than ever before. There were about five specialty DJ shops in and around Oxford Street, including Central Station, which was the biggest. Others started to specialise in different parts of the scene like deep house or techno, whereas Central Station was always very broad. It catered for commercial DJs as well. You could expect to find a bit of everything there.'

Radio

Radio was crucial in expanding the market for dance music in Australia. One of the earliest champions was a youth-formatted community radio station in Melbourne called Hitz FM, founded in 1992 by Anthony Gherghetta (aka Go-Go), who originally insisted on volunteers being under the age of twenty-one (later twenty-five).

Angie Young was one of those volunteers. She was a university student when she bumped into a high school friend on the train one day. This friend was Hitz FM's program manager and invited her to join the young crew who ran the station. 'So I helped out in the music library, going through record company promos every Saturday I could,' she remembers. 'I was studying full time, had two part-time jobs and played tennis, so there wasn't a lot of spare time, but I loved it. Their sound was nothing like any other station, and they definitely were a threat to commercial radio stations at the time. There were so many young and talented, creative and entrepreneurial types who were only teenagers. I'm still friends with many of them to this day. They were pro-active with their music and it was predominantly dance music. Everyone loved it!'

Excited by the success of his Melbourne venture, Gherghetta decided to take a shot at the Sydney market. At the time, JimmyZ had worked at a string of community radio stations up and down the eastern seaboard,

The Dance Media

Mark Dynamix and JimmyZ in their shared flat in Glebe, Sydney, circa 1994 (Photo by Rita McCulloch, courtesy of Mark Vick)

with his last port of call being 2RDJ 88.1 FM, based in Burwood in Sydney's inner west. Go-Go called, said he'd heard good things about him and asked if he wanted to get involved. JimmyZ jumped at the chance. Soon his 2RDJ FM colleague, Mark Vick (aka Mark Dynamix), also became involved. This was the pair who helped set up Wild FM.

An association called Sydney Youth Broadcasters Incorporated, with JimmyZ as vice-chairman, was created to apply for the test license. The newly established Australian Broadcasting Authority was making radio frequencies available on a test basis, so that aspiring community broadcasters could present their case for permanent metro-wide city licenses. In the end, both Hitz FM and Wild FM missed out on that prize and were forced to disband. They became too successful for their own good, ultimately failing to pass the non-profit test for a community station. But in their short-lived glory days, they sent shock waves through the commercial radio world, opening people's eyes to a huge slab of the youth market that programmers had neglected.

Gherghetta's partnership with Central Station Records provided the platform for those glory days, and JimmyZ – who says he has a 'knack for connecting and collaborating' – was one of the key instigators of this partnership. While at 2RDJ, Jimmyz had fallen in love with dance music, thanks to a certain charismatic and unique breakfast presenter on ABC Sydney's youth radio station Triple J FM – Maynard F# Crabbes. 'In amongst disco and Euro pop, he used to play these little Italo mega mixes,' says JimmyZ. 'The Italians had such a knack for making dance music accessible and fun, with lots of flair. I knew there was something going on with this music, and I wanted to find out more.'

After fellow announcer Mark Vick introduced him to Central Station (on Pitt Street at the time), JimmyZ started borrowing records for his two-hour radio slots on Friday afternoons. Shortly afterwards, he urged his 2RDJ colleagues to do likewise. 'Jo understood the power of radio – get the music out there and people would come find it. To get access to that music was like getting a gold key to the National Library. We would always give Central Station Records credits on air.' Jim would borrow the maximum records allowed – twenty-five – often selling on behalf of the music store, sometimes to DJs with similar tastes, like Nick Skitz.

Greater Burwood was a diverse multicultural locale and 2RDJ FM's audience had been predominantly the children of newly migrated Australians from Greece, Italy, Turkey and Lebanon. As he'd programmed, JimmyZ had kept a model listener in mind – a fictitious character called Effie, who was fifteen years old and lived above her parents' grocery store. Her older siblings and cousins would travel to and from Greece and bring back music cassettes from the dance party seasons on the Greek islands and Ibiza. 'I actually got to meet girls just like Effie,' he says. 'They would come in and volunteer to answer phones. I would ask them lots of questions, find out what they liked, what made up their essential profile. I took that sense of audience profiling on to Wild FM. My idea was to deliver music that listeners liked so much that they would never want to switch off.'

Gherghetta's new Sydney station went to air as Hitz FM on 6 November 1996. Three months later, it was rebranded as Wild FM with JimmyZ as music director. The fledgling station needed a lot of cash to buy equipment and studio space – much more than the sponsorship deals Central had previously offered media outlets. But Morgan saw potential. 'In a funny sort of way, I was the risk taker at Central,' he says. 'Jo worked *in* the business, and I worked *on* the business. I made contacts here and there, and he'd say, "OK, do some real work". So I set up the album we did with Sydney Mardi Gras. Then the government had this proposal for aspirant radio stations and I could see that it was an opportunity for us, so I brown-nosed my way around a few of these people. There was a gay radio station, Free FM, where I was the chairman. We had Free FM CDs and parties, with branding all over the place. I'd faff around doing that sort of thing, leaving a trail of

The Dance Media

destruction, and then Jo would make it work.'

Jo's version of the Wild FM story illuminates how he and Morgan operated. 'Basically Morgan came to me and said, "I've got this project I want to do" and I said, "How much money?" He said we'd need to advance this huge sum for studio equipment and so on. So I tossed the thing in my thinking bin.' After a lot of nagging from Morgan, Jo eventually did his thinking, coming to the conclusion that the only way Central Station could afford that level of backing was to collaborate with Go-Go on CD compilations.

In March 1997, an agreement was signed whereby Central Station provided a loan to Go-Go and his company to buy studio and transmission equipment and to construct studio facilities. A second agreement between the two parties provided Central Station with exclusive rights to CD releases. Two compilations appeared shortly afterwards – a single disc called *Central Hitz FM Vol 1* (in time for the station's very first month-long test broadcast) and a two-disc collection called *Wild FM Volume 1* (in time for the freshly retitled second broadcast).

Almost twenty years later, in May 2016, we meet in Sydney to reflect on the upshot of that deal. It's the day after Mark Vick and friends threw a tribute party at Home nightclub for the late DJ, Paul Holden.

Wild FM team members (clockwise from top left: Noah (surname unknown, Sponsorship Rep - USA), Kelli Schelfhout (Sponsorship Rep), Anthony "Go-go" Gherghetta (General Manager) and Michael Kilkeary

Six hundred people had come together on a Thursday night to raise money for the charities Holden had nominated in his will, and everyone present at our meeting is still on a high after the nostalgic event.

'It was an incredibly brave deal,' says JimmyZ about Central Station's involvement with Wild FM. 'Go-Go was a young, new face from Melbourne. But he knew he was onto something – a metro-wide license in Sydney that the government was letting go for free. 2RDJ only had a reach of about three to five kilometres, maybe fifteen on a good broadcasting day weather-wise. Jo had already seen how powerful community radio could be. Popular figures like Sharif Galal and Andy Glitre on Triple J and a young Nik Fish on 2SER had been extremely influential beforehand.'

In all, twelve volumes of Wild compilations were released under the Central Station label before the station closed down in 2001. (In fact, Wild CDs are still selling – helped by Wild Reunion dance events and new releases ever since 2001.)

'The way it worked was Jimmy would borrow records and review them,' explains Jo. 'He would play the ones he liked, and we knew what songs to put on the CD based on the reactions from the radio audience. We selected the titles together. Then Morgan got on the phone to license them. Like *Boom, Boom, Boom, Boom* by the Vengaboys. Basically it was the customers telling us what they wanted. We promoted the CDs with TV commercials, press and radio. Nicole from *3D World* was a great supporter. Shock Records Victoria was distributing for us nationally so we weren't just selling through our stores. We gave a percentage of the branded CD sales to the radio stations. We also did a lot of projects with clubs.'

'The risk paid off. They were selling like hotcakes, going double platinum,' adds JimmyZ.

Other radio station partnerships followed. In June 1997, Sydney's first 24-hour gay and lesbian radio station, Free FM, started broadcasting for a thirty-day trial period. Central Station offered a music voucher redeemable at the Oxford Street store to anyone taking out a $50 membership. Central Station also supported Joy FM in Melbourne, Fresh FM in Adelaide and Wild FM in Brisbane.

The two-disc format of the Wild FM compilations meant choosing forty tunes at a time. Unlike commercial radio stations, which relied on focus groups conducted in boardrooms to refine their programming, JimmyZ would guest DJ at dance parties in the inner west, so that he could meet people and understand what appealed to them. 'We had to license songs that were for the future, working three to six months ahead of the market. That wasn't easy. We had some infamous arguments,' he says.

Jo chimes in: 'You were reading a lot of magazines and you would say, "I want that song". The song hadn't even been released yet, so it wasn't easy. But I'd say, "I'll get you a copy. We'll see what happens."'

The conversation turns to Nick Skitz and how he came to be involved with Central. 'I remember this day,' says Jo. 'Nicholas Agamalis – a Greek boy, quite brassy – came in one afternoon. I'd done a CD with Pee Wee Ferris, which I had to push him really hard to do. It was called *Central Energy*, the first CD with the songs mixed together. Nick came in and said, "You're doing this shit for this guy. Why don't you give me a go?" He was seventeen or eighteen. I said, "Who the fuck are you, anyway?" He told me a few things and I said, "Well, if you're so good, give me something I can listen to". He went home, mixed something for me and I liked it. So I said, "Right. Here's the contract". Nick is a DJ and producer who became very successful with Central Station. He has a strong following and his Nick Skitz CDs sold very well. They still do.'

Not everyone was happy with the new music – Wild FM was blamed for noise pollution. 'When we started in 1996, it was nice, happy European dance music,' says JimmyZ. 'Then we progressed to a sound that was very popular with the Lebanese community. We called it "doik". *Kicking Hard* by Klubbheads, which Jo and Morgan released on Central, was probably the foundation song. Then it was on. The Klubbheads' sound would soon be heard emanating from the bodies of modified Subaru cars (Subies) with "fully sick sub-woofer" sound systems playing the Wild CDs from our actual broadcasts. Audio technicians had evolved amplifiers that would enhance the base frequencies, creating non-existent low-frequency sounds – like two octaves down – and with a whole lot of fancy compression and sound processing tools would pump this through a massive speaker array usually situated in the car boot, effectively using the car shell as a speaker box. The whole car would shake. You could hear house windows rattling as music lovers drove past. It was driving people nuts. It's likely the reason there are now laws prohibiting you from playing loud music from your car.'

But it wasn't the earthquake sound systems that killed Wild FM. The station folded in 2001 after missing out on the permanent community license – largely because of protests from commercial radio operators. 'They lobbied the government, saying they were paying huge license fees whereas Wild FM was paying nothing,' says Jo. Following an auction, a commercial station, Nova FM, took over the 96.9 frequency.

'Fresh FM 92.7 in Adelaide did get a licence,' says JimmyZ. 'It was run by an older consortium of people who were very careful not to rattle the cage, and who didn't want to appear to have any resolve to steal audience from other stations. We were kids and pushing the boundaries. Wild FM rated through the roof, taking about five per cent of the available listening audience. We ran a commercial-sounding station, with professional announcers and sponsorship managers. I managed to help invoke this long dream and it lasted until April 2001. A million dollars was brought in during the month of the final broadcast. I don't think Nova did that for many months. It was the end of an era.'

Meanwhile, back in Melbourne, rival dance-oriented stations Hitz FM and Kiss FM also missed out on permanent community licenses. Whereas Hitz disbanded forever, Kiss later reinvented itself as an independently funded community station in 2005, thanks to Timmy Byrne. The former club DJ became station manager shortly after the aspirant forerunner started in 1994. Modelled on London's Kiss 100 pirate station (which in turn had been modeled on New York's 98.7 Kiss FM African-American focused station), Melbourne's version was (and is) more focused on the style of music rather than the age of the audience, and should not be confused with the mainstream KIIS 101.1. Timmy laughs when probed about the station's place in the radio world. 'We're an oddity, actually. We are an independent radio station, operating on what are called low-power open narrowcast frequencies, which are down

Timmy Byrne with legendary DJ Frankie Knuckles at Sanity, Bourke Street, Melbourne, circa 1998

the left end of the dial. There was a Greek service using the frequency and we were able to negotiate the purchase of it. Later Mix FM tried to start broadcasting as Kiss, which we challenged them on, and in the end we were successful in negotiating a financial settlement for them to use the name KIIS. We have no relationship with them other than that.'

Asked how the station survives financially, he says: 'It's been an extremely wonderful roller-coaster ride. From the highs of standing in front of 20,000 people at the Sidney Myer Music Bowl for our event, Kiss My Grass, an all-Australian electronic dance music festival, to our fight with the name which was extremely stressful but in the end worked out for us financially.' Kiss FM also relies on memberships, advertising and sponsorship to stay afloat. A pioneer of online availability, the station has subscribers around the world and a massive Facebook following. Timmy is optimistic about the future of the model. 'Our listeners tend to be more intelligent. They're early adopters of technology and ideas, and they're looking for something to make the spark go off in their brains. That's why we try to do in the musical sense, and also what we talk about. It's all about curation. It's one thing for Spotify to throw up X million tracks, supposedly worked out from an algorithm of what you do and don't like. But people trust people who have music as a passion and have made a career out of it, who are leaders in their various areas.'

In Adelaide, Central Station was a long-time supporter of Fresh FM. 'We were sponsoring them every month to keep them on air and they are now a 24-hour music station,' says Tony Caraccia, the long-serving store manager. 'They've gone from a temporary licence and temporary times to twenty-four-seven. I'm proud of that.'

Television

Talk to any of the creatives featured in this chapter and you're certainly conscious of sparks going off in brains. They all have big ideas and even bigger ideals. An articulate and widely read law graduate, Mike Kerry argues passionately that the acid house movement changed the world as well as his own life path. Now running his own film creative and production company in Sydney (Danger Mouse Productions), he got his start in the film business by making videos for Central Station. 'Morgan bought some air-time on channel 31, a community TV channel in Sydney,' he says. 'He needed someone naïve enough to run around and make a TV show for him for free. It was a music video show, called *Tekno Station*, playing the Central tracks that *Video Hits* wouldn't play. We'd take

CDs, get some graphics and make our own videos. That was how I got into the film business. That was the fork in the road.'

Before this, Mike had been a top commercial DJ playing in suburban and regional clubs. 'It wasn't easy to get people on the dance floor at the start of the night in those venues. DJs worked harder. The crowd were just drinking alcohol and they were fickle,' he says. 'I had a girlfriend who was a raver. She took me to my first rave, which opened my eyes to the scene. What drives the acid culture around the world is the opportunity economy – people become DJs, promoters and entrepreneurs within the scene, bringing fresh ideas. I got involved with Central, we did *Tekno Station*, and through that I ended up at Channel [V] which at the time was looking for a dance music presenter.'

Mike is passionate about the impact of acid house in promoting cross-cultural acceptance. 'What the UK did better than anyone else in the second half of the twentieth century was export pop culture,' he says. 'Oakenfold, Rampling, Holloway, they go to Ibiza, take ecstasy at Amnesia, and bring that vibe back to the UK, where post-Thatcher Britain is primed for it. Dance music creeps up the charts around the world. The scene grows steadily through small radio stations in each capital city, a lot of cult shows. Then in Sydney, you have Wild FM which is the breakthrough. Now everyone is playing mix CDs and buying decks. The gay parties and Mardi Gras that were underground for years become something that straights want to go to because they have the best production and the best dance music. I've seen my friends become close friends with gays, transgender, anyone, and that's often because of dance parties and ecstasy. In a rave environment, the straight boys aren't threatened. Everyone is just loving the night and each other. Then in predominantly straight club nights, straight boys are imitating the gay boys' dance moves. Acid house was a massive leveler like that.'

In the mid 00s, Central Station teamed up with Channel 7 and an energy drink supplier to present two seasons of *Wild TV*, a dance music video program fronted by Mike and former model Chloe Maxwell at nightclubs around Australia. 'We covered DJs and did vox pops to give it a bit of colour,' says Mike. 'It was a decent enough show but we struggled to get some video clip clearance because of a ring-tone deal, which was big at the time. Without all the charting hits we were up against it and it didn't fly unfortunately.'

15. The Political Finish Line (1992-98)

'Central Station played a very interesting role in the copyright issues, but also the general positioning of music in Australia. I joined Sony Music is 1993. They were quite schizophrenic in their attitude toward imports. On the one hand, they didn't want to miss out, so they employed someone like me to tap into that market. But also they wanted to stop Central Station and other importers from controlling what they saw as their market. Central did put a lot of pressure on the major companies in terms of their distribution patterns and how they sold things. Sony might have a new release from Michael Jackson, for example ... It was a weekly battle. They would go out of their way to have the stock at the right price at the right time so that Central Station wouldn't beat them. But sometimes they'd want Central Station to bring product and do the promotion job for them. It was an interesting relationship. They would battle them on one occasion and be hand-in-hand with them on another.'
John Ferris

As disappointing as the Keating Government's 1992 decision to postpone changing the copyright law was, worse was yet to come. In effect, the government failed to deliver any change at all. Federal Cabinet was divided on the issue. In December 1993, it deferred a decision until February 1994, concerned about a consumer backlash in the lead-up to Christmas if it shelved plans to tackle CD prices. But February 1994

A 1994 'Financial Review' article about Central Station's battle with EMI and Virgin (Image reproduced with the permission of Fairfax Media Syndication)

came and went with no political action and no media pressure.

Many proponents of change lost heart, did deals or moved on to other things. Jo kept writing letters to the PM, Ministers and Senators (along with the media), but supporters were few and far between. Alan Oxley was one of those. Morgan remembers the former trade ambassador to Geneva for the GATT (General Agreement on Tariffs and Trade) coming to the Central Station store in Oxford Street. 'He was a big player and a wonderful guy. And we had his ear! It was a battle of principles for him.' In November 1994, *The Australian* published an article by Alan Oxley entitled *Turn a deaf ear to CD monopoly*, in which he castigated the Government for poor political judgment. The article was clearly informed by his visit to Central Station, emphasising that a generational change was underway in the popular music market.

On the day this story appeared, Oxley was interviewed on breakfast TV (*Good Morning Australia*). He also visited Canberra and met a host of politicians and advisers. A few days later, he faxed Jo and Morgan his analysis of the political situation: 'The issue is jammed over wide differences among officials, advisers and Ministers. It is not clear when it is supposed to go back to Cabinet. Duncan Kerr, Minister for Justice,

The Political Finish Line (1992-1998)

Michael Lee, Minister for Arts, and Peter Cook, Minister for Industry are supposed to bring a joint submission to Cabinet when they can work out an agreed approach.'

After thirteen years in power, the ALP lost the March 1996 election to the Coalition. John Howard became PM, and Peter Costello became Treasurer. Paul Keating resigned as Labor leader on election night.

'We slept on the floor until John Howard won,' Jo recalls. 'Then my business went up twenty-five per cent. I was serving behind the counter at the Oxford Street store in Sydney, and I saw all of these people coming down the stairs, people I hadn't seen for months coming out of the woodwork, and it felt like the black plague had finished – Paul Keating had gone. I remember that day very clearly.'

Given Coalition policy, you might imagine that amending the copyright law would have been a foregone conclusion. If so, you would be wrong. In October 1997, the Howard Cabinet met in Launceston and agreed to introduce legislation to open the recorded music industry to greater import competition. The spokesperson for ARIA, Emmanuel Candi, promptly vowed to fight change by convincing the minority parties in the Senate to block the legislation. After the House of Representatives passed the Copyright Amendment bill in November 1997, the Senate decided to defer voting on it, while it held seven public hearings between March and April 1998.

By May 1998, even the tabloids were taking note. In a story entitled *Rock on the rack* in Melbourne's *Sun-Herald*, Peter Holmes bemoaned falling CD sales as consumers turned to the internet for cheaper prices and more choice. In the end, the decision came down to four Senators – Bob Brown and Dee Margetts from the Greens, and Mal Colston and Brian Harradine, who were independents. In a late-night sitting, in the wee hours of 12 July 1998, the Senate finally passed the Copyright Amendment Act 1998. The Government took advantage of Colston's absence to ram it through with Harradine's support.

Jo was sleeping downstairs at the McMahons Point house when Morgan woke him up at five o'clock that morning to tell him the news. 'I remember it very well,' says Jo. 'It was a foggy day and I could hear the music from *The Mission*, Ennio Morricone, coming across the Harbour. I was absolutely exhausted. I'd already decided to give up fighting. Morgan said, "I've got some news for you". He was always trying to boost my morale. Phil Tripp has done this or the government has done that. When he told me that the government had put through the legislation the way

ARIA's campaign slogan

we wanted it, I said, "It's too fucking late. We don't need the changes any more". By then most of our income was from merchandise and clothing. It was a non-event for me. We had our own office in America and our own web site where you could download mp3 files.'

Although Jo felt underwhelmed by the win he had fought so long and hard for, his opponents hoped to sink the new legislation at the next election. On 14 July, *The Sydney Morning Herald* carried two scare stories: *Record company to drop local acts*, and *Young bands will be "crowded out by new CD law"*. On 17 July, Sydney's *Telegraph* reported that Shock Records had dropped a record label and four bands in the wake of the new law. But Michael Gudinski delivered the highest-profile statement. When announcing the sale of his fifty per cent stake in Mushroom Records to News Limited in September 1998, Gudinski took the opportunity to blame the new legislation for his decision. In a story headed *Murdoch music mushrooms as Gudinski sells out in disgust*, Pelita Clark reported that he had deliberately timed the announcement to coincide with the Federal election campaign so as to stoke anti-Howard sentiment.

A few days before the 1998 election, Jo sent a letter to Peter Costello wishing him the best. 'Despite all the noise created by ARIA, many in the music industry, especially retail and consumers, applaud your determination to govern Australia effectively,' he wrote. 'Please find enclosed copies of our single release *Here's Johnny* which should be the Coalition anthem when you retain Government on 3 October'.

In retrospect, Jo feels embarrassed about the song title, unaware at the time of the animosity between Peter Costello and John Howard. In any event, the Howard Government was returned, and we can be fairly

The Political Finish Line (1992-1998)

confident that Jo's suggested anthem wasn't played at the celebrations.

Looking back on his time as a political activist, Jo tells a story about meeting a lawyer who had once represented a multinational recording company and was then servicing independent players. 'We were both at this function. He got totally pissed and we were laughing. I raised the story about how the multinationals were trying to crush me. He told me that five or six of those lawyers had met one night and agreed that, "No money should be spared trying to get that man". That was me.'

Asked about the impact of being such a legal target, Morgan says, 'It was a mixture of fear at the legal bills mounting and the potential to lose the business any day. You realise that legal battles are a bit of a game of fox and the rabbit, and we were the rabbit in the headlights. You never knew what was going to happen next. It was very emotional.'

Acknlowledgements

Central Station Records wishes to thank the following, among others, for their support during the difficult battle to free up the Australian music market:

Richard Alston	Peter Costello
Gareth Evans	Professor Allan Fels
Ross Gittins	Gary Johns
Jeff Kennett	John Kerin
Paddy McGuiness	Alan Oxley

A Flipside advertisement from the late 90s

16. Devolution (2000-2007)

Back in the mid 1990s, Jo began 'franchising' the stores in Melbourne, Adelaide and Brisbane to employees he trusted. 'When I decided that I didn't want to do this any more – it was too hard, the business was too big for me to control, and I'd had enough of doing the same thing every day – the idea was to involve our best employees and give them ownership into the business,' he says. 'The stock might have been worth $400,000. I would say, "Fine, have it for $150,000. Get the pain off my back". So they took the leases, and they ran the stores.'

Sometimes things worked out; but often they didn't. Tony Caraccia remained at the helm of the Adelaide store until 2005, but the Melbourne and Brisbane stores went through several changes. Jonce Dimovski, for example, had jumped at the chance to take over as franchisee in Melbourne in the mid-90s. He had introduced new clothing and computers into the product offering, and lived his music industry dream for a while, until the business had slowly disintegrated. He blames differences with his business partner and his own divorce for the downhill slide.

By the late 90s, the stress of running his legal and political battles had taken a huge toll on Jo's health. 'I was overweight and starting to develop high sugar levels. My blood pressure was through the roof,' he says. 'I went to a herbalist who introduced me to the concept of blood types and nutrition. After reading *Live Right for Your Blood Type*, I realised how much genes determine behaviour, not just physical aspects.'

In what was a major turning point for Jo, he threw himself into the subject and developed an enduring passion for managing physical and mental health through nutrition. And not just his own – he began to apply his ideas in managing the Central Station team. 'The efficiency of employees was decreasing,' he says. 'The output was non-creative and messy. There was a lot of absenteeism, especially after long weekends. I couldn't tolerate it. I was the boss and I used to work seven days a week, but other people were taking a day off every two weeks. So I decided to import testing kits and insisted that everyone use them to find their blood type. After that, I gave each employee tasks according to their blood type. For the O group, I gave them more adventurous things – out of the office, meeting people, political things, propaganda, marketing, all skills that don't require sitting at a desk and concentrating on a subject. The A group loves to sit down and do meticulous data entry. The B Group is extremely creative but also very temperamental, so don't put them in a group or they will clash. So I knew how to maximise everyone's energies and talents. Efficiency went up within a short time. Instead of disturbing people on a daily basis, I kept pigeonholes for each employee and filed paperwork there for weekly meetings with them about training.'

Then, little by little, Jo and Morgan began pulling back from the day-to-day running of the stores and labels. They could see the writing on the wall – downloads were coming – and decided to cultivate a new generation of managers with the energy and foresight to tackle future challenges. 'Business is like chess,' says Jo. You've got to work your moves ahead of time. We were getting number one hits, but I could also see that we were getting slack, living off the work that had been done before. You've got to keep digging, keep hungry. At the shop level, the

Central Station Records 'class of 2000' (courtesy of Stevie Bourk)

label too became tired of winning. "Hey guys, let's relax." I could see that coming. You have to plan the hits so that you make the same or a bit more than your basic costs. You can also change your cost structure but that's very hard, very slow. The only way to survive is to increase your income. So look ahead.'

To Jo's horror, however, a new battlefront opened up, and it was all the more disturbing because of its closeness to home. He'd always supported rival independent labels Pro DJ International and Colossal Records when choosing tracks for the Wild CD compilations, and he'd long dreamed of building a great Australian indie label by joining forces with them one day. But suddenly Pro DJ and Colossal began licensing tracks that Central Station had been selling, and they chose to send Jo the same sort of threatening letters that the multinationals had used. This perceived betrayal was a heavy blow. Then, in 2000, Tim McGee, Central's A&R manager, resigned to establish Ministry of Sound Australia.

Feeling surrounded by negativity, Jo took a walk on the beach at St Kilda to try his usual trick – summoning up the 'energy'. Morgan was in Sydney, so he was alone as he sat on some rocks and looked at the waves, feeling angry with himself and with Australia. 'Why is this happening?' he demanded of the universe. The answer suddenly dawned on him. 'Hang on, wait a sec. I didn't create this problem,' he muttered, pointing his finger at the sky. '*You* created this. *You* fix it! I'm just acting on your behalf.' As had happened before in his life, the minute Jo decided he didn't want to win any more was the very minute he started to do so. The 'energy' turned in his favour. The legal challenges melted away, with both Pro-DJ and Colossal distracted by other problems. At this point, Jo started putting together a plan to take Central Station into the future.

Strengthening the team

The first step was to promote Jamie Raeburn into the role vacated by Tim McGee. Had Central bothered with such titles, he would have been known as A&R director. Similarly, had Central been a hierarchy-bound organisation, Ashley Gay would have reported to Jamie when Morgan poached him from Pro-DJ to do A&R. Instead, the Melbourne-based Ashley reported directly to Jo and Morgan, and Jamie and Ashley somehow agreed on who did what.

Ashley's first task was to set up a new retail and office space in Melbourne. After the first franchise had gone under, Melbourne had been without any Central Station presence at all. Then Jo and Morgan bought an old amusement parlour in the basement of a building on Swanston Street and charged Ashley with fitting it out as the new store, with an office at the back for his own use. On top of his A&R role, Ashley ended up looking after the computer networks for the offices and stores because of his interest in technology. This interest also inspired him to ensure that Central was an early adopter of digital distribution. 'Jo let me join us up as one of the first Apple iTunes suppliers in Australia, and from there we did direct digital deals with all of the main platforms as they started up,' he says. 'We were placed very well with digital distribution of our content worldwide.'

Between them, Jamie and Ashley made the most of their new signings at trade fairs like MIDEM and Pop Komm. 'It was a bit of a hustle,' says Jamie. 'We'd just run around the place, looking for new labels, new content, listen to them and try to sign them on the spot. A lot of it was done in bars, on napkins, at three in the morning. Handshake deals. We picked up a lot of shit as well. That's one of the problems with those impulse events.'

Almost twenty years after coming to these shores with his Australian-born girlfriend, Jamie retains a thick Scottish accent. He also retains a trace of culture shock, after his induction into Central Station's 'free-form' style. 'The first day I met Jo, I rocked up for a meeting at their house, and he answered the door butt naked. There's an intro for you,' he laughs. In his experience, there is no exact equivalent of Central Station outside Australia. Most tastemaker stores in the UK started labels, he says, but very focused ones. No one covered the field like Central Station. He worked on some of the label's biggest acts, from the Vengaboys to 'all the trance stuff'.

Another key figure in the new national team in this era was Angie Young. After finishing high school, Angie had started work at a law firm, but volunteering at Hitz FM in Melbourne had sparked a passion to work in the music industry. Someone had suggested talking to Jo and Morgan about possible opportunities. 'I met with the guys, just to have a chat,' she recalls. 'They said, "Well, we don't really have anything going, but we can see that you're very passionate about music and we'd like to work with you somehow. Would you move?" and I said "Yeah, of course". A month elapsed. Then I moved to Sydney in March 2000, right before the Olympics. Initially, it was all up in the air. I was helping Jamie go through demos. They'd get piles and piles of CDs from overseas and local artists and I'd go through them, make comments and flag the ones that were of interest. And I'd give feedback to the artists in the No pile too, because I'd want that if I was in their shoes. You'd have to be very diplomatic, of course.'

Around 2003, Angie Young was elevated to the job of national promotions manager. 'My role was to take music to radio, TV and print. There was no online press at that point. I was the middle person between the artist and the media.' She remembers doing a lot of promos for the Wild CD compilations, targeted at dance radio stations, print press and street press. 'They were really successful, especially Volume 9 which was many people's favourite. Mine too,' she says.

But Angie's favourite memory of her time at Central was doing the tour promo for Darude and DJ Sammy who both had massive hits at the time. 'I'm still in touch with them today and they both have a fondness for Australia as it really was a huge part of their success,' she says. 'Darude's *Sandstorm* had a resurgence recently as Peking Duk dropped it at Stereosonic in 2014 and the crowd went nuts. As a result of that,

The Central Station Records team welcoming Jay-J (a house music DJ from San Francisco) and vocalist Latrice to Australia in 2007. Back row from left: Matt Nugent, Tom Mason, Alison Eaton, Mike Witcombe, Kamila Borkowska, Jo Phelps, Angie Young. Front row from left: Matt Handley, Jay-J, Latrice. Front: Jamie Raeburn (courtesy of Angie Young)

Darude toured Australia a few months later and came back again in 2016. Sammy played at this awesome Austereo-run event called Rumba, which had massive artists from all over the world. It was at the peak of *Heaven* and *Boys of Summer* and he was one of the most energetic acts on the day. People loved him.'

Unlikely bedfellows

Just as friends could turn into enemies, so could enemies become friends. 'In later years, even major labels approached us to put stuff out,' says Morgan. 'For example, there was an artist called Armand van Helden. We recognized that he had great potential for our market, but the local branch of his label, EMI, showed no inclination to release his work here. So we went to London and met with the parent company, and they said they'd prefer to have us release it anyway – because EMI had so much product, that it would get lost there, whereas we would love it and care for it. EMI also owned a German label called Interchord that chose to deal with us rather than EMI in Australia to make sure they were promoted properly.'

So how did Jo feel about working with the multinationals he had fought for so long? 'I didn't trust when some of them wanted to do business with us,' he says. 'But we were ahead of them and we had the hits so they had to work with us. We became a niche market for them. So we had to modify our behaviour as well. We were not the radicals, the antagonists, the activists any more. Morgan's focus was a combination of direct sales and third-party licensing. So we started doing business with a whole range of players.'

The negotiations

Although the record labels and Flipside were going well, Morgan and Jo were worried about the retail side. They still directly employed fifteen people in the stores. 'The shops weren't doing so well and we could see the trends towards digital sales,' says Morgan. 'That's why we moved more into accessories and clothing. A lawyer I knew came up with a proposal for selling the record label and we decided to consider it. There were some pretty heated conversations. It was horrible. Tears. It was a big deal for Jo, but I could see he was getting sick. He was wearing himself out. I just had to fight through that pain barrier.'

That lawyer mate of Morgan's was called Robert Scard. When Jo first heard his proposal to sell, he wanted none of it. Central Station was his life and he had no idea what he would do with himself without it. In the end, though, what pushed him into considering the idea was hearing some disturbing news about the financial state of Shock Records, Central's distribution partner. 'The market was deteriorating for everyone,' remembers Jo. 'Everybody was trying to survive ... consolidate, cut costs and happy ever after. The retail situation was difficult, especially trying to compete with big groups like Sanity that commanded big discounts from suppliers. But distributor problems meant checkmate – we had to sell the business. No distribution, no sales. Robert said Sony could be interested, because they were trying to buy content. Fuck, I had to move my queen!'

Jo, Morgan and Robert met Sony management at the Sydney HQ. 'Denis, the chairman, was there and Emmanuel Candi, business manager,' recalls Jo. 'It was an afternoon and we had a beer. Denis put his arm around my shoulder as he showed me his Rolling Stones jackets, his guitars, his awards – all those music things he liked hanging on the walls. I kind of fell for him, because I always admired his skills and his ability to do things others couldn't.'

In non-hostile talks like this, it's customary for potential buyers to undertake a process called 'due diligence' – when auditors sift through numbers and documents in order to finalise the offer price. 'There were lots of complications,' says Jo. 'They took all the information they wanted and then came back to me with an unrealistically low number.'

Around this time, a Central Station artist was nominated for a 2003 ARIA Award, so Morgan booked a table at the awards presentation night. It was not to be a happy occasion. In the lead-up to the event, Jo discovered that Sony had applied for the 'Central Station' trademark in New Zealand and Europe as part of its global PlayStation ambitions. Rightly or wrongly, he began suspecting that Sony had only proceeded with acquisition discussions to extract information and was now exploiting vulnerability discovered through that process. Making matters worse, he also learned that Sony was trying to lure away one of his top artists. By the time the ARIA Awards night came around in October, Jo's fury had reached fever pitch. As luck would have it, Sony's two tables (full of top brass and their guests) were located only about twenty metres away from Central's table in the huge Olympic Stadium at Homebush.

'I was very nervous and uptight because I knew what was happening behind the scenes,' remembers Jo. 'I tried not to drink too much. I didn't go around and meet people.'

But one particular artist at the Central Station table kept winding Jo up, boasting about Sony chasing him. Suddenly, all of Jo's childhood rage bubbled up and he went off like a volcano.

'I'm ashamed to say that my behavior that night was unsavoury,' he confesses. 'I wanted to let Sony's management know that I felt betrayed and that I would do everything I could to foil their trademark application. But I didn't handle the conversation well. I felt impelled to make them understand my anger. Tables were shaken, some glasses fell on the floor and I used a lot of foul language until security guards grabbed me and threw me out. The next morning, I woke up thinking, "Fuck! What have I done?"'

Jo couldn't explain his behavior to Central Station staff, because it would reveal his sale intentions, so they were left feeling confused and concerned. 'We're doing business with Sony. What's up?' All day long, the phone ran hot. An anonymous thug made threats. Industry folk wanted the low-down.

Although Jo shot off a letter of apology to Denis Handlin, and sent a bunch of flowers with a hand-written card to his wife begging forgiveness for his uncharacteristic behaviour, newspaper gossip columns kept the embarrassment going and ARIA banned Jo for life from attending its awards ceremonies.

Fortunately, Robert Scard had located another potential suitor, the Home Leisure group, which owned MRA, a Brisbane-based company with a huge holding of old recordings. A lunch meeting with a broker in a golf club on the Gold Coast kicked off discussions.

Jo remembers it vividly: 'Morgan and I went into this swanky golf club. James Packer and all these big shots played there. We were shown to our table – beautiful white tablecloth, four different glasses for water and wine, and this dealmaker sitting there. I've been working all my life like a dog. I've resisted having all that luxury. I don't like watches. I don't like gold. I don't wear anything expensive. I only buy things that I can use to improve myself. So this man could see that I was kind of peasant-looking.'

Feeling like the underdog, Jo sized up the man he'd come to meet. He saw someone astute and intelligent but 'sick in the body', and told him straight out what he thought his blood type was and what ailments were troubling him. The dealmaker was so surprised by the accuracy of the analysis that he dropped his knife and fork. Then he returned the favour, telling Jo that he'd studied Central Station's legal structure and found problems. Central's lawyers had failed to file the right paperwork back in 1983 when capital gains tax was introduced, so there were nasty tax implications for prospective buyers. The two men decided to help each other.

The sunset of the stores

Because the buyer was only interested in the Central Station and Wild trademarks, all of the stores had to be franchised ahead of the sale. Ironically, while he had been the one to instigate the whole process, bringing Jo along kicking and screaming, Morgan was the one who blinked at this point. 'I thought these iconic shops were still viable,' he says.

Eventually, though, the job was done.

Stevie Bourk took over in Sydney, moving the store upstairs to a smaller location, near the entrance to Q Bar nightclub. Some years before he'd had a casual conversation with Morgan about buying the store if that possibility arose: 'Then lo and behold, a couple of years later, they called me to their house at McMahons Point. They remembered what I'd said and wanted to know if I was still keen. I was blown away.'

Andrew Parkes assumed Stevie's old role in the vinyl department, having retained 'an absolute passion for vinyl' while being still fully aware that the downturn was underway. With his good memory for artists and tracks, he says that he was 'quite handy with ordering', but it had been Jo's example that had really showed him how to sell records. 'I think we all learned a thing or two off Jo,' he says. 'It was always like, "I see you've bought that track. You should buy the other track by him. Very, very good. Ah, everyone's been buying this track. All the big DJs have been playing this." That was Jo for sure.'

In Brisbane, Murray Brown had been 'a bedroom DJ trying to get gigs around Brisbane' when Matt Nugent had given him a job at the big Elizabeth Street store in 2003. Having already managed one of his parents' record stores in Ipswich, he became the obvious choice for franchisee when Jo and Morgan began preparing Central Station for sale. Deal done, Murray also chose to move to a smaller space – about ten shops down Elizabeth Street – while simultaneously boosting the wall space for vinyl. 'It was pretty much wall-to-wall records,' is how he describes it.

Most people overseas were starting to buy their music in a digital format by this stage, but Brisbane DJs still had a passion for vinyl and kept shopping at local record stores.

Music Wars

Three friends – Jim Kontogiannis, Andee Frost and Janette Pitruzzello (aka JNett) – decided to take on the Melbourne franchise.

'I went up to Sydney and hung out with Jo and Morgan and they showed me the ropes up there,' says Jim. Asked what he picked up from those sessions, he says, 'They've always been so much fun, so I learned to have fun the whole time'.

Unfortunately for Jim, he didn't pick up any of Jo's shrewdness. 'It was something we did as a passion. Sales were the last thing on my mind ... which was pretty stupid in hindsight,' he says. 'It was a transitional phase when DJs were shifting from vinyl to digital. I've seen graphs of vinyl sales, and they go up in the 70s and 80s and then decline right through the 90s and 2000s, so I think the worst period before this current renaissance was the exact time when we owned that store.'

Meanwhile, the metal shop did more than its fair share of moving around too. The last and biggest location was in the Banana Alley vaults opposite the dance music store at 340 Flinders Street. Eventually, Jo sold the shop to Greta's first-ever hire. Greta herself had left Central by

The Brisbane team in a photoshoot for the cover of 'Scene' magazine in 2007

At very back: Steve Kecskes (aka Seventy-7) of the hardcore department

From left middle row: Sean Hughes (Seany B) of the hip hop department and previous manager Harry Katsanevas (Hakka)

From left at front: Antony Partridge (Baby Gee) of the trance department and Murray Brown (Murray Brown) of the house department and store-owner

(Photo by Mark Duffus, courtesy of Murray Brown)

The heavy metal shop in the vaults in Banana Alley (courtesy of Greta Tate)

this stage, but came back to work for the new owner under a new brand, Metal Labyrinth.

Ray Herd became franchisee in Perth. 'The shop in Perth was a replica of the Adelaide store, with a lot of twelve-inch singles, merchandise, equipment, T shirts, everything that people wanted to buy,' remembers Jo. 'It was a very successful store. Ray Herd did well with promotions with clubs and DJs. I do miss him. We don't know where he is. Last time I spoke with him was about three or four years ago. We've tried to locate him but so far have been unsuccessful.'

The sale

After exiting the retail business, Central Station made a huge loss, but it was now in shape for sale. 'So it came down to price,' Jo recalls. 'I had my number in mind, and he had his number. I was a little bit higher and he said, "This is what we can afford to give you." I said to Morgan, "Let's take it" so we formulated contracts.'

As a formal transaction, the sale took place on 11 November 2003 – the anniversary of Ned Kelly's execution in 1880, Armistice Day in 1945, and the Whitlam Government's dismissal in 1975. Spookily, it was also the anniversary of Jo's departure from Italy in 1967, and the opening of JIST Records in 1975. You decide which anniversary is most fitting.

When Jo signed the contract at a fancy office in Australia Square, Sydney, the former outlaw announced, 'I am getting out of the music industry forever'. He and Morgan were required to stay for two years to oversee the merger's success, but Jo was happy to leave earlier. 'I didn't think they needed me any more – this old man in between. Jamie Raeburn took over. I wanted them to be able to do what they wanted to do without interference. I left Jamie with a bunch of wonderful people.'

The new business employed twenty-seven people, with twelve in the head office, and it assumed responsibilities for all legal stoushes, including successfully contesting Sony's trademark application in New Zealand. Ironically, Sony later became the distributor for the new entity.

The outlaw and the hombre retired to a cattle station in the Sunshine Coast hinterland in Queensland. They were now comfortably well off, thanks to a lean-and-hungry approach to business. Over the years, they'd taken very little profit out of Central Station, investing everything they could into development. Sadly, as Jo later realised, Home Leisure was not interested in continuing to develop the labels that he and Morgan had created. 'They wanted the cash and franking credits we'd built up,' he says.

Reality bit for the Central Station storeowners too. As the vinyl market continued to decline, they adapted as best they could. Shortly after becoming franchisee in the mid-90s, Tony Caraccia moved to Rundle Mall. The last location was on Diagonal Road, Oaklands Park. He kept the business going until 2005, and is proud of the fact that he outlasted Sanity in town. In partnership with Tony, two brothers, Paul and Mim Mitolo (owners of the St Paul's venue) opened a Central Station store in a shopping centre in Marion, south-west of the Adelaide CBD, which eventually closed around 2007.

Stevie Bourk ran the Sydney store for about four years, before selling to DJ Bella. The ultimate closure happened around 2007.

Murray Brown remembers the precise moment that he witnessed the start of the trend against vinyl in Brisbane. It was December 2008. 'Erick Morillo came to play at Family and all the local residents DJs were there,' Murray explains. 'Everyone at that time was talking about people DJing with CDJs overseas, and he came to town and absolutely tore the place upside down. All the DJs were like, "Wow, I can't believe he can play like this on CDs", and everyone triggered, "I've got to be able to do what he did". So then they all put more effort into learning how to play on CDs. From that gig forward, things started to shift toward CDs.'

Eventually, and very sadly, Murray closed the doors of Central Station in Brisbane in 2009, but decided to keep the local DJ competition, Central Battle, going to discover new DJs. Winning the

Left: The entrance to the last Brisbane store

Below: The interior of this store in 2007 (courtesy of Murray Brown)

comp himself in 2001 had really helped him get ahead as a DJ and he felt this was his way of giving back to a community that had supported the store so much. 'I put a lot of effort into helping up-and-coming DJs get noticed by local venues. I'd invite all the promoters and booking agents down to the heats and grand final, so they could see all this new talent. Of the top ten finalists, generally eight or more of them would get gigs and their first taste of playing in a venue. The competition helped to launch careers for guys like Tydi and Nick Galea, who are both still prominent members in the music community.'

Eventually, however, Murray was forced to stop the Central Battle as sponsors became harder to find without the presence of the store.

He says Jo is 'amazing at cultivating people's inner spirit': 'He always put effort into helping people who had a passion for what they were doing.'

'Central Station was like the hub that kept the community together, not just Central but that whole record store culture,' he adds with real fervour in his voice. 'Everyone would come in on a Thursday, because that's when shipments were in. And they'd all see each other in the shop. Back then, if you wanted a track, you'd have to wait to get it. Now you can hear it on the radio, Shazam it on your phone and download it within a minute. To this day, it still amazes me that this is possible.'

Over in Perth, Ray Herd had taken up the franchise. Rudy James was his full-time manager until 2003, when he started an architectural practice from home and dropped back to part-time. By 2007, the shop was slowing down and Rudy left to concentrate on his practice. 'It ended up closing in 2010,' he says. 'Ray scaled back everything, and did some renovations. The store lost the street vibe, and became more focused on the CD market. The download market took a fair bit of the vinyl trade, but we never made money on vinyl anyway. It was more of a service. Music became very disposable after the mp3 market came in. Mail ordering became a big thing too – people used to source their own music.'

One shop at a time, record store culture disappeared ... for the time being, anyway.

A business meeting at Central Station. Morgan Williams is at far left, and Ray Herd is in the foreground, twisting to face the camera.

17. The Phoenix Rises

During the 90s, Professor Fels recommended Jo as a speaker at a Monash University student seminar. Jo worked hard preparing himself for a presentation about his business and vision, but when he tried to print his notes on the day, the printer kept jamming. Jo calmed himself down by meditating. Luckily, when the computer restarted, he was able to print three pages, but he was running very late.

After being introduced, Jo went to the front of the classroom with his notes and some show-and-tell items – cassette, vinyl and T-shirt. At the last minute, though, he decided to ditch his notes and speak from the heart. Afterwards, students asked him where he wanted to take the business in the future. 'My ambition is to float on the stockmarket by the year 2000,' he said. Then he summed up his philosophy: 'If you're starting a business, there's no point trying to divide yourself from it. You are the business. If you want to have extra shareholders, you can do that at any time. Choose a name and register it. Select and register a trademark too. And then you may be able to sell something once the business is viable. But don't put all your eggs in one basket/company.'

Jo has good reason to be grateful for separating his egg baskets. When he was most vulnerable to financial ruin from court action, QC Leslie Glick advised him to restructure his business interests as a defence. When he sold Central Station to the Home Leisure group, the dealmaker helped him clean up the structure of entities. And when Destra Corporation (which subsequently bought Central), went under, he and Morgan were able to save a crucial basket of eggs – the one holding all of the Central Station trademarks. To understand that rescue, we need to backtrack a bit.

After the sale, Jamie Raeburn ran Central Station Records as a business unit within the Home Leisure group, working closely with fellow unit MRA which handled distribution. 'They moved to a place in Crows Nest,' says Jo. 'They did amazing things, more than I could believe. But I was retired, and focusing on cleaning up my affairs.'

'We got big offices and hired a number of staff,' Jamie recalls. 'We were doing really well, selling a lot of physical units, with quite a lot of hit singles going on. At that point, we had to start digitalising all our assets because iTunes was coming online. We spent years converting all of our CDs to mp3s and of course a few years later everyone wanted WAVs. We also had to change all of our physical contracts to digital agreements. At the same time, we were dealing with a group of bosses that had not a clue about the music industry and were literally only interested in the bottom line. While that gave me a great insight into running a proper corporation – much of which I still gratefully use today – it was painful trying to explain to a board of directors why some hit record you signed didn't actually become a hit on the day the budget said it would.'

Ashley Gay moved from A&R to focus on establishing the digital platform, and Matt Nugent took responsibility for label management, working out of MRA's office in Brisbane. 'I was there twelve months, basically being the middle man between the Central Station label and the MRA distribution people, so that everyone understood what was going on, that we had enough stock coming through enough display material,' he says. Later he moved to Sydney and became marketing manager.

Meanwhile, Jo and Morgan developed their clothing business with Shawn Yates. Shawn had been only seventeen years old when he'd started working for them. One day, he'd said he wanted to take the operation to the next level, focusing on the Carhartt label. 'Shawn had proven to be a careful and studious businessman, so we set up a separate business with him,' recalls Jo. 'It was time for him to take a share of the business. So we formed a company, Flipside Distribution, with Shawn as MD owning fifty per cent. Flipside now has three stores in Sydney (two Carhartt and one Supply) and one (Carhartt) in Melbourne, wholesaling nationally, and even some exporting. The business employs close to forty people in Melbourne and Sydney, and Morgan and I are very proud of their cutting-edge work.'

Over the years, Jo and Morgan had put every spare cent into savings. Jo explains his approach: 'If you have extra cash in the business, don't take it out and buy yourself a Mercedes Benz. Keep it in the business.

The Phoenix Rises

Because those businesses can't survive forever. Music is going through a very difficult period and the only ones that will survive are those capable of adapting to the future. The others will become obsolete.'

What happened next in the Central Station story highlights the wisdom of their approach. A public company, Destra Corporation, borrowed heavily to buy several music and publishing businesses, including Central Station, which then began reporting to a new set of corporate bosses. Several years later, in the midst of the global financial crisis, Destra went into forced administration. Jo and Morgan lost almost half of the agreed price for Central, because the share component of the package became worthless. More importantly, many Destra employees lost all of their entitlements as well as their jobs. The Central Station team fared better than most because the unit had been trading well and had cash at hand.

There were other heartaches, though. 'When Destra fell flat on its face, thirty years of business went down the spout,' says Jamie Raeburn. 'The vultures moved in, taking all of the label deals we'd developed over the years.'

'The administrator offered us the opportunity to buy Central Station assets,' says Jo. 'So we formed a company with Jamie Raeburn, Tim

Jamie Raeburn and a few mates celebrating the rebirth of Central Station Records

McGee and Richard Mergler to continue with the Central Station name.'

Jamie expands on this development: 'When Jo and Morgan bought back the trademarks, they needed someone to go out in the market and get all those deals back. I'd already decided to do this with them, and then we thought it might be a good idea to have Tim involved as well, because he's quite savvy. That's how the joint venture happened. It was very much me running it, with the others being silent partners.' Jamie spent his first year and a half with the new Central Station 'pretty much renegotiating all our old label deals and trying to hang onto as much as humanly possible'. Thanks to strong relationships and reputations, most people came back on board, despite the financial losses and 'bad taste in the mouth' that Destra's demise had left them with.

His first hire was Archie, a well known DJ who tells people, 'I'm like Prince or Madonna. I don't really have a surname'. Having worked on Central compilations in the early 2000s, Archie slotted nicely into the A&R role. 'I was brought into the label at a really interesting time when iTunes was getting big and CD sales were dropping off,' he says. 'Now the industry is being flipped on its head again. It's all gone to streaming and labels are being forced to readapt. I've had to learn a lot on my feet, and not rely on what I thought I knew.'

Archie, Central Station's current A&R manager (Photo by Wes Nel, www.wesmel.com, courtesy of Archie)

18. The Dance Scene 2000+

> 'We carried no less than nine or ten twelve-inch record crates to every gig, just to be sure that we could cover every genre and track request imaginable. And when CDs became the new thing, we loaded up a mixture of record crates and CD boxes and folders that filled the boot of my father's old Valiant when I drove to gigs. We were the educators ... it was our job to take the crowd on a musical journey. Requests were not very common in those days [early 00s] as the public were generally willing to wait and see where their night would end up, and what new monster track the DJ would drop at the height of the experience. Every time I played a dance floor filler, the common question was, "Where can I buy that track?"... My proud response was, "Central Station Records."'
> **Richard Rinaudo**

In the dance world, everything became bigger and slicker in the new millennium – the events, the touring, the stardom and the accolades. DJs and producers became household names and frequent flyers. But, as the digital revolution marched on, the economics and power politics of the music industry changed beyond recognition. Artists have never had it so good in some respects – they can access sophisticated technology at a fraction of previous cost, produce their tracks at home, and press a few buttons to send their work to a label. Barriers to entry have tumbled. Recording companies are no longer the all-powerful gatekeepers. And unknowns can become YouTube stars literally overnight. But low entry barriers bring their own problems. Apart from a few megastars, no one

DJ Rich (right) and DJ Mark Pellegrini (left) at their weekly event at the Grand Hyatt, Collins Street, Melbourne circa 2000-2002 (courtesy of Richard Rinaudo)

makes money out of selling music any more. 'The whole game's changed,' says Steve Hill. 'You make your income from merchandising, performing, putting on events and YouTube hits as opposed to record sales. Having said that, I had three million hits on Spotify and I think they cut me a cheque for twenty-two bucks or something!'

Starting in 1991, back in his hometown of Wellington in New Zealand, Steve played house music at clubs like Clare's, Ecstasy Plus, Paradiso and Tatou. As a sideline, he organised launch parties for recording companies, which is how he came to meet Morgan. When Steve decided to move to London in 1997, Morgan told him to keep in touch. The adventurous Kiwi had no job lined up, but he knocked on a few doors and eventually Pure Groove Records hired him to develop its mail-order business. 'In the first two or three months, we had out first top twenty record, so it just went crazy from there,' he says. Pure Groove was known for 'the harder side of the spectrum' of dance music and Steve immersed himself there in a 'band of genres' that he has stuck with for the rest of his twenty-five-year history as a DJ and producer.

'In the UK, I played at a night called Frantic and they were booking all the biggest venues over there – Brixton Academy, Camden Palace,' he says. 'I played at the End, Ministry of Sound, Bagley's. I played all over, but I was mainly based in London ... and I would fly and play at festivals like Dance Valley in Holland, Qlimax ... I'd play in Japan, Europe, Ireland, South Africa.'

The Dance Scene 2000+

Steve Hill (courtesy of Steve Hill)

In the midst of all this activity, Steve acted as Central Station's London contact, alerting Morgan to hot tracks and checking out potential licensing deals. When he decided to quit London in 2004, he opted to live in Sydney and took on the role of business manager for Central Station, working on the Wild-branded TV program and energy drink while also mixing compilations for the label and continuing to DJ far and wide.

He laughs when nominating the pittance Spotify recently paid him – he's a realist. Nowadays, he makes most of his living appearing at festivals around the world, and believes that Australia is on a par with Europe in terms of attracting the biggest acts and showcasing the latest ones, thanks to homegrown promoters. 'The big rave promoters from the 90s became the big festival promoters of the 2000s,' he says, pointing to people like Richie McNeill (aka Richie Rich), who ran Hardware parties at Melbourne's Docklands in the late 90s, Two Tribes events at Homebush in the early 2000s (in partnership with Future Entertainment), and then Summerdayze and Stereosonic around Australia post 2000. (Richie sold his Totem Onelove Group to American company SFX in 2013.)

Like many successful DJs and producers, Steve has started his own events – as co-owner of the Masif Saturdays nightclub in Sydney.

Another young gun on the Central Station label, Alex Karbouris (aka Alex K) skipped school as much as he could get away with from the age of fourteen and hung around radio stations instead – New Wave FM

99.3 to begin with and then Wild FM. 'I always knew that music was the thing I wanted to do,' he says. 'It wasn't even about DJing. It was about making music, like promos and doing things with editing.'

By age seventeen, he was production manager at Wild FM and hawking his NRG songs to Central Station. 'I started making dance albums with them,' he says. 'They were called *Kickin Hard*. They went really well back in the day – 1998 to 2003 ... It was good for me. Tim, Jo and Morgan have been in my life so long that they feel like family. I grew up with that company. A lot of good times along the way. Struggles too. Music is like that – ups and downs.'

To promote his music, he played live broadcasts for Wild FM in clubs along Oxford Street. After the station closed down, however, he moved to the UK for a few years, to capitalise on the popularity of his style there. He was signed by All Around the World, released several *Ultimate NRG* albums, and played 'in some pretty extreme places'. On his return to Australia, he went back to releasing with Central Station.

Asked what he thinks about the state of music today, Alex is characteristically laconic. 'I'm never one to say like the old days were better. Today's the day and you've got to adjust. I embrace it. If this is how it's going to go, I'll go with it. You can produce everything with one computer. You don't have to fork out tens of thousands of dollars

DJ Alex K (courtesy of Alex Karbouris)

for equipment, microphones and all that stuff. It's very easy to do, so it opens up avenues. You don't even have to leave home. You can send it out to 500 labels at once. All the social media stuff is great. You can get your stuff out there.'

BeXta's career took an unusual route. She started as a producer, performing her own material early on, and only turning to DJing around 1997. From 1993 until the last few years, she headlined festivals, raves and clubs all across Australia and overseas. In fact, she claims more Big Day Outs that any other DJ. So it's fair to say that she would have an excellent understanding of how crowds vary from city to city. 'Back then, every city had a distinct flavour,' she says. 'They all had different ways of dancing. It was fascinating. Brisbane people would use their arms when dancing but not their legs. Sydney people would use arms and legs, but in a different way from Melbourne, which had the shuffle. I used to wonder how it could be so different in the same country ... They'd wear the Converse One Stars in Sydney, while Melbourne had the fat pants, those fluffy fluoro gaters. I thought that was kinda cool.'

BeXta herself was very conscious of visual impact. 'When I was doing the live shows, I'd get costumes made up,' she says. 'I'd have dancers as well, so we'd coordinate costumes. I used to have a thing called "Live BeXta Cam", which was around the size of a matchbox which I'd fit over one of my eyes. So when I was playing live, people could see what I was doing – they'd project it onto the screen, mixed with original video content by video artist JMG13. I liked to embrace the theatrical side of things. It's a bit of fun.'

As his style of music grew in popularity, Kid Kenobi's career took off, culminating in his being voted Australia's favourite DJ for a record three years (2003-2005) in the annual inthemix.com DJ poll. 'For ten years, it was just bigger, bigger, bigger,' he says. 'You'd go from

> **Best of the festivals**
>
> For many years, Australia was spoilt for choice in terms of electronic dance music festivals – including (but by no means limited to) the Big Day Out, Falls Festival, Future Music Festival, Harbourlife, Laneway Festival, One Love, Parklife, Splendour in the Grass, Stereosonic, Summadayze and the Sydney Gay and Lesbian Mardi Gras. Although many of these mega-festivals no longer operate, new and exciting boutique events have appeared.
>
> For up-to-date info on festivals, see http://www.everfest.com/australia

Kid Kenobi (Photo by Stephen Govel, courtesy of Kid Kenobi)

organising little parties yourself to someone asking you to do their parties in the back room, then in the main room. Some of the bigger, more commercial clubs decide they're going to do something around the music you're playing. So you get embraced more in the mainstream. Ministry then got involved and wanted me to do a CD. I started to play overseas at big clubs and festivals. All these factors came together.'

In the middle of his twentieth anniversary tour and mix tape series, Kid Kenobi was still able to squeeze in time for producing side projects (some of them secret) while also running his own label, Klub Kids. 'It's a small independent label, but it does really well,' he says. 'It's a good access point for talented artists who will go on to do bigger things or get on to majors. It's like a lunching pad.'

Although Kid Kenobi continues to be his main identity, he uses other names for side projects, such as *Original Rude Boy*, a 90s-inspired breakbeat EP he was busy working on when interviewed for this project. 'I don't use my real name for anything,' he says, laughing. Whatever the name, the impression Kid leaves is consistent – an entrepreneur brimming with enthusiasm.

So let's look at what some of our other characters have been doing since we all partied at the end of 1999.

Melbourne

John Course has played many major stages in Australia, including closing Summerdayze twice. 'A pretty amazing experience when there's 55,000 people at Sensation White at Ethiad Stadium with the roof closed and everything,' he recalls. 'When I started DJing, I had no idea there would be a point when I'm playing to 25,000 people at an event, because that whole DJ movement hadn't happened yet. When I started, DJs were just the guys who knew how to play good music. They hadn't produced music. And they didn't travel the world. Les Toth or Stan Michael would become well known in their city, because the club was big. But a kid in Frankston didn't know the name of the DJ that played in the Chevron. Move forward twenty-five years and the kid in Frankston knows the name of Will Sparks, who used to live in suburban Melbourne and now tours the US and headlines stadiums of 10,000 or 15,000 people. Because the world works like that now.'

Ken Walker is still going strong after an illustrious career playing big stadiums and festivals, supporting touring superstars like Jay Z and Missy Elliott, and hosting radio programs. When Prince toured Australia in February 2016, not long before his untimely death, Ken played at the Melbourne after-party. He stuck to underground funk from 1979 and 1980, 'the rarest of rare grooves, nothing commercial at all', and his choices hit the mark. 'That was an amazing experience,' he says. 'A valet who spoke for Prince came up to ask me about the tracks, and he ended up buying a bottle of Cristal for me and the other DJs who played.'

Ken had a lot of success in the 90s licensing old disco tracks. The idea came to him while having a haircut. 'Kenny, where can we get all the dance music we used to listen to?' his Italian barber had asked. 'We can't get it on CD.' At the time, Ken had been working for the Pro DJ label and teamed up with one the owners, Geoff Sturre, to license disco

John Course (Photo by Andrew Raszevski, courtesy of John Course)

Ken Walker (courtesy of Ken Walker)

tracks from the late 70s and early 80s so people could reconnect. 'We scoured every DJ until we got a good pressing and then had it transferred from analogue to digital. Geoff sat in the studio and cleaned out all the pops and clicks you get from the vinyl, and then we released those tracks onto CD for the first time. But what we did was put together a megamix – a fifteen-minute mix of tracks. I said, "If we get Sanity to play this in their shops on a Friday night and Saturday morning, they will go gangbusters". And that's exactly what happened. We didn't put one cent of advertising into these CDs but each of them sold about 30,000 copies.'

Nowadays, Ken is remixing the same era of music: 'Basically what I do is take a lot of the old disco tracks that don't have the right energy levels for today or weren't produced very well. So I modify old tracks to bring them up to the energy levels of what I'm playing now, to fit in with my set. I'll take an old track, extend the intro, and put a drum loop over the top to give it a bit more meat.'

Another prominent Melbourne player, DJ JNETT, believes that the local scene has never been healthier. 'Melbourne is a city that the rest of the world seems to be paying attention to,' she says. 'I did an interview recently with a New York internet radio station, and the interviewer said that they're straight on to whatever comes out of Melbourne. Talk about a turnaround. I never dreamed that would be the case. There's certainly a lot more people producing and they seem to be less afraid now. We don't look at ourselves as lesser-thans.'

There's one thing sure to rile DJ JNETT – describing her as simply 'a female DJ'. 'I just don't want it to be about my gender alone,' she

DJ JNETT with Frankie Knuckles back in the day (courtesy of JNETT)

says. 'It's like all those customers at Central Station who would say, "Yeah, JNETT, she's a really good female DJ" and you'd go, "What the hell does that have to do with it?" Suggesting men were better, but she's pretty good as a female! But I am certainly proud to be a female in this industry and consider myself nothing but equal!'

To impress her is also straightforward. 'If there's a great sound system, I don't care what or where the club is,' she declares. 'You can mould it how you want to. Certainly the best system I've ever played on was a Hardcore 900 party in the late 90s, playing on the same system the Rolling Stones had just used on their Australian tour.'

JNETT generally sticks to vinyl for her gigs, which feature a mix of house, disco, funk, Afro and reggae. Influenced more by the independent underground house music imported during her record store days (see chapter 16), she steered clear of the big tracks that were once top-sellers. 'It seems what was once considered side room music, seems to be more of a main room vibe now!'

Like JNETT, Greg Molinaro is enthusiastic about the quality of music coming out of Melbourne these days. Local productions account for a sizeable proportion of the new vinyl he sells at his HUB301 Records store in Abbotsford, Melbourne. 'There are currently many talented kids living in the area who have got their own studios and record labels and they're pressing vinyl, and selling them worldwide as physical copies,' he says. 'Melbourne has its own movement happening. We are the next Berlin or Detroit in the making. I have no doubt we will one day be known as a music capital.'

Having been in the record retailing business almost continuously since 1987, Greg has experienced several cycles throughout his career. 'Music is this non-discriminating, liberating form of entertainment. Then, all of a sudden, with the birth of the digital age and file sharing, things changed dramatically. You could see the rapid decline of vinyl sales throughout the world. Within a short period, it just imploded and collapsed – to the point where I was ringing distributors that I'd dealt with for over twenty years, including my time at Central, and they wouldn't pick up their phones because they'd literally gone out of business. At the same time as you saw physical sales decline, you saw the commercialisation of music, clubs and festivals worldwide. Music just wasn't the same. There was a moment where it seemed as if it had all stopped. Or maybe I got tired of it. I folded everything up and virtually gave my last shop to one of my staff members who then ran it on a smaller scale. I was no longer inspired by the music scene.'

After seventeen years of Rhythm & Soul Records, Greg opened a little bar called Two of Hearts in South Yarra. There he offered gigs to local DJs and slowly regained his faith, making connections with a new generation of underground talent and a new 'micro world' of music. The 'movement' that excites Greg is largely powered by well educated, humble young musicians who have combined electronic elements with classical instrumentation to create a sound signature that is unique to Melbourne's landscape. 'There's no aggression in it at all,' says Greg. 'They've pulled back the tempo and it's quite atmospheric and open-sounding, just like our landscape. Many labels around the world are looking at Melbourne, seeking out the talent that is amongst us. It's a very niche thing, and you're either connected to it or you're not. I've always been interested in the underground and what no one backs. When I left Rhythm & Soul, that was the end of a cycle. Now I feel we are at the birth of another cycle which excites me.'

Sydney

Upstairs from Central Station in Sydney, Q Bar started an event at four o'clock on Friday afternoons called Qushi. Friends of the owners who weren't really DJs were asked to come along and play a few tunes while free sushi was served. In 1998, actor, model and musician Mark Gerber was one such friend, and a good response from the crowd set him on a new path. Soon he was playing alongside Stephen Ferris in Q Bar's VIP Bar (in the Exchange Hotel), and being asked to reinvent that venue's Lizard Lounge. 'It was a lot of fun,' says Mark. 'It had almost a Studio 54 vibe. A lot of models, actors, glitterati were involved.' As well as DJing himself, Mark did marketing and publicity for the Q Bar and ran parties for Fashion Week and New Zealand magazine *Pavement*. Then he reinvigorated the early evening offer at the Exchange. 'That's how Spectrum came about. It was successful almost immediately and turned into a renowned small live music venue.'

The former musician from the indie alternative three-piece band, Scapa Flow, wasn't afraid of mixing up genres. 'I could jump from funk to Michael Jackson, to the Chemical Brothers, to the Smiths, to you-name-it,' he says. 'When I progressed to the beat mixing and house music, playing in the early hours of Saturday morning at the Lizard Lounge, I used to drop the Gorillas, ACDC and all manner of rock and roll into the middle of a house set, and the whole room would erupt and go mad.'

Mark Dynamix has always followed his own taste rather than seeking popularity. About 2007, he moved to Berlin for a year to explore his passion for the city's sparse tech-house sound. There he started a record label called Long Distance Recordings, and began producing and remixing a more European sound on it. From 2010, he decided to temporarily hang up the headphones for a few years, after relentlessly touring for more than fifteen years. So he steered his company towards film and TV, composing and producing music and recording live audio. Nowadays, he's back behind the decks, playing at his own events, Jack the House. 'It felt like the right time to slowly ease back into it in 2014, and then start the event promotions the following year,' he says. 'At Jack The House, we play a lot of music which harks back to the 1988-to-1992 period and which Central Station was paramount in introducing me to. We have DJs playing who were pioneers at the time (and still are), as well as DJs who started a few years after this period and continue to make a massive contribution to the Australian music scene, such as Phil Smart, John Ferris, Kate Munroe and Robbie Lowe. Some of these DJs were putting parties on when I was eighteen. To have them play at my event is quite surreal but absolutely humbling.'

Mark happily admits that the night is 'completely indulgent and, if you like, nostalgic' but points out that the music has come full circle. 'When you play those records now, many of them sound fresh again because the style at the moment is similar – it's basically house music with rap – which is what hip house was back in 1988. And I'm sure that all the genres that aren't deemed fashionable at the moment will

Above: Paul 'flex' Taylor playing at a fundraiser for the Multiple Sclerosis Society at the Abercrombie (on Broadway in Sydney) in 2012 (courtesy of Paul Taylor)

Left: Nik Fish (courtesy of Nik Vatoff)

eventually come around again in ten years' time. That's why I never get rid of the great classic records.'

Also driving down memory lane, Steve Bourk has been organising parties with a mate for the last five or six years. When interviewed, he was still high after their sell-out, 650-strong event at the Midnight Shift on Oxford Street the previous Saturday night. 'I've been looking at Facebook all day and there are so many people commenting about how good the night was,' he says. Steve promotes the events through Facebook pages boasting thousands of followers, but maintains the vibe of an exclusive community. 'Some people deposit the money in my account and

I register-post the tickets. And some people will drive to my house or I'll drive to theirs on a weekend. It's all hand-picked. We like to work out who's coming.'

The age group is thirty-plus, and the music is all Wild FM classics. Asked what songs got the best response, Steve nominates *Magic in You* (Sugar Babes), *Because We Want To* (Billie), and three or four songs by the Klubbheads. All pre-2000 stuff.

In 2000, Nik Fish moved to Home nightclub in Darling Harbour. Along with BeXta and Jumping Jack, he also toured nationally. 'We became a bit of a crew. We'd go to all capital cities, even as far as Perth and Darwin, and we'd play these big venues and big sound that the kids wouldn't normally get to hear. If we played at the wrong venue we could easily clear the dance floor. No matter what kind of weaponry, skill and charisma, at the end of the day, if you don't have the right music ...'

Adelaide

From playing in every single nightclub in South Australia, DJ JoSH progressed to doing massive parties in Sydney and Melbourne, and became one of the most recognised and well travelled of South Australian DJs. Ranked number eight in Australia in the first inthemix.com.au dance music awards in 2002 (and number one in South Australia for four years running), she doesn't hesitate when asked to nominate the reasons for her success. 'I was just determined to become a DJ in a male-orientated world and to be treated as an equal,' she says. 'And it was the people who got me there. My sets just uplifted everybody. I said to myself, "One day I'm going to play at Mardi Gras", and everything just fell into place after that. It took me ten years of submissions to get there, and I'm the only South Australian to have been major-billed at Mardi Gras, not once, not twice, but three times. I also got to play three Sleaze Balls in Sydney.'

JoSH has had a long connection with Central Station. 'I shopped with them throughout my entire DJ career,' she says. 'I was also the event coordinator of the Central Station Dance Music Awards. My interaction with them was from the very beginning until the very last – I closed the doors as manager at the Marion store. When Central came to Adelaide, all the Italo house and house music from Europe started coming in. They were the outlet for all these kids to become who they were – the HMCs, the Simon Lewickis, myself. We all shopped there. We'd hang out there. We'd share vinyl. I think Central Station probably played the

One of the CDs released by JoSH on the Central Station label

biggest role in importing European dance music into Australia.'

In 1999, JoSH released *Sessions 002* on the Central Station Records label. Then, in 2004, she also released a JOY FM compilation album on Central – *Mardi Gras*. After a lull in her DJing career, when she encountered ageist attitudes from some promoters, she began organising her own events. Her fiftieth birthday retrospective event in 2016 sold out at 700 heads, for example, and her boat parties on the Port River attract around 300 people each month from October to April. 'I've found my tribe,' she says. 'That generation of people have had kids and those kids are now old enough to stay home. Now all the old heads are coming out again and they want to party their arses off, so it's kind of like a natural progression. "OK, let's do this again. Everybody's ready for it."'

Brisbane

While working at Central Station's store, Matt Nugent was DJing at a bunch of venues – Fever in Paddington plus Family, The Monastery and Empire in the Valley. He says that the house music scene in Brisbane really improved around 2000 when the Empire became a lot more popular. 'That's when guys like myself and Matt Kitshon, Chris Wilson, Freestyle, Mark Briais, Jason Morley and Jason Rouse became popular in the clubs. The sound went from the harder stuff into house. Baby Gee was also super popular from about 2002 until 2010. He was the main trance DJ on Friday nights at Family with Tydi and Skye. Tydi has now gone on to be a big success internationally. Miss Tracy who worked at Central Station was an important rave DJ in the early 2000s playing at System 6 parties promoted by DJ Thief. Jason Morley played at Family

Rudy James playing at the Black 01 Afterparty at Geisha in Northbridge, Perth (courtesy of Rudy James)

with me on Saturday nights and was quite popular too.'

Murray Brown won the Central Station DJing competition (called Central Battle) in 2001, but didn't get commercial gigs until 2002, when he started playing at The Monastery during the week. At the end of 2004, he started playing at the Gold Coast, with one three-year residency at Quest followed by another at Platinum. Back in Brisbane, he played at GPO for two years before becoming the main-room resident at the Met for six years. Asked about his genre, he says, 'A tough commercial house was more my style. It had to have chug. I always like to have vocals in my set – things people can sing along to and feel as if they are a part of the journey.' And what about the current dance music scene in Brisbane? 'There is a trend towards putting on one-hour sets, and turning DJs into promoters, which I think is not sustainable for a business. It creates a lack of consistency in the music throughout the night,' says Murray.

Perth

In the 00s, DJ Kenny L played at festivals, as well as at clubs and bars. One of his main gigs was at The Church. To promote the club and the Wild brand owned by Central Station, he and fellow resident DJ Riki hosted a popular radio show on Groove 101.7 FM called *Wild Nights*. It was a natural progression for Ken, having previously worked with Colin Bridges on RTR FM. Unfortunately, as with Wild FM in Sydney a few years earlier, Groove's community radio licence was eventually revoked because it failed the non-profit test.

For more than a decade, Ken also ran a store, The DJ Factory, supplying equipment as well as vinyl. 'We closed in 2014. From 2010, we saw a very rapid decline in vinyl sales. All the young people wanting to get into DJing were moving into Tractor and Serato [vinyl emulation software] or CDs,' he says. Nowadays, he has a weekly residency at one bar and does guest spots at other venues. 'I've never pigeon-holed myself,' he says. 'I'm a jack-of-all-trades musically, although I've gained recognition as a purveyor of certain genres at different times. As dance music has evolved, I've evolved as a DJ.'

The former rave DJ has seen a resurgence in 'rave-orientated' events in Perth. 'There are a few crews around now that are trying to relive the old school vibe and playing the music from those days,' he says. At the same time, he is worried about the current state of the scene in Perth. 'Like everywhere in the country, the late-night club scene has been affected by changes in licensing laws, but we are a smaller city so it's affecting us more,' he says. 'This new generation simply won't pay a door charge. All the nightclubs have had to become free. And they're trialling these lockout restrictions and the removal of shots – which is destroying nightlife. We have a lot less clubs than ever. At the same time, with the economy in a lull, young people just can't afford the prices that the festivals got up to. We've seen some of the national promoters go down.'

Auckland

An indigenous New Zealander himself, Philip Bell doesn't like to 'stereotype brown people' but he points out that Auckland has the world's biggest city-based Polynesian population and that's what drives the huge popularity of hip hop and reggae. 'Reggae in New Zealand is absolutely massive,' he says. 'Bob Marley is somewhat of a cult figure of everything, not just musically. I hate to put people in boxes, but the struggles are really relatable. I watched this documentary a couple of months ago and it said that the reason why people like West Coast hip hop is because of the funk that's inside the music. They use funk as the backbone. Other parts of America use really hard beats, but the West Coast ... that's why a lot of music these days has got some reggae involved ... it's a reggae feel but updated.'

When interviewed for the book, Philip had just released his latest album of hip hop and R&B. 'We shipped a couple of thousand hard copies as well as releasing digitally,' he says. It's amazing that people

Philip Bell aka DJ Sir-Vere (courtesy of Philip Bell)

are still buying hard copies. But it's all about touring. Nino Brown on Universal is quite similar. We release the albums to tour them because club culture is where it's at.'

Now resident DJ and promoter of Code, Sam Hill spins 'punk, funk, nu wave, rock and roll, fucked up house, sleazy electro and mutant disco'.

'I'm still a house DJ, but there's such a wide variety of what you would call "house" nowadays,' he says. 'Because of my age – I'm forty-eight now – I'm not super comfortable being in a club with a whole bunch of eighteen-year-olds, even though it goes down well. I'm more comfortable playing to people who are thirty or forty. They're tapping their toe and having a beer and not necessarily jumping around until four in the morning, but out at midnight, maybe having a dance.'

It's difficult to imagine Sam ever being uncomfortable – he seems such an easy-going guy on our FaceTime call. 'Sometimes I just play backgroundy stuff,' he says. 'But I get booked for top forty, very commercial, where I'm literally playing Calvin Harris all night. If I'm playing to a cool club crowd, I might be playing something like Rufus.'

Collateral for the Wild Reunion of November 2016 ...

and for the Metal for Melbourne event of January 2017

19. Full Circle

The more things change, the more they stay the same. On a beautiful Spring day, Google maps lead the way to a beaten-up door in an obscure Melbourne laneway. The mission is to meet Andee Frost, generally called Frosty, a former Central Station staffer and franchisee. The door is locked and aloof, with no buzzers or signs to welcome visitors. Ten minutes elapse as the occasional courier or clerk passes. Then a man arrives with a bunch of keys.

'Frosty?'

'No,' he replies.

Which is not a surprise – he's too old to fit the frame. The surprise is that he hasn't heard of Andee at all.

'This is a private lodge,' he says. 'No one here of that name. But there's a nightclub upstairs. Maybe he belongs there. You're welcome to wait if you like.'

There's a wooden bench in the little foyer. The place feels like a down-at-heel country pub – full of hose-down tiles, dark and sticky timbers and musty smells. When Frosty arrives to show us upstairs to his nightclub, the vibe moves on a few decades, from the 30s to the 60s, but the mustiness remains. There is a long bar at the entrance, and then curtained booths before you come upon a small dance floor, a tiny stage and a set of turntables.

'You can feel the ghosts here.'

He laughs. 'It was dead space. We leased it off the Raob-Gab lodge for three years and run it as a nightclub. It's called Hugs & Kisses. Before that it was called the Buffalo Club, and it used to be called Mouse Trap, back in the day, a long time ago.'

In his mid-30s, Frosty is one of the youngest people interviewed for this book, but he's no novice. Barely into his teens, he became involved with community radio – Eastern FM in Croydon – helping a young Ashley Gay do his club show. Too intimidated to venture into the cliquey Central Station world, he built up a record collection by shopping in the suburbs, and started out as a mobile DJ. Later playing at a local nightclub called Jooce, which held underage events, he met established DJs like James Ash and Ivan Gough who helped him hone his craft. Before long, he was doing club gigs in the city. Then Ashley Gay got him a job at Pro-DJ and took him along when he switched to Central Station in the early 00s. Jo and Morgan had recently re-established a presence in Melbourne with a basement store in Swanston Street. A few years on, when they were preparing the business for sale, they broke some earth-shattering news.

'Jo and Morgan were like, "We're going to close the store down" and we were like, "Arghh". That's all we knew what to do. So we decided to take it and run with it, set it up in another spot,' remembers Frosty. So he and colleagues Jim Kontogiannis and Janette Pitruzello took on the franchise, and moved to a smaller location in Somerset Place. They changed the name to Hear Now BC (Brown Cow) Vinyl Boutique, and had fun until the stress of running a business in a vanishing market became too much to handle.

'At the time, Janette was having her second kid. Jim was over it. And I was exploding into a DJ career,' says Frosty. 'So we decided it was too hard. Let's just get rid of it. There was a massive debt. At the same time, all the distributors were going bust ... Everything was changing. The public's overall mood was that digital was going to kill vinyl ... It's funny now, because vinyl is still there. Streaming is popular and tapes are coming back at the moment. But CDs are gone, and vinyl is still there.'

Melbourne is brimming with new independent record stores, particularly in Northcote and Collingwood, and even the huge JB Hi-Fi store in the city where Jim Kontogiannis now works has a massive vinyl section. When friends want to jump into this pond and ask Frosty for advice, he laughingly tells them, 'Don't do it! Save your money'. 'Obviously it's a bubble and it's going to burst at some point,' he says. 'I've been making this joke all year: vinyl stores are the new juice bars, or the new frozen yogurt stands. A lot of people are trying to go after the same market. So it will be interesting to see how long it lasts this time. But the upside is that some amazing stores are out there right now.'

Full Circle

Having been burnt in the dawning of the digital age, Frosty is happy with his current patch. 'Anything you can't do online is good,' he says. 'That's why nightclubs are good. You can't really go to an online nightclub and drink.' Until a year or so ago, he was DJing in big venues and festivals, but he opted out of the mainstream. 'I wasn't really in love with the music I was having to play, and I wasn't in love with going interstate and playing average gigs when I could be at home in Melbourne playing amazing gigs,' he says. As well as owning Hugs & Kisses – a members-only club with an RSL-style license – he runs Saturday nights at The Toff in Town (in Curtin House), a monthly party called Animals Dancing, and smaller events at late-night rave caves like Mercat (at the Queen Victoria Market).

He feels at home in the underground scene. 'Everything's a little bit hard to find, a little bit secretive,' he says. Indeed, the actual entrance to Hugs & Kisses is even more obscure than where we came in – just a black door, nothing else. There's no signage and no marketing. It's all word of mouth, and social media. Unpretentious little venues like this – off the beaten track, with no foot traffic – make for cheap rents and the economic freedom to offer innovative music.

The problem for people like Frosty is that the mainstream keeps trying to freeload on their efforts. 'There are certain promoters who are just about money, and they steal from the underground and try to cherry pick the acts they want,' he says. 'I am constantly fighting people like that. You bring acts out – and I tour people as part of my job – and all of a sudden a big promoter throws their bankbook at them. Thankfully, a lot of acts, because of personal rapport, will turn around and say they're not interested, and they stick with the people who are doing it for the right reasons.'

The more things change, the more they stay the same.

Wars happen. In Sydney, Brisbane and Perth, venues feel under siege from lockout laws. Local DJs are outraged about nanny-state, knee-jerk reactions to media-hyped problems. 'Lock-out laws have decimated the club scene,' says Cadell Bradnock. 'It's a bit hard to swallow when we know what's really going on – a lack of transport and a lack of police.' Although no longer DJing and therefore not directly affected, Sydney-based Paul 'flex' Taylor is equally fervent in his criticism: 'My heart bleeds for this city. It's totally screwed now. I'm so glad that I got to play in nightclubs where there weren't these restrictions, and there was a scene. It doesn't exist any more. There's a blanket over everything. Where are all the DJs going to play? The clubs have closed and the restaurants that made money on the back of nightclubs have gone too. Promoters, singers, bartenders, everybody in the entertainment industry are getting new jobs. Imagine having a passion for something and having no outlet for it? That's unhealthy.'

At the Oxford Art Factory, where Central Station once lived, Mark Gerber has changed what he can to survive. 'I don't wait for the avalanche to come over me. I saw this coming and I've put measures in, cut costs, made my business model even more diverse and inclusive,' he says. He has also got on the front foot politically, trying to get an alliance together to argue the case for responsible venue-owners.

Cut costs. Diversify. Lobby. Does that story sound familiar?

That's exactly what Jo and Morgan did, of course. They won their battle to keep Central Station alive, and in so doing helped to nurture Australasia's dance scene as a whole, as well as many individual careers.

Central Station V2 lives on, with Jamie Raeburn at the helm, ably supported by Archie in A&R, Amanda Jenkins in PR, Ben Morris in club promotions, Andrew Boon in digital marketing, and Kate Fuery in business affairs. This lean little team (with Ashley Gay looking after digital distribution) has taken the label into a new era of success, not just licensing tracks from overseas but developing Australian talent in the global market. Bombs Away is a good example. Two brothers from Perth sampled a YouTube clip in their lounge room and created a catchy club record called *Big Booty Bitches*. Archie happened upon the track, thought there was potential and signed the duo. 'From there it's been huge, one of our biggest earners. Not just here in Australia, but in the US and Europe,' he says. 'It turned into a bit of a cult record.'

Odd Mob is another example. 'They sent me a demo a couple of years ago,' continues Archie. 'I heard something really special. There's been a bit of work developing their sound, but now it's very recognisable. They're really talented. For two young guys to have ten additional labels around the world pick up the record is quite a big thing.'

Another recent success story is Starley, an unknown Sydney artist that Archie discovered in late 2015. '*Call on Me* has been one of the biggest hits to come out of Central Station Records. As of early December 2016, the song has already clocked up a whopping 80 million streams on Spotify, alongside being a top ten single on iTunes here in Australia – amazingly without any major radio additions just yet. It's looking like it will be a global hit for us.'

'The industry has changed so much,' observes Jamie. 'In the old Central Station model, all we had to care about was what was happening on radio in Australia. Now we have to worry about the playlist in Latvia, and a local translation of an artist's poster in Korea. You need adaptability. The nerds have taken over. You're not really selling music any more. You're selling how many views you can get. How many followers your artist has.'

Indeed, Jamie admits that he's weary of the pace of change in the music industry. 'It's really hard to stay abreast. There is virtually a new DSP [digital sales platform] launched every week. I'm less interested in developing new platforms than in focusing on new music. Thankfully I've got a team of really good folk here who are keen and willing to embrace new technology.'

On the other hand, Jamie is excited about the growing popularity of streaming services. 'This year [2016], the Australian music market stopped declining and started increasing. That's going to be a worldwide trend, now that pirating is null and void from streaming. People are getting used to signing up and paying these monthly amounts.'

Archie has converted to streaming for his own music needs. 'I definitely prefer the physical format,' he says. 'Being able to go into your collection and handle a record has much more value than the digital format. In the same breath, I'm really excited about the streaming format because it gives people an opportunity to discover a whole bunch of music that they might not have come across before. There are pros and cons.'

Although Central Station V2 operates very differently from V1 – it's a high-volume, global-reaching digital game nowadays – the label shows the clear stamp of its heritage. As Archie points out, Central Station is distinctive for its 'immense catalogue of old classics that stem from the record store days', and its core activity (alongside developing new talent) continues to be licensing in of songs from other worldwide partners.

Jamie rattles off some bragging points: 'We had a four-times platinum single with a guy called Qwote. We had a top five album with Hardwell. And we had a number one single with a UK trance act called Above & Beyond. They're huge, selling out everything from the Hordern to the Sydney Opera House. They hit number one on iTunes in 2015 even though they had never been played on national radio here.'

'We look after Defqon, which is a Dutch music festival brand,' adds Archie. 'We also work with Tomorrowland, another massive festival brand in Europe. We are a bit eclectic in what we do as a label. We're diverse too — gay, hip hop, house. That's where the whole ethos of Central Station works. We are open to anything that's good and that we feel passionate about.'

Cultivating the tastemakers is as important today as it ever was for Central Station. As with everything else, though, the task has become more complex. There are more channels, and digital savvy is essential. 'Clubs and dance radio are still really important for us,' says Archie. 'But we're very proactive promoting our music across all media. The people who curate the music on Spotify are really important these days. They can sometimes help to break a record.'

'The music industry was one of the first sectors to be hit by the internet,' observes Jo. 'Considering all the changes it has been through, I think the current form of Central Station has excelled. I keep in the background. Sometimes they ask for my ideas, but overall they've had the freedom to do what they're doing. Congratulations to all of them.'

The more things change, the more they stay the same. Nowadays, when most people of their age and financial position tend to be taking it easy, Jo and Morgan are still tackling new frontiers. On the business side, they're involved in several joint ventures other than Central Station: NextStation, VRStation, Ambition Entertainment and Flipside Distribution.

'NextStation and VRStation are businesses involved in streaming content from nightclubs and dance events,' explains Morgan.

Jo goes on to explain how he and Morgan became partners in Ambition Entertainment: 'Robert Rigby, ex Warner Music, and Brian Harris from EMI are very capable people in the music industry. Morgan came to me one day and said they needed some funding. So we got involved, along with Greg Shaw and Seb Chase (from MGM), to form Ambition Entertainment. It deals with contemporary music, everything from James Morrison to The Everley Brothers.'

Former foes going into business together says a lot about how far the various partners have come from the horror days of the music wars. 'Forgiving and moving on is a powerful thing,' says Morgan. 'It's like a load coming off -- very energising.'

Although they travel to Sydney regularly to look after business, Jo and Morgan spend most of their time at their compound in the Sunshine Coast hinterland – jokingly dubbed the Black Mountain Nudist Colony. There they shelter a few refugees (economic or political), host a motley stream of visitors, and personally tend to their beloved chooks, dogs

Full Circle

and permaculture plots. They live humbly. When cooking, Jo wastes nothing, throwing stalks and all into his vegetable wok-ups ('good fibre'). Supervising his fruit trees and systems for animal feed, composting and recycling keeps him busy.

Having read this book, you may have formed the impression that the two of them are instinctive operators who've never opened a business book in their lives. But they are both avid readers and deep thinkers. Jo reads every issue of *The Economist* and *Self Realization Fellowship* ('a magazine devoted to healing of body, mind and soul'), while Morgan subscribes to dozens of online news services. In his own way, each is still lobbying for change: Jo sends policy suggestions to politicians and Morgan dashes off articles to friends.

Jo still cares passionately about public policy and lists a raft of changes he would like to see happen before he dies, including more affordable public transport (he suggests $3 per day anywhere), the decriminalisation of drugs, second-tier industrial law for the small business sector, assisted dying, and a green army to protect our forests, lakes, rivers and seas. He also argues that money currently spent on fireworks should be redirected to hiring artists and performers for free concerts in parks across Australia.

That's *The Economist* side of Jo speaking. The *Self Realization* side is also apparent: 'If you're in business, put your idea of getting rich away. Focus on what you know, what you have a feeling for. Check out your competitors. Look at all the possibilities and cost them out. Once you're

Jo and friends (Photo by David Hannah)

decided which way to go, visualise your product, and how you're going to sell it, before you do anything. When you get to a difficult stage, there's no point surrendering. That's a dead end. So pull back and move onto something else. Think a hell of a lot. You might have a thousand ideas. But then you realise that only one will work. Just keep at it. Work on difficulties, and you will learn how to deal with other situations. When you succeed, remember that money is a responsibility. If you don't do anything with it, you're wasting that energy. You have to use it to create and to invest in other people.'

The social worker side of Morgan is equally apparent. Jim Kontogiannis tells a story that highlights this: 'I had dinner with Morgan recently, and I mentioned that I was teaching myself upholstery. Out of the blue, I got a message from him saying that his neighbour is an upholsterer and would like to train me up. He offered for me to spend a month up there with them to train!'

The more things change, the more they stay the same. Greta Tate is still championing Metal for Melbourne gigs. JimmyZ is still connecting people, nowadays mostly to promote 'a different level of uplifting living' via the relatively new concept of eco villages. Stephen Allkins has retired from paid work, but still does a handful of charity gigs in aid of mental health, women's refuge or youth causes. 'I do it in that old school way, about bringing people together for dance, because dancing is a really important spiritual thing for me,' he says.

The tribe that led the dance revolution in Australia and New Zealand remains both idealistic and broad-minded. People express sadness about the commoditification of music, and the nanny-state attacks on youth having fun. At the same time, they are philosophical and optimistic about change. Timmy Byrne strikes a common chord: 'Dance music is always evolving. People are coming up with new labels and new sounds. But are they really new sounds? Or just being labeled something different? There are so many music schools now, and many more avenues for people to make a living out of music, whether it be writing for a video game or a corporate event. Ever since the synthesiser and electronic music were invented, they've never gone away and never will.'

Asked to nominate his favourite memory of Central Station, Jo seems taken aback – as if he has never contemplated the concept. When urged to say the first thing that pops into his head, he gives a surprising answer – it was when Morgan threw himself into marketing *Here's Johnny*. 'Before then, Morgan was blah blah about promoting Central Station ...

not full-hearted. Then he started sending all these faxes out to the radio stations, disconnecting our phone line to do that. I said to him, "For goodness sake, get two lines". But he did a good job. It was Morgan who created that monster hit.'

Jo could never be accused of showering Morgan with praise. He's more likely to upbraid him for being typical of his blood type – O – flinging around words like 'hubris' and 'excessive' about him. They are hilarious together – an odd couple that works. When Jo is being particularly blunt or blinkered, Morgan rolls his eyes and grumbles, 'Total Asperger's'. They know that they are each stronger for having the other, but don't waste words or gestures showing it. Shared values tie them together as much as shared history.

In contrast to choosing a favourite memory, Jo has no hesitation when asked about his proudest moment. 'It's when we shared our businesses with other employees, and continued as if nothing had happened. Also when I gave the land here back to nature. They were my best moments in life.' He and Morgan have undertaken a process called 'voluntary surrender' whereby most of their 500-acre property – barring the plateau where the accommodation sits – has been permanently protected as a wildlife sanctuary.

Jo and Morgan at the entrance to their property in the Sunshine Coast hinterland, which they have protected from development in perpetuity (Photo by David Hannah)

'At a DJ Association meeting in Melbourne many years ago, someone asked me what I was going to do with all my money when I'd made it,' remembers Jo. 'I promised I would give at least ten per cent of my money towards the environment. When we found this property, I knew straight away that it was the one I wanted. All of this beautiful forest, no one around, pure nature. And now it's a protected area, one of the biggest in this region. We've had a lot of support from the Noosa Council.'

Like Jamie and Archie, Jo is excited about the benefits of streaming. Typically, though, he emphasises the environmental pay-off: 'The way we are consuming resources, we are going to burn this planet before too long. We should focus on producing only those physical things that we truly need. We must cut down waste and stop destroying the planet.'

Jo and Morgan want any profits from this book to go towards developing artists and reversing environmental damage. Currently, they support the Australian Wildlife Conservancy (www.australianwildlife.org), Land For Wildlife (http://www.lfwseq.org.au), and the Wildlife Land Trust established by Humane Society International (http://wildlifelandtrust.org.au). 'We are also looking out for other non-profit organisations that support Aboriginal people's involvement in land conservation,' says Jo. 'I have always been attached to the environment. I saw the destruction in Italy – people throwing everything in rivers from dead chickens to old mattresses and sewerage. It really impressed upon me. When I was about ten, I asked my teacher, "Do we have enough oxygen the way we are going?" He said, "I can't answer that question", and he looked at me as if thinking, "Where are you from?"'

Jo laughs. It's that strange, raspy laugh that shows that he gets it – he's always been a bit of a misfit.

But he certainly found his niche in life. As the old slogan goes: Everything to Dance To. Everything to Dance For.

Appendix 1 - Last Word: Professor Allan Fels

(By email 28 July 2106)

I am pleased you are writing a book about Central Station Records and Giuseppe Palumbo.

In reply to your questions, as Chairman of the Australian Competition and Consumer Commission, I have had to deal with many very difficult competition questions. Typically very large amounts of money are involved in decisions and so the resistance to change and the introduction of true competition is strongly resisted. I would rate the opposition by the record companies as amongst the strongest of all. One special reason for that is that it was the giant multi national companies that were driving the campaign from abroad. Their interests are not restricted to Australia, although they are quite substantial in Australia. Their interests were to oppose Australia introducing the changes because they feared they would then spread to Europe and even possibly to the United States.

What they thought to do was to hide behind local performers. Local performers had strong incentives to support their record company sponsors because of their relationship with them. They also did not understand the issues.

I found it very disappointing that most of the local performers who opposed the changes did not lend an ounce of support to our quite radical proposals to give performers the right to copyright and associated changes that would have greatly strengthened the position of performers. They also failed to recognise that many performers buy CDs themselves and should not have to pay the excessively high prices that we had.

Giuseppe Palumbo played a very important role in the struggle to free up the music market in Australia. He understood the situation a lot better than many other people did but he also had the courage to fight for change and to take all the risks including financial, that this involved. There was high risk of retaliation and punishment by the big record companies.

When a body like the ACCC is seeking change, it needs support from some people in the industry. Part of the struggle is for the government body to gain knowledge of exactly what's happening in the market and what the exact consequences of parallel import restrictions are. The ACCC got much of its knowledge from Giuseppe and from others. They explained to us how the market worked and this put us in a much stronger position to argue credibly for change.

As to performers who say that the changes in the law may have impaired their careers, I feel that they are the victims of the old propaganda of the record companies. Like most areas of deregulation, freeing up this market expanded it considerably and created greater opportunities, especially for local performers. If there were performers gaining from the old system it was predominantly international performers overseas whose loyalties improved as a result of the high prices in Australia. There is fairly little flow on or trickle down to Australian performers. The situation could be compared with telecommunications reform. When Telstra had a monopoly, people working there complained they would suffer from the changes, but in fact as everyone knows, once the market was freed up, there was a massive expansion in terms of employment and sales as new products and services flooded the market and created boundless opportunities. Something similar is happening now with the advent of Uber in the taxi industry. There is a similar story to tell about CDs.

I hope this is helpful.

Kind regards
Allan Fels

Appendix 2 – The Players

Stephen Allkins (aka [Love] Tattoo) One of Australia's most celebrated and original DJs and producers, most famous for his sets at Patchs and Sydney's Gay and Lesbian Mardi Gras. Recognised by a 2001 Dance Music Award for Outstanding Contribution to Dance in Australia. Now semi-retired and focusing on charity gigs.

Mark Alsop Celebrated Sydney DJ, best known for playing at Hordern Pavilion, Toybox, Inquisition and Honey parties as well as at the clubs along the Oxford Street strip. Co-managed Central's Pitt Street store 1989-90. Still playing locally and nationally. www.markalsop.com

Jo Altman (aka DJ JoSH) Adelaide-based DJ, best known for playing trance music between 1995 and 2005 in Sydney and Melbourne as well as across her home State – including a ten-year residency at ARQ in Sydney. Ranked number eight in Australia (number one in South Australia) in the inaugural inthemix.com.au dance music awards in 2002. Played three Mardi Gras parties and three Sleaze Balls. Has hosted many radio shows and appeared regularly on channel [V], including in the *20 years of DJ Josh* special in 2004. Now a full-time gym manager and personal trainer, while also running her own dance events. www.djjosh.com

Archie A well known DJ who worked on compilation CDs for Central in the mid 2000s. Now A&R manager for Central Station Records.

Kevin Attwood Co-owner of the Xchange, a famous gay venue in Prahran, Melbourne, for 25 years from 1986. Now runs his own online radio station called *Rhythm City*, and produces and directs shows for Channel 31.

Philip Bell (aka DJ Sir-Vere) Known as 'a South Pacific hip hop pioneer', Philip is a nightclub DJ and radio host who has sold more than 250k mix CDs under the *Major Flavours* brand. Former editor of *Rip It Up*, New Zealand's longest running music magazine. Also previously did A&R for BMG in NZ. Now program director for Mai FM, Auckland's number one radio station. Also tours extensively in Australia and NZ. https://www.facebook.com/djsirvere/

Stevie Bourk (aka Stevie B) Former vinyl manager at Central's Oxford Street store who took over the franchise in 2003. He now organises parties for over-thirties who want to dance again to the Wild FM era of music. Also owns Easy Test, which has the Australian rights to import drug testing kits from Amsterdam, a business he inherited from Central.

Cadell Bradnock (aka DJ Cadell) Based in Sydney and still DJing after 22+ years. Has played at rave parties, gay clubs and mainstream clubs around Australia; also Ibiza, Mykonos, Asia, Malaysia, New Zealand and USA. ARIA chart DJ for twelve years. Has a radio show on Bondi Beach Radio (*Late Nite Shopping*). www.djcadell.com

Colin Bridges Long-standing presenter of a five-hour dance music program (*Beats Per Minute*) on 6UVS FM 92.1 in Perth, judged 'Best Hi-NRG dance music radio program in the world' by *Dance Music Report* in 1989. Big mail-order customer for Central Station.

Murray Brown Franchisee of Brisbane store. DJd at various venues between from 2002 and 2015, including the Monastery, GPO and the Met in Brisbane; and Quest, Platinum, Bedroom and Shooters on the Gold Coast. Now responsible for the operations of a food and beverage import wholesaler.

Timmy Byrne DJd at many Melbourne clubs in the 80s and 90s, including residencies at the Underground and Redhead. Now station manager, program director, music director and announcer for Kiss FM, an independent dance radio station with an international subscriber base. http://kissfm.com.au

Gavin Campbell Ran many nightclubs in Melbourne in the 80s and 90s, most famously Razor. Founded Razor Records, which later became a subsidiary label of Mushroom Records. As a member of Filthy Lucre, achieved international success with a dance remix of Yothu Yindi's *Treaty*, the fifth biggest-selling Australian record of 1991 and Song Of The Year at the 1991 ARIA awards. Recently relaunched Razor Recordings. www.razorrecordings.com

Emmanuel Candi Executive Director of ARIA during PSA enquiry

Tony Caraccia Managed Central's Adelaide store from 1989 to 2005, including as franchisee from the mid 90s. Also started the Perth store.

John Cassar Prominent Melbourne DJ and early Central Station employee. Sadly no longer with us.

Danny Corvini Editor of *3D World* from 1996 to 1999, and now a freelance journalist for *Domain*, the property section in *The Sydney Morning Herald*. He runs a Facebook page called 'I Partied in Sydney in the '90s' for kicks.

Peter Costello Treasurer of Australia (1996-2007)

John Course DJ and producer, famous for playing big stadium gigs as well as major clubs. Signed to Ministry of Sound as a DJ throughout the 2000s, he has sold more than a million mix CDs in Australia alone. Co-founded independent label Vicious Vinyl with Andy Van.

Jesse Desenberg (aka Kid Kenobi/Original Rude Boy) Voted Australia's favourite DJ for a record three years (2003-2005) in the annual inthemix.com DJ poll. Has remixed for some of the world's biggest names in dance, pop and rock, and played at top nightclubs around the world. In 2016, celebrated his twentieth year behind the decks with a national tour and mixtape series (*20 Years a Kid*); also launching a breakbeat EP as 'Original Rude Boy'. Runs his own label, Klub Kids, which focuses on bass, electro house, deep house and trap.

Jonce Dimovski First manager of Brisbane store; later was manager at 340 Flinders Street, Melbourne. Melbourne franchisee in the mid 90s. Now coach's assistant and video analyst for the Melbourne Storm.

Susan Dowler For many years strategically managed Central Station's legal defence against suits brought by the major recording companies. Now a Melbourne-based QC.

Nick Dunshea Former employee in Central Station's distribution centre 1988-90. Later worked for Shock Records, where he instigated the distribution arrangement with Central. In 2006, founded Liberator Music, a music label within The Mushroom Group. http://liberatormusic.com.au

Gareth Evans Attorney General in the Hawke Government (1983-1984)

John Ferris Sydney-based DJ, club promoter, radio DJ, and producer, known for his genre diversity. Awarded 'Outstanding Contribution To Dance Music' in the inaugural Australian Dance Music Awards in 2000. Headed the SonyDance label for Sony Music Australia from 1993-2001. Still very active in club music and the music industry in general, including working with Ministry of Sound Australia as Head of Sync and Licensing, chairing the APRA Committee on Club Music, and serving on the ARIA Club Chart Committee.

Nicole Fossati Editor of Sydney's 'dance music bible', *3D World*, from 1994-97. Later worked on a TV show about dance music on SBS called *Alchemy*, as a drive host on Triple J, and editor in chief of the Music Network. She veered into video production and set up her own company for a few years, and is now working on the 46th floor of the MLC building for a multinational corporation as the head of content.

James Fraser Worked for Central Station from 1989 to 1995, when he left to DJ full-time. In Sydney, he played at the Flinders, Exchange, DCM and Midnight Shift as well as Mardi Gras and other major dance parties. In Melbourne, he held residencies at 3 Faces and The Market Hotel for more than ten years, while also appearing at Red Raw and Winterdaze. He has supported touring DJs (such as Louie Vega, Frankie Knuckles, David Morales & DJ Spen) and bands (including Fleetwood Mac and Coldplay). As a record producer, James works under the artist name, Stereolove. He had a #8 hit on the *Billboard* Dance charts in 2015 with Los-Angeles-based singer Sara Loera, and has worked with Grammy award winning singer Matt Alber. http://www.stereolove.com.au

The Players

Andee Frost Former Central Station employee and franchisee. Has renounced playing at big clubs and festivals in favour of running underground events in Melbourne, including at his own Hugs & Kisses nightclub. Resident at 'The Toff In Town' on Saturday nights ('The House de Frost'). Formerly hosted a weekly radio show, *no way back*, on Melbourne's Triple R station.

Angus Galloway (aka DJ Angus, DJ Bribe) Brisbane hip hop DJ and later rave DJ, regarded as one of the most important pioneers of the city's dance music scene. Sadly, he passed away in 2008. The subject of a documentary called *Flow* due for release in 2017. For more information, search 'Flow - DJ Angus aka DJ Bribe documentary' on Facebook.

Ashley Gay A&R manager for Central Station from 2000 to 2009. Started Xelon Entertainment, 'Australia's premier digital music distribution company' in late 2009. http://xelonentertainment.com

Mark Gerber Former indie musician, house DJ, party/venue promoter, having a long association with Q Bar and the Exchange Hotel. Now runs the Oxford Art Factory in the site once occupied by Central Station Records in Darlinghurst, Sydney, and active in the campaign to fight Sydney's draconian lock-out laws. http://oxfordartfactory.com

Leslie Glick Melbourne-based QC who helped Jo and Morgan see a way out of their legal strife

Mikel Goodman (aka DJ Fenix) Sydney-based DJ, promoter, radio host and rave flyer designer who worked around Australia during the 90s. Now runs his own internet-based promotional gear business, specialising in plastic cards, lanyards, drawstring bags and more. www.pr.com.au

Stephan Győry Runs The Record Store in Crown Street, Darlinghurst (previously the site of BPM Records)

Denis Handlin Chairman & CEO of Sony Music Entertainment Australia & New Zealand and President, Asia. Also current Chairman of ARIA (as at February 2017).

Brian Harris Previously general manager at EMI. Now one of Jo's and Morgan's business partners, via Ambition Entertainment.

Ray Herd Long-term Central Station employee in Melbourne and storeowner in Perth.

Sam Hill Auckland-based house DJ and former co-owner of Bassline Records. Has released several successful dance compilations. Voted #2 DJ in 2003 NZ music awards. Now resident DJ and promoter of Code.

Steve Hill NZ-born DJ and producer, known for hard dance, hard trance and hard style. From 1997-2004, lived in the UK, where he worked for Pure Groove Records and was Central Station's local contact. Was later business manager for Central Station in Sydney. Has notched up more than 300 productions, including two artist albums and five UK top 20 remixes. In 2005, he started The Masif Organisation, a record, publishing and events company which he continues to head, including running Masif Saturdays (a weekly nightclub in Sydney), as well as touring the world. www.djstevehill.com

Jim Hirst (aka JimmyZ) Music director of Wild FM, who worked with Central Station to select tracks for the Wild compilation CDs. Later a DJ and dance presenter on the Nova FM network. Launched his own CD brand, Foreplay, and toured 'White' parties.

David Hitchcock (aka Hilda) Famous DJ in Melbourne and Sydney remembered for mixing gay tunes with audio-cassettes. Now deceased.

Paul Holden Prominent Sydney DJ, a pioneer of the city's rave culture of the late 80s and 90s. Was honoured by a tribute party at Home nightclub after his accidental death in March 2016.

Clyde Holding Federal MP for Melbourne Ports (1977-1998)

Paul Jackson Club and radio DJ in Melbourne, who created the Hardware Club and ran a popular show, *Blame it on Disco*, on Triple R in Melbourne in the 80s. Managed Central Station's Sydney stores until his untimely death.

The Players

Rudy James (aka DJ Rudy) Worked at Central Station's Perth store. Played US house music at many Perth clubs and raves during the 90s. Now runs his own architectural practice. www.arjaidesigns.com.au

Alex Karbouris (aka Alex K) Sydney-based producer, singer, songwriter, DJ and promoter, known for pioneering the NRG style. Has sold over 600,000 albums worldwide, including *Kickin Hard* compilations via Central Station.

Harry Katsanevas (aka Hakka or Harry K) Former manager of the Brisbane store. Has run Family, a 2000-capacity nightclub in the Valley, since 2001. Named DJ of the Year in Brisbane's 2016 gay awards, for his starring role at Family's gay night, Fluffy, on Sundays.

Paul Keating Treasurer of Australia (11 March 1983-3 June 1991); Prime Minister (20 December 1991-11 March 1996)

Andrew Kelly Former Brisbane store manager who became CEO of Central Station's American operations in 1988

Mike Kerry Top commercial DJ in Sydney in the 90s. Founded Evolution Under 18s at Dee Why, and Sounds on Sunday at the Greenwood Hotel. Produced a community TV show for Central called *Tekno Station*, hosted *Club [V]* and *Room 208* on Channel [V] from 1999 to 2005, and *WILD TV* on Channel 7 from 2005 to 2006. Now runs his own film creative and production company, Danger Mouse Productions. http://www.dangermouseproductions.com.au

George Klestinis (aka George Vagas) Pioneer of acid-house in Australia, who created and ran the legendary Le Rox nightclub in Adelaide and later played at major 90s raves in Sydney. Was the first DJ/promoter to tour all of the top international hardcore DJs to Australia. Now produces short films, documentaries and music clips; also regularly uploads archive band footage from the early 80s. See 'Grunge Tee Vee' on YouTube.

Jim Kontogiannis Joined Central Station in 1992 and worked in a few Melbourne stores, before joining forces with friends to become franchisee in 2005. DJd at clubs and raves from the 90s through to 2009. Now works for JB Hi-Fi's Elizabeth Street store.

Simon Lewicki (aka Groove Terminator) A prominent DJ in Adelaide who had considerable success as a producer of dance singles, TV show themes and film scores. As a member of the Chilli HiFly group, he produced *Is It Love?*, a No. 1 US *Billboard* club smash in 2001. Now runs 120 Publishing.

Katie M Little (aka Plus One) Sydney-based DJ, promoter and lighting tech who was prominent in the 90s rave scene. Still runs the design business, One Of A Kind, that she and husband Tim Poulton (aka Mach V) originally set up to design rave flyers and CD covers. Has also written a memoir about growing up with her celebrity mother, Jeanne Little, and has a blog called *Going to Seed*. http://goingtoseed.blogspot.com.au

Ken Lockhart (aka DJ Kenny L) Perth-based radio and club DJ, who also owned The DJ Factory, a vinyl and equipment store catering for DJs

Wes McDonald DJ and long-time Central Station employee, who worked in both Melbourne and Sydney. Now works for the Body Shop in Melbourne.

Tim McGee Worked for Central Station Records in the 90s, firstly managing the Oxford Street store, and later running A&R. Left Central to establish and head up Ministry of Sound Australia, which is expected to be rebranded following Sony's 2016 acquisition of the London-based Ministry of Sound Recordings.

Gil Matthews Former drummer with Billy Thorpe and the Aztecs and record shop owner (Stacks of Wax, Melbourne) who fought to open up the music market in Australia. Enjoyed a successful business career.

Maynard (aka Maynard F# Crabbes) Came to the attention of Triple J as a member of the Castanet Club cabaret group, and worked for the youth-oriented radio network from the mid 80s to the mid 90s, most famously as host of the flagship *Breakfast Show*. At home on multiple platforms (stage, radio, TV and podcast) and in both public and commercial media outlets, he has assembled a CV of epic diversity. Along the way, he released two compilation CDs on the Central Station label: *Maynard's Classics 1995-2000* and *Maynard's Classics 2000-2005*. maynard.com.au

The Players

Greg Molinaro Employee at Chapel Street (Melboune) from about 1987 to 1993, who then went on to open Rhythm & Soul Records on Greville Street, Prahran. The business expanded to include two shops, distribution operations, a recording label and a touring company. He later ran the Two of Hearts bar in South Yarra and opened HUB301 Record Shop in Abbotsford in 2016.

Edwin Morrow (aka DJ Edwin) Legendary Brisbane DJ, mixer, songwriter and producer who created the Halloween and Adrenalin dance parties. Died in 2014.

MRA Entertainment Group Pty Ltd The music division of the Home Leisure group, which acquired Central Station in 2003.

Matt Nugent Popular Brisbane DJ in the 00s. Former Central Station store manager, who remained with MRA after the merger to work on label management and marketing. Later DJd in Sydney at the Chinese Laundry and One Love clubs. Recently launched Double Up Records and artist management service. https://www.facebook.com/doubleuprec

Emilio Palumbo Worked at Central Station in Melbourne for seven years during the 80s, including managing 340 Flinders Street. Now runs a motor mechanic business specialising in servicing European cars.

Andrew Parkes (aka Andrew James) Played all styles of house music (acid house, UK garage and some hard house) at many Sydney venues from the 90s to the 00s, ranging from The Duke of Cornwall to Home. Worked his way back into carpentry by doing work for nightclubs. Still does the Sublime annual reunion parties.

Janette Pitruzzello (aka DJ JNETT) Melbourne-based DJ who plays house, disco, funk, Afro, soul and reggae and has supported the likes of Frankie Knuckles, Theo Parrish, Moodymann, Danny Krivit, Sadar Bahar, St Germain and Floating Points. Presented the ABC live TV show *Recovery* in the late 90s. Her debut EP *Wildlife* was released in 2016 via Maurice Fulton's BubbleTeaseCommunications. Also hosts PBS.fm radio show *Are You Ready?*

Rebecca Poulsen (aka BeXta) Trance and hard dance producer and DJ. The first female DJ in Australia to tour nationally, and has played across the globe in her career. Has supported and headlined with many touring internationals, including Prodigy, Underworld, Fat Boy Slim, Carl Cox, Showtek, and Paul Van Dyk. Also has remixed many hard dance artists from around the world like Lisa Lashes and Kidd Kaos. Released several *Mixology* compilations and original tracks under the Central Station label. Currently taking some time to enjoy being a mum and a post-graduate research student, and plays occasional reunion parties in Sydney. www.bexta.com

Kris Prpa (aka Ms Krystal Pussy Cha Cha) Melbourne-based DJ who managed Central's Chapel Street store for many years

Trent Rackus DJ and former Central Station employee. Now works for Ministry of Sound Australia, managing Soapbox Agency and the touring side of the company.

Jamie Raeburn Joined Central Station in 1998 as assistant A&R, after working for a UK label called Clubscene. Later became A&R director when Tim McGee left. Has run Central Station since the sale and re-emergence as a joint venture. See www.centralstation.com.au

Graham Richardson Senator for New South Wales (1983-1994)

Richard Rinaudo (aka DJ Rich) Former DJ and producer who now runs the Star Music group, including recording labels, a publishing company and artist management services. http://www.starmusic.com.au

Vivien Rogers An early Central Station hire, who originally managed the Chapel Street store before initiating the 'alternative' store at City Square

Justice Sheppard Chair of the Copyright Law Review Committee. Now deceased.

Nick Skitz Nicholas Agamalis, better known as Nick Skitz, began working for dance label Pro-DJ International in the early 90s, and later became involved with the Central Station Records label, featuring on

Wild and Skitzmix compilations. Best known for his remixes of the *X-Files Theme*, *Excalibur*, *Funky Choad* (which made the top 10 in the UK charts) and many more productions. See http://nickskitz.com

Michael Smellie Managing director of Polygram who helped Jo and Morgan at key points in this story

Brian Smith Managing director of RCA Records of Australia Pty Ltd from 1979 to the mid 80s

Peter Snow Independent record storeowner in Melbourne. Former treasurer of the Australian Recordsellers Association who appeared before the Copyright Law Review Committee and the PSA inquiry into sound recordings. Now has fingers in a number of entrepreneurial pies.

Cameron Stirling DJd in big clubs in Melbourne (including Sheiks, Madison's, Chasers, Underground) during big times for those venues (80s). Now works in executive recruitment.

Greta Tate First Central Station employee, running Metal for Melbourne. Later co-managed Metal Labyrinth. Keeps in contact with many former customers via Facebook. Now semi-retired and living in Ballarat.

Paul Taylor (aka Paul 'flex' Taylor) DJd in Sydney, Melbourne and Surfers Paradise from the late 70s through to 00s including at the Underground in Melbourne and the Hordern Pavilion in Sydney. Now a customer service representative by day, while playing music and book writing after hours.

Alan Thompson Central Station manager and graphic designer

Les Toth Long-serving Melbourne DJ (42 years), best known for playing rock at pubs such as the Ferntree Gully Hotel and supporting major mainstream acts like Midnight Oil, Cold Chisel and INXS. Now semi-retired.

Phil Tripp Phil's company IMMEDIA! published the AustralAsian Music Industry Directory for twenty-three years. Wrote many freelance articles about criminality in the music industry. Later ran a PR company. Now retired. http://philtripp.com

Paul Turner Managing director of Warner Music in Australia from the late 70s to late 80s. Now deceased.

Nik Vatoff (aka Nik Fish) Former employee at Central's Pitt Street store, who became a club, rave and radio DJ. Hosted *Musiquarium* rave show on 2SER for seven years in the 90s. Later played at Sublime and Home nightclubs in Sydney, as well as touring nationally. Released compilation CDS under the Central label. Now assistant manager at Store DJ in Sydney, while still playing the occasional gig.

Mark Vick (aka Mark Dynamix) DJ and producer with more than thirty mix CDs, ten original releases and many remixes to his name. Has toured nationally and internationally. Voted Australia's #1 DJ by *3D World* in 2001 and #2 by inthemix.com.au members in 2002/3/4. Now divides his time between his recording label, Long Distance Recordings, running dance parties and composing music and producing audio for film and TV. http://www.longdistancerecordings.com and http://www.facebook.com/djmarkdynamix

Jac Vidgen Promoter and business leader of the Recreational Arts Team (RAT), which threw forty RAT parties in Sydney between 1983 and 1992. Currently based in Manila, teaching people Buteyko's method (optimal breathing practices which reverse chronic illness). Search for RATrospective group on Facebook.

Ken Walker Started DJing in 1977, aged sixteen. First club gig at age seventeen (Bunnies in Footscray). As a producer, has sold well over half a million albums. Now music director for eight Melbourne venues, DJs five nights a week, and mixes and produces an international radio show (*Blow Your Speakers*) that airs in twelve countries.

John Wall DJ and director, creative director and head of marketing for Fuzzy, a major Sydney event promoter best known for Parklife, Field Day, Shore Thing and Harbourlife.

Jim White MD of Festival Records from the late 70s to late 80s

The Players

Jon Wicks Hosted a Sunday night dance show, *D-Mix*, on 2 Triple S FM, a full-power community radio station in Canberra. Ran events and DJd at clubs in Canberra in the late 80s to late 90s, before moving to Sydney and the early rave scene. Now a voice-over artist and producer.

Peter Wilson Singer, songwriter and producer, who has written tracks for acts such as Amanda Lear, Carol Jiani and Nicki French, as well as performing and releasing under his own name. His latest album, *Overdrive*, on UK label Energise Records was released in January 2017. www.energiserecords.com

Shawn Yates Runs Flipside Distribution, in a joint venture with Jo and Morgan

Angie Young Worked for Central Station from 2000-2007, mostly as national promotion manager. With business partner, Petrina Convey, she now runs her own publicity, artist and event promotion company, Xposed Media. http://www.xposedmedia.com.au

From left: Mandy McCourt (Jo's assistant), Trevor Courtney (producer), Lisa Edwards (talent) and Stephen Robinson (Central's first A&R manager)

Appendix 3 – Employees

Jo took great care in listing the following names and dates, extracting information from different hard copy and digital records. However, owing to the nature of the records, mistakes may have been made, including missing names altogether. Should you wish to make amendments, please write to giuseppepalumbo@gmail.com
The format is First Name/s SURNAME (Year commenced)

Thomas Lewis ABBOTT (1993)
Nigel ABELA (1987)
Parwin AKHUNDZADAH (1989)
Mark ALIADAS (1988)
Doug ALLAN (1987)
Tim ALLISON (1997)
Mark Adrian ALSOP (1988)
Bill ANDRIOPOULOS (1987)
Kyle ARMSTRONG (1997)
Shnoosee BAILEY (1990)
Simon BANKS (1989)
Paul Graeme BARNES (2000)
Sonia Maria BASILE (1993)
Mark Steven BATES (1989)
Kathleen Patricia BATHGATE (1989)
Ian Lawrence BATTEN (1993)
Heidi Elizabeth BAUCHE (2002)
Jason BAYLEY (1999)
Steven Mark BELL (1989)
Emma BELLAMY (2000)
Adam BLACK (1998)
Tony BLACK (1989)
Andrew BOON (2010)
Kamilla BORKOWSKA (2006)
Steven John BOURK (1999)
Michael BRADLEY (1990)
Tracy BRENNAN (1997)
Bruce BRIGHAM (2000)
Murray Edwin McArthur BROWN (2003)
Cameron BROWN (1997)
Vernon Kevin BRUCE (1987)
Jason David BURTON (1987)
Sam CANNALONGA (1986)
Tony CARACCIA (1989)
James CARDONA (1988)
John Francis CASSAR (1978)
George CATHELS (2016)
Karen CATT (1989)

Angus CHAPEL (1997)
Ping CHEN (2003)
Terence CHIN (2001)
Adam CHOCKER (2002)
Marc CHRISTIE (1994)
Lorna CLARKSON (1999)
Andrew P COLLINS (1988)
Peter COMBES (2016)
Patrina CONVEY (2000)
Tom COTTER (1998)
Matthew CRAWFORD (2000)
Aaron CROCKER (1990)
Patrick CRONIN (2001)
Shawn John CROWHURST (1987)
Jamille CUMMINS (2003)
Nicole CUPIC (1999)
John DANCE (2001)
Bernard DE BROGLIO (1992)
John DEBLASIO (1992)
Loretta DELFINO (1998)
Chris DEMOS (1987)
Bruce Nicholas DEVCICH (1992)
John DI PIERRO (2000)
Tass DIAKAVASILIS (2008)
Jo DICKISON (1993)
Luciano DIMASTROMATTEO (1990)
Jonce DIMOVSKI (1988)
Damien DONATO (1991)
Alison DOWNS (1988)
Jeff DRAKE (2007)
Mary DRIVAS (1987)
Nicholas Roger DUNSHEA (1988)
Giuseppe DURSO (1986)
Samuel Alexander DUTCH (1999)
Alison EATON (2002)
Peter Simon ELMALOGLOU (1994)

Pearse Connolly Rua ELTON (2002)
Nalan ERGUL (1988)
Nigel EVANS (2004)
Michael Alexander FIELD (2001)
Mark Edward FISHER (1988)
Gerard Gabriel FLETCHER (1981)
Jason FORETTI (2000)
Antonella FORMOSA (2003)
Chris FRASER (2000)
James Fenwick FRASER (1989)
Andrew Dale FROST (2000)
Jacqueline Louise GAIBOR (1992)
Angus Warwick GALLOWAY (1989)
Michelle GARCIA (2000)
Annabelle GASPAR (1994)
Ashley GAY (2000)
Vincenzo Renato GIGLIA (1987)
David GILLARD (2000)
Anthony Michael GOURLAY (1989)
Guilio GRANDINETTI (1998)
Nick GRAY (2001)
Zachary GRAY (2003)
Trent Andrew GRIMES (2002)
Tina GRUNDMAN (1999)
Mauro Celestino GUARNACCIA (1988)
Lisa Jane Perry HAM (1986)
Hamish David HAMPTON (2003)
Russell John HANCORNE (1991)
Matthew HANDLEY (2000)
Andrea HANIC (1995)
Jacqueline Ruth HANSON (1985)
John Moran HARDIE (1970)
Patrick HARRIS (2000)
Hannah HAYWARD (2002)
Karen Judith HEFPS (1989)

Khalil HEGARTY (2000)
Ryan Edward HENDERSON (1993)
Raymond Kenneth HERD (1980)
Kristian HERNANDEZ (2000)
Robbie Ian HINTON (1990)
David Charles HITCHCOCK (1991)
Samantha HORTON (1998)
Gina HOUSE (1994)
Kristian HOUSELBERGER (2000)
Chris HRONOPOULOS (1999)
Pamela Jane HUBRUCK (1994)
Barry John HUDSON (1989)
Kathleen Robyn HUGHES (1988)
Nathan HUGHES (1997)
Sean HUGHES (2004)
Daniel IRVINE (1994)
Lisa JACKSON (1997)
Paul Francis JACKSON (1982)
Karen Anne JAMES (1989)
Rudy JAMES (1996)
Naomi JAMIESON (1999)
Amanda JENKINS (2016)
Jaime Alfonso JIMENEZ SARTA (1989)
Jessica JONES (2002)
Tristan JONES (1990)
Jennifer JUCKEL (2002)
Christine KAKAIRE (2002)
Harry KATSANEVAS (1991)
Adalet Ashley KAYA (1988)
Stephen Craig KEAT (1988)
Steven John KECSKES (2001)
Josh KELLET (2016)
Andrew Hilton KELLY (1990)
John KERNAGHAN (1992)
Scott KIMBALL (2001)
George KLESTINIS (1993)
Ryan KONDRAT (2000)
Jim KONTOGIANNIS (1994)
Theodoros (Aki) KORMANOS (1988)
Nicole Mireille KOSKY (1989)
Christia KOULOUNDI (1989)
Svetlana KRASINSKI (1984)
Jeffrey Michael LAKE (1991)
Ann LEE (1988)
Stanley LEUNG (2000)
Susie LIBERMAN (1988)
Suzanne LINDLEY (1995)
Brentan LLEWELLYN (1996)
Annie LUO (2000)
Paul (aka Archie) MAGLIULO (2003)
Julie Frances MANDS (1988)
Brett MARTIN (1989)
Antony William MARTINI (1987)
Tom MASON (2004)
Lachlan McDonald McAULEY (1988)
Mandy Kim McCLOUD (1988)
Wesley James McDONALD (1986)
Tim McGEE (1994)
Louise McGREGOR (1999)
Christine McINTOSH (2001)
Peter John MENSFELD (1990)
Colin Henry Jaraslav MICHALEK (1984)
Jackeline MIFSUD (1998)
Brook MILLER (2000)
Jacynta MIRMIKIDIS (2000)
Jesse MITCHELL (2002)
Gregory MOLINARO (1988)
Edward James MONTANO (2002)
Ben MORRIS (2013)
Edwin Campbell MORROW (1990)

Adrian John MULLINS (1983)
Jerome NASSIF (2000)
Joe NEHMA (1999)
Gary Francis NEWMAN (1981)
David NISSANI (2001)
Lee David NORRIS (1989)
Matthew James NUGENT (2000)
Bridget Ann O'SULLIVAN (1995)
Cait O'SULLIVAN (1995)
Louis OBERLEUTER (2001)
Michelle OWEN (2001)
Emilio PALUMBO (1983)
Giuseppe PALUMBO (1975)
Leonarda PALUMBO (1986)
Con PANTZIDIS (1989)
Andrew James PARKES (2002)
Antony PARTRIDGE (2004)
Marqueritha E PATTON (1992)
Margaret PAVLIDIS (1982)
Dominy Christine PEACOCK (2002)
Shane PETROVIC (1999)
Joanne PHELPS (2004)
Alex PIERIAS (1987)
Wayne PINA-ROOZEMOND (1992)
Janette PITRUZZELLO (1993)
George PLAYFAIR (2016)
Suzana POPOVKSA (2000)
Adam Benjamin POWNALL (1992)
Kristina PRPA (1985)
Justin Charlie QUAY (1987)
Jamie RAEBURN (1998)
Jermia RAJASEKARAM (1988)
Stephen John RALPH (1975)
Christian RALSTON (2002)
Kavi Raj RAMNANI (1998)
John Daniel RANDLE (1989)
David REID (2002)

Nigel REYNOLDS (1997)
Brian RISELEY (1996)
Kellie RITCHIE (1995)
Gabriel RIZZA (2000)
Stephen Patrick ROBBINS (1986)
Michael Clark ROBINSON (1987)
Stephen John ROBINSON (1988)
Vivien Patricia ROGERS (1983)
Jason ROSS (1998)
William ROSS (2009)
Kenneth Victor ROSSER (1983)
Caterina RUSSO (1989)
Melanie RUTHERFORD (1999)
Melina SAMARIAS (1987)
Angus Christian SANDERS (1994)
Jeremy SCOTT (2000)
Flynn James SCULLY (2002)
Louise SERGENT (2006)
Nancy Elizabeth Andrea SERRA (1989)
Simone Lesley SEYMOUR (1998)
Roger Wayne SHELDON-COLLINS (1988)
Melinda SHI (2000)
Kathryn SILAS (2000)
Aaron SINES (1997)
Vanessa SIROLA (2001)
Jamie SKUNTOUROGLOW (2000)
Stephen John SONIUS (1996)
Shane George SOUTHBY (1989)
Matina STAMATACOS (1987)
Karyn Michelle STEELE (1989)
Fraser STEWART (2005)
Leanne STEWART (1996)
Cameron STIRLING (1980)
Adam STIVALA (2016)
Cory Mathew STOCK (1993)
Anders SUNBERG (1987)

Sheena SWAN (2005)
Aniela SWIATEK (2011)
Greta Florence TATE (1979)
Dearne Michelle TAYLOR (1990)
Jules TAYLOR (1985)
Shayne THOMAS (1988)
Alan Charles THOMPSON (1986)
John THOMPSON (1999)
Petar Ivan TOLICH (1988)
Trevor Matthew TOWE (1988)
Simon George Allan TOYER (1998)
Peter Kaman TSOI (1991)
Souli TSIOLIS (1998)
William Stewart TULLOCH (1980)
Guy Desire UPPIAH (1987)
Dale Grant VAN DEN BOOGAARD (1994)
Nicholas VATOFF (1990)
Louie VELESKI (1988)
Pamela VERITY (1988)
Agnes Marie WACLAWIK (1989)
- Rebecca WADE (2000)
Steven Edward WATSON (1996)
Zoe WATSON (1997)
Shu-Tao WEI (2002)
Carl WEST (1999)
Chad WESTON (1999)
Michelle WEIR (1993)
Tracey Ann WILKINS (1988)
Talei Elvira WILLIAMS (1990)
Morgan Evan WILLIAMS (1988)
Paul WINEGGE (1995)
Mike WITCOMBE (2007)
Eric WOO (2001)
Carolyn WORSLEY (2000)
Addie Lee WORTH (1993)
Shaun YATES (1995)
Jennifer YEALES (1996)
Angie YOUNG (2000)
Anna Estelle YOUNG (1999)
Leslie YOUNG (1983)
Tony Ron YOUNG (1991)
Jamie ZARZYCKI (1998)

Appendix 4 – Addresses

Giuseppe (Jo) Palumbo
giuseppepalumbo@gmail.com

Morgan Williams
morgan@centralstation.com.au

Central Station Records
www.centralstation.com.au

Music Wars – The Sound of the Underground
www.centralstation.com.au/musicwars
www.musicwars.com.au
Also search for 'music wars' on Facebook and Instagram

Carhartt
http://www.carhartt-wip.com.au

Supply
E: online@supplystore.com.au
F: facebook.com/supplystore
Follow us on Instagram @supplystore
http://www.supplystore.com.au

Ambition Entertainment
info@ambitionmusic.com.au
http://www.ambitionentertainment.com